あなたも通訳ガイドです

英語で案内する

# 大阪・奈良・神戸

柴山かつの 著
Katsuno Shibayama

英文校閲 Paul Dorey

the japan times 出版

## 日本を好きになってもらいたい

　コロナ禍が収束し、大阪・関西万博の開催など明るい話題も増えてきた今日この頃、海外からのお客様が大幅に増加し、美しき日本文化を伝える機会が増えました。本書『あなたも通訳ガイドです　英語で案内する大阪・奈良・神戸』はシリーズ第3弾です。私の経験に基づき、通訳ガイドと海外のゲストとのリアルな会話形式にしました。私自身の喜びと驚き、そして失敗などの**経験を素直な気持ちで伝えた実況中継本**でもあります。

　最近は、大阪のミナミや奈良を歩いていると海外にいるような錯覚さえ覚えます。私の通訳ガイドデビューの場所は、四天王寺、大阪城、道頓堀　道具屋筋、黒門市場などでした。新人ガイドの頃は歴史等を説明するのに必死でした。ゲストが何を求めていらっしゃるのか見極める余裕がなかったので、ゲストを退屈させてばかりいました。

　ところが、人形浄瑠璃の発祥の地が大阪であることを説明した後のことです。**道頓堀のくいだおれ太郎**の前で眉毛と目を動かし、首を振って人形のまねをしてみせると、ゲストの皆さんは笑顔になってくださり、ツアーの雰囲気がとても良くなりました。セサミストリートの**マペット**が人形浄瑠璃からアイデアを得て作られたことを説明すると、熱心に聞いてもらえました。道具屋筋では、ゲストに**大阪弁**を教えながら買い物をしました。本書には、そんな実体験をたくさん盛り込んでいます。

　「**仏教のデパート**」と呼ばれ、愛されている四天王寺では**仏教の基本**を学び、住吉大社では**神道の基本**を学べる構成にしました。四天王寺では**仁王様**の前で、あうんの呼吸を説明するだけでなく、It signifies the entire life span of a human being. A baby was born crying "Ah Ah Ah," and when we get old, we die peacefully, saying "Un."（人の一生を意味します。赤ちゃんは『あああ』と泣きながら生まれ、私たちは年を取ると『うん』と言ってあの世に行くのです）と話しています。やや大げさなジェスチャーを入れ、言葉に抑揚をつけて話すと、興味を持ってもらえるのです。住吉大社の象徴・**太鼓橋**を背景に進む神道式の花嫁行列は、時代絵巻のような美しさですので、ゲストにもご覧いただければと思っています。

大阪城では、**豊臣秀吉公**のことをご存じの海外ゲストが多いのに驚いたことがありました。「**武士はどのようにして生まれたか?**」といった質問にうまく答えられなかったり、戦国三英傑（three unifiers during the Age of the warring States）の織田信長、豊臣秀吉、徳川家康について詳しく質問されてドギマギしたこともあります。

　奈良の**東大寺**で延べ260万人の人が協力して創建した大仏様の話をすると、感動されるお客様もいらっしゃいました。シカが大好きでシカの話で盛り上がったゲスト、**春日大社**で屋根を突き抜けている木に驚かれ、神道の説明をすると感動されたゲストもいらっしゃいます。

　興福寺では仏像好きなゲストが、国宝館の三面六臂の**阿修羅像**が少年の顔、思春期の顔、青年の顔を持っていることなどを説明してくださいました。そのような場合は上手な聞き役に徹します。ガイドには**臨機応変さ**が大切なのです。興福寺南側には**町家**を改装したレトロな店舗が並ぶ「**ならまち**」が広がっており、興福寺を拠点に観光を楽しんでくださる方も多いです。

　中には、寺社仏閣や城にあまり興味のないゲストもいらっしゃいます。そんなときには、世界初の連結超高層建築である**梅田スカイビル**、四季の花々を楽しめる万博記念公園、海遊館、神戸の街並みをご案内できるように本書で紹介しました。

　また、本書で学んでいただくと、豊臣秀吉、松下幸之助、安藤百福、江崎利一氏のように**クリエイティブで不屈の精神をもって努力し、成功した偉人**について説明できるようになります。逸話では**一寸法師**などを取り上げています。

　近年、ロングツアーが増え、海外ゲストをご案内する場所が広がりました。廃城の危機を乗り越えよみがえり、人々に生きる勇気を与えた不戦の**姫路城**、自然と手を取り合って生きる人々と日本の原風景に感動できる**白川郷**、太古の歴史を刻む憧れの**伊勢神宮**、世界で初めて真珠の養殖に成功した**真珠島**、仏教体験ができる天空の聖地・**高野山**も本書に収録しています。さらに、**厳島神社**の大鳥居をはじめ、建築物の中にある**先人の知恵**についても本書で学び、ガイディングしていただければ幸いです。

広島の**平和記念公園**を訪れる海外ゲストが増加していることも、とてもうれしく思っています。小鳥のさえずりが聞こえる美しく整備された公園で、私たちが原爆で亡くなられた人たちのことをどれだけ大切に思っているか、**平和の大切さを海外ゲストの方々に感じ取っていただければと思います**。原爆ドームの周りでは、被爆者や親族の方々がボランティアで、自分たちに起きた出来事を平和への祈りを込めて話してくださいます。広島を訪れると、**通訳ガイドの仕事は平和への懸け橋**の役割も担っているのだなとつくづく感じます。

　本書は通訳ガイドとして仕事をされている方だけでなく、通訳ライセンスを取得するために勉強されている方、また、英語に興味がなくても日本語だけでも楽しんでいただけます。関西旅行のガイドブックとしてもお読みいただけると思います。

　本書をこの世に出すにあたってご協力くださった寺社仏閣、城、各種施設の方々には、大変お世話になりました。また、編集者の西田由香さん、英文校閲者の Paul Dorey 先生は読者目線で最後まで忍耐強く編集、校閲してくださいました。心より感謝申し上げます。皆様の温かい励ましと優しさのおかげで、念願の一冊が産声を上げることができました。

　本書が、読者の皆様のお役に立つことを心より願っております。

平和への祈りをこめて　　　柴山かつの

# 目　次

はじめに **...** 002

本書の使い方 **...** 009

音声のご利用案内 **...** 010

## Chapter 1　大阪

1. 大阪〈1-10〉 **...** 012

2. 大阪城〈1-12〉 **...** 036

3. 住吉大社〈1-8〉 **...** 070

4. 四天王寺〈1-8〉 **...** 090

5. 梅田スカイビル〈1-4〉 **...** 110

　　海遊館〈5-6〉 **...** 118

　　万博記念公園〈7-8〉 **...** 122

その他の名所めぐり

　①中之島 ... 128

　②御堂筋のイチョウ並木と彫刻 ... 129

　③菅原道真を祀る大阪天満宮 ... 130

　④日本三大祭りの一つ、天神祭 ... 130

　⑤百舌鳥・古市古墳群と仁徳天皇陵 ... 131

　⑥サンタマリア号で大阪湾周遊 ... 131

　⑦高速道路が貫通している TKP ゲートタワービル ... 132

　⑧勝尾寺 ... 132

　⑨日本で 2 番目に高い skyscraper、
　　あべのハルカス 300（展望台）... 134

## Chapter 2 　奈良

**1.** 東大寺 〈1-10〉 **...** 136

**2.** 春日大社 〈1-8〉 **...** 160

　　奈良のシカ 〈9-10〉 **...** 176

**3.** 興福寺 〈1-3〉 **...** 184

その他の名所めぐり
　①ならまち ... 192
　②法隆寺 ... 193
　③若草山の山焼きとその理由 ... 194

## Chapter 3 　兵庫

**1.** 神戸の街 〈1-3〉 **...** 196

**2.** 姫路城 〈1-10〉 **...** 204

その他の名所めぐり
　①灘の酒 ... 228
　②明石海峡大橋 ... 229
　③メリケンパーク ... 230
　④布引ハーブガーデン ... 232
　⑤有馬温泉 ... 232

# Chapter 4 大阪から日帰り旅行

**1.** 宮島 〈1〉 **...** 234

厳島神社 〈2-6〉 **...** 236

平和記念公園 〈7-11〉 **...** 246

**2.** 伊勢神宮 〈1-4〉 **...** 258

ミキモト真珠島 〈5-6〉 **...** 266

**3.** 白川郷 〈1-4〉 **...** 276

**霊場　高野山とは** ... 286

1. 高野山 ... 288

2. 壇上伽藍 ... 288

3. 金剛峯寺 ... 291

4. 奥之院 ... 294

5. 宿坊 ... 296

索引 **...** 299

カバーデザイン・本文レイアウト　姉崎直美
DTP組版　朝日メディアインターナショナル株式会社
編集協力　田中大輔、株式会社ファイブ・スターズ・ジャパン　福島 美千子

ナレーション　Chris Koprowski（米）& Nadia McKechnie（英）
録音・編集　ELEC録音スタジオ
音声収録時間　約3時間45分

## ●●● 本書の使い方 ●●●

◉ **本書の構成**

全4章からなり、各章は以下の5つのパートから成り立っています。

> ①英文ダイアローグ
> ②ダイアローグの日本語訳
> ③単語の小箱
> ④瞬間英作文
> ⑤玉虫の宝庫　　　1. 見学の手順
> 　　　　　　　　　2. 通訳ガイドからのアドバイス
> 　　　　　　　　　3. 通訳ガイド体験日記
> 　　　　　　　　　4. 通訳ガイドお役立ち英語表現

## ●●● 効果的な学習法 ●●●

本書の①英文ダイアローグは、通訳ガイドと外国人プライベート観光客との会話で成り立っています。

①英文ダイアローグに入る前に、④瞬間英作文を学習してもよいでしょう。左下のヒントを使い英作文にチャレンジすると、本文のダイアローグが理解しやすくなります。

それから、③単語の小箱をチェックし、②ダイアローグの日本語訳から①英文ダイアローグに訳せるようになりましょう。

⑤玉虫の宝庫は情報満載のコラムです。

1. 見学の手順では、寺社仏閣の観光する場所の情報を日本語で復習します。

2. 通訳ガイドからのアドバイスで、①英文ダイアローグがもっとすんなりと頭の中に入ってくるようになります。

3. 通訳ガイド体験日記では、失敗談などが正直に語られています。ガイディングの参考にしてください。

4. 通訳ガイドお役立ち英語表現では、主にダイアローグの関連表現を紹介しています。

## 音声のご利用案内

本書の音声は、スマートフォン（アプリ）やパソコンを通じて MP3 形式でダウンロードし、ご利用いただくことができます。

### 📱 スマートフォン

1. ジャパンタイムズ出版の音声アプリ「OTO Navi」をインストール
2. OTO Navi で本書を検索
3. OTO Navi で音声をダウンロードし、再生

3秒早送り・早戻し、繰り返し再生などの便利機能つき。学習にお役立てください。

### 💻 パソコン

1. ブラウザからジャパンタイムズ出版のサイト「BOOK CLUB」にアクセス

https://bookclub.japantimes.co.jp/book/b658354.html

2. 「ダウンロード」ボタンをクリック
3. 音声をダウンロードし、iTunes などに取り込んで再生
   ※ 音声は zip ファイルを展開（解凍）してご利用ください。

# Chapter 1

# 大阪

大阪城、住吉大社、梅田スカイビルなど、見どころ満載の大阪。市内をめぐりながら、エネルギッシュな大阪らしさをゲストに楽しんでいただきましょう。

（上）道頓堀（i viewfinder/Shutterstock.com）
（右）大阪城（Aman Arykbaev/Shutterstock.com）
（下）住吉大社の太鼓橋（Pumidol/Shutterstock.com）

# 1-1　大阪

関空、大阪弁、開拓精神、商人の街、水の都、綿糸と薬品について

**On the train to Osaka, after introductions at Kansai International Airport**

G: Now we **are heading for** Osaka. It takes about one hour.

T: I've heard Japan's **public transportation system** is highly developed, so this is exciting for me. I liked Kansai International Airport, too.

G: The passenger terminal was modeled after a glider which has just landed. It was designed by the famous Italian architect Renzo Piano, who also designed The Shard in London. Kansai International Airport was built on **reclaimed land**.

T: I'm from London. The Shard is an 87-story building and is the highest in Western Europe. By the way, I've always wanted to visit Osaka. I want to pick up some Japanese words, especially some Osaka dialect, during my stay in Osaka. So, Osaka is famous for its talented merchants?

G: Yes. Osaka people are known for being good at making money (laughing). There's a famous Osaka dialect greeting, "Mōkarimakka?" (laughing), which means "Are you making money?" "Bochi-bochi denna" means "So-so." It's a **stereotypical** Osaka merchants' greeting.

T: Can I try? "Mōkarimakka?" (laughing)

G: (Laughing) Bochi-bochi denna. Osaka people are said to be **enterprising**. Osaka is close to the sea and there are many rivers, so Osaka citizens built canals and bridges. Osaka was called the "Water Metropolis." However, Osaka people filled in the waterways to build highways and streets. Now, Osaka is winning back its name "Water Metropolis" by holding festivals along the waterways and promoting cruising. Osaka people are willing to take on challenges. This environment **fostered** independent, industrious, and interesting townsfolk. Osaka was also called the "Manchester of Japan." Do you know why?

T: Manchester was famous for its **cotton yarn**. Osaka, too.

G: Right! At the end of the 19th century, Osaka produced 90 percent of Japan's total cotton yarn production. Osaka is still the biggest center of the **textile industry** and **pharmaceutical production** in Japan.

G：通訳ガイド　T：観光客

## 関西空港で互いに自己紹介してから大阪までの電車の中で

**G：** 今、大阪に向かっています。1時間ほどで着きます。

**T：** 日本の公共交通機関は高度に発達していると聞いているのでワクワクします。関空も好きになりました。

**G：** 乗客ターミナルは、到着したばかりのグライダーをモデルにデザインされています。ロンドンのシャードのデザインをした有名なイタリア建築家、レンゾ・ピアノにデザインされました。関空は埋め立て地に建設されました。

**T：** 私はロンドン出身です。シャードは87階建てで、西ヨーロッパで一番高いビルです。ところで、私はずっと大阪に来たいと思っていました。大阪滞在中に日本語、特に大阪弁を少し覚えたいです。大阪は有能な商人で有名ですよね？

**G：** はい。大阪人はお金もうけがうまいことで有名ですよ（笑）。有名な大阪弁の挨拶があります。「もうかりまっか？」は「お金もうけをしていますか？」という意味です。「ボチボチでんな」は「まあまあです」を意味します。典型的な大阪人の挨拶です。

**T：** 言ってみましょうか？　もうかりまっか？

**G：** （笑って）ボチボチでんな。大阪人は企業心に富んでいると言われています。大阪は海に近く、多くの川があったので大阪人は運河や橋を造りました。大阪は「水の都」と呼ばれていました。ですが、高速道路や通りを造るために水路を埋め立てました。今、大阪はまた水路の周辺でフェステイバルを開催したり、クルージングをプロモーションしたりして「水の都」の名前を取り戻しています。大阪人は進んで新しいことに挑戦するのです。環境が独立心のある勉強熱心な面白い住民を作り出しました。大阪はまた日本のマンチェスターとも呼ばれていました。なぜだかわかりますか？

**T：** マンチェスターは綿糸で有名です。大阪もですね！

**G：** その通りです。19世紀の終わりに大阪は日本の総綿糸生産の90パーセントを占めていました。大阪は今でも日本の繊維産業と薬品生産の中心地です。

## 単語の小箱

- □ be heading for ... …に向かっている　□ public transportation system 公共交通機関
- □ reclaimed land 埋め立て地　□ stereotypical 型どおりの　□ enterprising 企業心に富む
- □ foster …を育む　□ cotton yarn 綿糸　□ textile industry 紡績産業
- □ pharmaceutical production 薬品生産

# 1-2 大阪

### 松下幸之助氏、発明の街、カップヌードルついて

**T**: I'm a manager of a boutique. In the future, I want to set up an apparel company, and I'm also thinking of becoming a restaurant owner and building up a chain. In a book I read, it said Osaka has produced many **entrepreneurs**.

**G**: Right! The most famous entrepreneur was Kōnosuke Matsushita, who set up the present-day Panasonic Co. Ltd.

**T**: He's world-famous. Mr. Matsushita is called "the god of management." I'd like to know more about him, though.

**G**: He had to drop out of elementary school because his father's business failed. He was sent to Osaka to work as an **apprentice** at a shop, and at the age of 15 he got a job as an apprentice worker at an electric lighting company. He was very studious and quickly got promoted to inspector. He designed an improved light socket, but few people were interested in it. At the age of 23 he set up his own small company with very little **capital**. His sockets didn't sell well. However, luckily and unexpectedly, the company received a **bulk order** for electric fan parts. He invented many products and expanded his company into the world-famous Panasonic.

**T**: Mr. Matsushita was an inventor as well as an entrepreneur!

**G**: Yes! Mr. Matsushita once said, "Just think. Use your **ingenuity**. If you fail, you can try again."

**T**: I see. If I'm afraid of doing new things, I'll never be able to create anything new.

**G**: Right! Instant noodles were also invented in Osaka, by Momofuku Andō, who established the Nissin Food Co.

**T**: Oh, really? I love cup noodles!

**G**: After World War II, due to food shortages, many people suffered from **malnutrition**. He was shocked to see many people waiting in long lines on freezing cold days to eat a bowl of ramen at a black market **stall**. He wanted to help other people. Also, from a business point of view, he felt there was a demand for instant ramen. He decided to invent instant noodles.

G：通訳ガイド　T：観光客

T：私はブティックの店長をしています。近い将来、アパレル会社の設立を考えています。また、レストラン経営者になってチェーン店をつくることも考えています。大阪は多くの起業家を生み出したと書かれた本を読んだことがあります。

G：その通りです！　一番有名な起業家はパナソニックの設立者の松下幸之助氏です。

T：松下氏は世界的に有名ですね。経営の神様と呼ばれています。もっと詳しく松下氏について知りたいです。

G：松下氏はお父さんの事業の失敗で、小学校を中退しなければなりませんでした。お店で丁稚奉公するため大阪に送られ、15歳で見習工として電灯会社に就職しました。彼は勉強熱心だったので、検査員にスピード昇進しました。改良された電気ソケットを考案しましたが、興味を持つ人はほとんどいませんでした。23歳で松下氏はほとんど資本金なしに小さな会社を設立しました。彼の考案したソケットは売れませんでした。しかしながら、幸運にも期せずして、扇風機の部品の大量注文を受けました。彼は多くの製品を考案し、自社を世界的に有名なパナソニックへと発展させました。

T：松下氏は起業家であるだけでなく、発明家でもいらっしゃったのですね。

G：松下氏はこのように言いました。「とにかく考えてみることである。工夫してみることである。失敗すればやり直せばいい」

T：なるほど。新しいことをすることを怖がったら、何も新しい物は作れませんね。

G：その通りです！　インスタントヌードルも大阪で発明されたのですが、日清食品を設立した安藤百福氏によってなんですよ。

T：ええ、そうなんですか？　私はカップヌードルが大好きです。

G：第二次世界大戦後、食料不足で多くの人が栄養失調で苦しみました。彼は凍えるほど寒い日に、闇市の屋台で多くの日本人が一杯のラーメンを食べるために長い列を作って待っているのを見てショックを受けました。彼は人々を助けたいと思いました。彼はまたビジネスの観点からも、インスタントラーメンの需要があると感じました。彼はインスタントヌードルを発明する決意をしたのです。

## 単語の小箱

☐ entrepreneur 起業家　☐ apprentice 見習い　☐ capital 資本金
☐ bulk order 大量注文　☐ ingenuity 創造　☐ malnutrition 栄養失調　☐ stall 屋台、露店

## 1-3 大阪

日清食品のカップヌードル、江崎グリコのキャラメルについて

G: After a process of **trial and error**, Andō's instant noodles, named "Chicken Ramen," **were released** on to the market in 1958. Mr. Andō also developed the entire production method. At first they didn't sell well, but became popular because consumers loved the taste and convenience. Above all, they took only two minutes to cook!

T: I'm curious to know when and how cup noodles were developed.

G: Mr. Andō went on an inspection trip to America. He saw how Americans ate noodles by breaking the noodles in half, putting them into a cup, and pouring hot water over them. They also ate the noodles with a fork. Then, he **hit upon the idea of** making cup noodles. Cup noodles made their debut in 1971. They became a big hit and a global food!

T: That's surprising! Mr. Andō got the idea from American consumers!

G: Cup noodles are sold in about 80 countries. Cup noodles are sent to poor countries and **disaster areas** as food aid. Both cup noodles and Mr. Andō have been loved by so many people all over the world. When he passed away in 2007, he received high praise as an inventor and an entrepreneur in an **editorial** in *The New York Times*. The headline was "Mr. Noodle."

T: So, by creating cup noodles, Mr. Andō contributed a lot to people's survival.

G: Right! The founder of Ezaki Glico also had Osaka connections. His son was a **sickness-prone** child. Mr. Ezaki asked the university hospital to **analyze** oyster **broth**, and the analysis showed that it contained about 40% glycogen. After receiving permission from a doctor, he started giving oyster essence to his son. His son gradually became healthier. He hit upon the idea of mixing glycogen and caramel. After a process of trial and error, Mr. Ezaki succeeded in making a nutritious glycogen caramel. He shortened glycogen to "Glico." The Ezaki Glico Company was born.

T: Osaka people are really creative!

G: Exactly! Osaka is the home of many other inventions, too.

G：通訳ガイド　T：観光客

G：安藤氏は試行錯誤の実験の後に、「チキンラーメン」という名の安藤のインスタントヌードルを 1958 年に発売しました。安藤氏が生産方法をも開発したのです。当初、売れ行きは良くなかったのですが、消費者がその味と便利さを絶賛したので人気が出ました。何といっても、ほんの 2 分間で調理できたのですから！

T：いつ、どのようにしてカップヌードルが開発されたかにとても興味があります。

G：安藤氏はアメリカへ視察旅行に出かけたのです。安藤氏はアメリカ人がヌードルを半分に切ってカップに入れてその上からお湯をかけているのを見たのです。またアメリカ人たちはヌードルをフォークで食べていました。それで彼はカップヌードルを作るというアイデアを思いついたのです。カップヌードルは 1971 年にデビューしました。大ヒットし、グローバルフードになりました。

T：驚きました！　安藤氏がアメリカ人消費者からアイデアを得ていたとは！

G：カップヌードルは約 80 か国で販売されています。カップヌードルは貧しい国々や被災地に食料援助として送られます。カップヌードルだけでなく、安藤氏は世界中の多くの人に愛され続けています。2007 年に安藤氏が他界されたとき、『ニューヨークタイムズ』の社説で彼は発明家として、そして起業家として非常に高く評価されました。ヘッドラインは「Mr. Noodle」でした。

T：安藤氏はカップヌードルを発明し、人々の生存に貢献したのですね。

G：その通りです。江崎グリコの創始者も大阪ゆかりの人物です。彼の息子は病気にかかりやすい子供でした。江崎氏は大学病院にカキ汁の分析を依頼し、分析結果からカキ汁には約 40％のグリコーゲンが含まれていることがわかりました。医師から許可を得て、彼は息子にカキのエッセンスを与え始めました。彼の息子は次第に元気になりました。彼はグリコーゲンとキャラメルを混ぜ合わせるというアイデアを思いつきました。試行錯誤の末、江崎氏は栄養価のあるグリコーゲンキャラメルつくりに成功しました。彼はグリコーゲンを短縮して Glico としました。このようにして、江崎グリコ社が誕生したのです。

T：大阪にゆかりのある人は本当にクリエイティブですね。

G：その通りです。大阪はその他多くの物の発祥の地でもあります。

## 単語の小箱

- [ ] trial and error 試行錯誤　　[ ] be released 発売される
- [ ] hit upon the idea of ... …というアイデアを思いつく　　[ ] disaster area 被災地
- [ ] editorial 社説　　[ ] sickness-prone 病気がちな　　[ ] analyze …を分析する　　[ ] broth だし汁

# 1-4 大阪

グリコの看板、カニの看板、大阪弁について

### Pointing at the Glico signboard

G: This is Dōtonbori Street. Please take a look at the Glico **signboard**. This sign is modeled on a famous runner. The catchphrase is "One piece, three hundred meters." If you eat one piece of candy, you can run 300 meters.

T: I see, but I don't want to gain weight, so no thanks (laughing).

G: This phrase means that one piece of candy is very nutritious. The first signboard was put up in 1935, and this 2014 one is the 6th version, with 140,000 LEDs. The **reflection** of the neon lights on the river at night is very beautiful. Some say this area is flashy, but it's a popular place. This is a popular photo spot! Many people **imitate the pose of** the Glico sign like this and take a picture (making a pose). Shall I take your picture?

T: (Laughing) Please do!

G: This bridge was famous as a place where boys picked up girls (laughing).

T: I see. Many young boys and girls are walking around here.

### In front of the crab sign

G: Look at the crab sign.

T: Wow! That's interesting! It's moving its hands and legs!

G: It's inviting customers in by moving its hands. Do you want to try **steamed crab bun**?

T: Wow! I'd love to.

G: Here you go. Try some. How do you like it?

T: Good! It has a real flavor of the sea. By the way, what did you say to the **shop assistant**?

G: I said, "Nanbo desuka?" It means "How much?"

T: Nanbo desuka? How do you say "arigatō" in Osaka dialect?

G: Ōkini! Osaka is a food paradise. It's also a water metropolis. River-cruising is a great way to enjoy Osaka. We don't have time for it today, though.

T: Ōkini for teaching me so many things.

G：通訳ガイド　T：観光客

## グリコの看板を指さしながら

G：これが道頓堀筋です。グリコの看板を見てください。この看板は有名なマラソンランナーをモデルに作られました。キャッチフレーズは「一粒 300 メートル」です。キャラメルを一つ食べたら 300 メートル走れます。

T：なるほど。ですが、私は太りたくないので食べるのをやめておきます（笑）。

G：このフレーズは、キャラメル一つにとても栄養があることを意味しますよ。最初の看板は 1935 年に作られ、現在の看板は 2014 年に作られ 6 代目で、14 万個の LED を使っています。夜にネオンライトがこの川に光るときれいですよ。派手な場所だという人もいますが人気のある場所です。写真撮影に人気のある場所です！　多くの人が看板をまねてこんな感じでポーズをとって写真撮影しますよ。（ポーズを作って）写真を撮りましょうか？

T：（笑って）お願いします！

G：この橋は男の子が女の子をナンパする橋として有名でした（笑）。

T：なるほど。たくさんの若い男の子と女の子が歩いていますね。

## カニの看板の前で

G：カニの看板を見てください。

T：わあ！　面白いですね！　手と足を動かしていますね！

G：手を動かしてお客様を招待しているのですよ。かにまんを食べたいですか？

T：わ〜！　ぜひ食べたいです。

G：どうぞ。お召し上がりください。いかがですか？

T：おいしいです！　海の味がします。ところで店員さんに日本語でなんて話しかけていたのですか？

G：「なんぼですか？」と言いました。「いくらですか？」を意味します。

T：「なんぼですか？」（笑）「ありがとう」は大阪弁で何と言いますか？

G：「おおきに！」です。大阪は食べ物天国です。大阪は水の都でもあります。リバークルーズは大阪を楽しむ素晴らしい方法でもあります。今日は十分な時間がないのですが。

T：たくさんのことを教えてくれておおきに。

### 単 語 の 小 箱

□ signboard 看板　□ reflection 反射　□ imitate the pose of ... …のまねをする
□ steamed crab bun かにまん　□ shop assistant 店員

# 1-5 大阪

天下の台所、大阪・京都・神戸人の比較、文楽とセサミストリートについて

### Looking at various restaurant signs

**T**: This area looks like an amusement park of signboards! There are many good restaurants. I can see why Osaka is called the kitchen of Japan.

**G**: I see what you mean. Rice is Japan's **staple food**. Osaka became the central market for the rice trade in the 18th century. Waterways were developed, so foodstuffs from other areas were brought here, and Osaka **prospered** as a food **distribution center**. Therefore, Osaka began to be called the kitchen of the country. It's said that Osaka people go bankrupt by **overspending on** food, Kyoto people on clothes, and Kobe people on shoes. There's an interesting expression about Osaka: "Kuidaore." It means "Eat until you drop."

**T**: I want to eat until I drop!

### In front of Kuidaore Tarō

**G**: Look at Kuidaore Tarō beating his drum.

**T**: (Laughing) Kuidaore Tarō! The way he moves his eyebrows, eyes, and neck is interesting!

**G**: When I was a child, I used to imitate his way of moving his eyebrows like this (laughing). The **founder** of the restaurant thought that this shop needed a symbol. Osaka **was the birthplace of** Bunraku puppet shows and is still the center of Bunraku. It's said that he hit upon the idea of using a puppet and made it with the help of a Bunraku puppet maker. Kuidaore Tarō is said to be one of the most popular symbols of Osaka. It is said that the producer of Sesame Street got the idea for the Muppets when he saw a Bunraku puppet show.

**T**: That's surprising!

G：通訳ガイド　T：観光客

## レストランのさまざまな看板を見ながら

**T**：この街は看板の遊園地みたいですね。たくさんのいいレストランがありますし。大阪がなぜ天下の台所と呼ばれるのか、その理由がわかります。

**G**：あなたがおっしゃっていることがわかりますよ。お米が日本の主食です。大阪は18世紀に、お米の取引の中心市場になりました。大阪は水路が開発されていたので、ほかの地域からの食料が大阪に集められました。そして大阪は食べ物の流通の中心地として栄えるようになりました。そして天下の台所と呼ばれるようになったのです。大阪の人は食べ物にお金を使いすぎて破産する、京都の人は服に、神戸の人は靴にと言われています。大阪について「食い倒れ」という面白い表現があります。それは「倒れるまで食べる」を意味します。

**T**：倒れるまで食べたいです。

## くいだおれ太郎の前で（文楽とセサミストリート）

**G**：ドラムを叩いている、くいだおれ太郎をご覧ください。

**T**：（笑って）くいだおれ太郎！　彼の眉毛、目、首の動かし方は面白いですね！

**G**：私は子供の頃、この眉毛の動かし方をこんな風にまねたのですよ（笑）。レストランの創始者はこのお店のシンボルが必要だと考えました。大阪は文楽の発祥の地で、今も文楽人形劇の中心地です。彼はこの文楽人形のアイデアを使おうと思いつき、文楽人形のメーカーの助けを得てこの人形を完成させました。くいだおれ太郎は最も人気のある大阪のシンボルの一つだと言われています。セサミストリートのプロデューサーが文楽を鑑賞したときに、マペットを作るアイデアを得たと言われています。

**T**：びっくりです。

## 単語の小箱

□ staple food 主食　□ prosper 栄える　□ distribution center 流通の中心地
□ overspend on ... …を使いすぎる　□ founder 創立者
□ be the birthplace of ... …の誕生の地である

# 1-6 大阪

### 文楽（人形浄瑠璃）、法善寺、たこ焼きについて

T: By the way, what's Bunraku?

G: Bunraku is one of Japan's traditional performing arts. It started in Osaka in the 17th century. It has **been designated as** an **Intangible Cultural Heritage** by UNESCO. One puppet is handled by three people. (Using gestures) The main **puppeteer** controls the head, the upper portion of the body and right hand. His first assistant handles the left hand. His second assistant handles the legs. When I see their movements, I feel as if the puppets are living. It **is accompanied by** a kind of music called "Jōruri." Jōruri is performed by a Jōruri narrator (singer) and a shamisen player. The Jōruri narrator (singer) chants the story in a unique tone. You can enjoy it with an English language earphone guide. The National Bunraku Theater is in this district.

T: I wish I had enough time to see a show.

### Hōzenji Temple and Hōzenji Alley

G: People who come to Hōzenji Temple pray for good fortune by **pouring water** on the statue of Fudō Myō-ō with a **ladle**.

T: Wow! This statue of a god is covered with moss!

G: Water is the source of all life. Fudō Myō-ō always accepts your prayers with his whole body.

T: Great. I'll pour water over it and pray for good fortune.

G: Hōzenji **Alley** is located in the entertainment district; however, this area retains a nostalgic atmosphere. There's a variety of restaurants.

### At a takoyaki restaurant

G: Osaka is the birthplace of takoyaki, **grilled octopus dumplings**. Shall we try some?

T: OK. It's very interesting to watch them making the takoyaki. Their hand movements are so quick. Wow! Here comes the takoyaki!

G: Let it cool down for a couple of minutes. If you want to eat it now, you'll need some water to **put out the flames**. (laughing)

G：通訳ガイド　T：観光客

T：ところで、文楽人形劇とは何ですか？

G：文楽は日本の伝統舞台劇の一つです。17 世紀に大阪で誕生しました。UNESCO
に無形文化遺産として指定されています。人形が３人の人形遣いによって扱われ
ます。（ジェスチャーを使って）主遣いは頭部と体の上部、右手を操作します。
左遣いは左手を、足遣いは足を操作します。私は動きを見て人形が生きているよ
うに感じます。浄瑠璃という名前の音楽が伴奏されます。浄瑠璃は、ナレーター
（歌い手）と三味線を演奏する人によって演じられます。浄瑠璃のナレーターは
独特の節回しで歌います。英語のイヤホンガイドを使って鑑賞できますよ。この
地域に国立文楽劇場があります。

T：鑑賞する十分な時間があればなと思います。

### 法善寺・法善寺横丁で

G：法善寺に来る人は、不動明王像に柄杓（ひしゃく）で水かけして幸運を祈ります。

T：わあ！　この神様のお像はこけで覆われていますね！

G：水はすべての命の根源です。不動明王は全身であなたのことを受け止めてくだ
さっているのです。

T：すごいですね！　水をかけて幸運を祈ります。

G：法善寺横丁は娯楽街の一角にありますが、この地域には昔懐かしい雰囲気が漂っ
ています。いろんな種類のレストランもあります。

### たこ焼き屋で

G：たこ焼き、グリルしたたこの団子は大阪が発祥の地です。たこ焼きを食べましょ
うか？

T：はい。たこ焼きを作る様子を見るのはとても面白いです。手の動きはとても速い
です。わ〜い！　たこ焼きがきました。

G：２、３分冷ましましょう。今食べたいなら、（口の中の）火を消す水が必要です
よ（笑）。

## 単語の小箱

□ be designated as ... …として指定されている
□ Intangible Cultural Heritage 無形文化遺産　□ puppeteer 人形遣い
□ be accompanied by ... …に伴奏がつく　□ pour water 水をかける　□ ladle 柄杓
□ alley 裏通り、路地　□ grilled octopus dumpling たこ焼き
□ put out the flames 火を消す

23

# 1-7  大阪

なんばグランド花月、漫才、吉本新喜劇、健康を増進する笑い、落語について

G: Yoshimoto Shinkigeki comedy shows are performed here 365 days a year. You can enjoy "Manzai" and "Rakugo" story-telling performances here.

T: What's Manzai?

G: Manzai is Japanese comedy, usually performed by two comedians: a **straight man** and a **funny man**. The funny man does stupid things and tells jokes. The straight man **points out** what's strange about the funny man's actions and words. They **throw jokes and puns back and forth** and tell funny stories. Manzai comedians mix their dialog with actions to entertain the audience. They touch or hit each other **affectionately** (laughing). This looks strange to some foreign tourists.

T: I see. In my country, stand-up comedians tend to perform monologues for the audience.

G: Yoshimoto Shinkigeki comedy shows are very interesting to most foreigners, even if they don't understand Japanese. Osaka has produced many popular comedians, probably because Osaka people are straightforward and frank. Also, the Osaka dialect is said to be funny.

T: You're a kind of comedian. You really entertain me a lot.

G: Laughing a lot is good for your health. It'll decrease your stress and **activate your NK cells**!

T: Ōkini. (laughing) I'm lucky to be in Osaka.

G: Next, I'll explain Rakugo. Rakugo is **sit-down comedy**. Rakugo comedians wear traditional Japanese kimono. One person performs two or more different roles by using different voices. They also make gestures; for example, with a folding fan called a "Sensu" and a hand towel. They can be used to represent many things and **stimulate** the audience's imagination. Rakugo comedians talk in the simple language of the common people. Their verbal skills are superb, because it requires years of training to become a professional Rakugo comedian. The number of English Rakugo clubs has been increasing in local communities as well as universities. It improves **interactive skills**.

T: I'd like to try English Rakugo too.

G：通訳ガイド　T：観光客

G：吉本新喜劇コメディショーは1年365日、ここで上演されます。あなたはここで漫才や落語などを楽しめますよ。

T：漫才って何ですか？

G：漫才は日本のコメディーで、たいていはツッコミ役とボケ役の2人で演じられます。ボケ役の人がアホなことをしたり、冗談を言ったりします。ツッコミ役の人がボケ役の人の言葉や行動のおかしな点を指摘します。彼らは、冗談や洒落を飛ばしながら面白い話をします。漫才コメディアンは観衆を楽しませるために会話にアクションをつけます。親しみを込めてお互いに体を触ったり叩いたりします（笑）。これは海外からのお客様の中には不思議に思う方もいらっしゃいます。

T：なるほど。私の国では、スタンダップコメディアンは聴衆に語りかけます。

G：吉本新喜劇は、日本語を理解しない海外のお客様にとっても面白いようです。大阪は多くのコメディアンを生み出しましたが、多分これは大阪の人が単刀直入で率直だからです。また、大阪弁は面白いと言われています。

T：あなたはコメディアンみたいですね。本当にたくさん私を楽しませてくれます。

G：たくさん笑うことは健康に良いです。あなたのストレスを減らしNK細胞を活性化させます！

T：おおきに（笑）。大阪に旅行できて幸せです。

G：次に落語について説明しましょう。落語は座って演じるコメディーです。落語家は日本の着物を着用します。異なった声質を使い、1人で2人以上の役割を演じます。「扇子」という名前の折りたためる、扇と手ぬぐいを使って、ジェスチャーをします。観客の想像力をかき立てるために、扇と手ぬぐいは多くの物の代わりに使われます。落語家は普通に使われている庶民の言葉を使って話します。落語家はプロになるために長年の修行が必要なので、話術に長けています。英語落語クラブが大学でも地域社会でも増えています。落語は対話技術を向上させます。

T：私も英語落語に挑戦したいです。

## 単語の小箱

- □ straight man ツッコミ役　□ funny man ボケ役　□ point out ... …を指摘する
- □ throw jokes and puns back and forth 冗談や洒落を飛ばす
- □ affectionately 親しみを込めて　□ activate *one's* NK cells NK細胞を活性化させる
- □ sit-down comedy 座って演じるコメディー　□ stimulate …を刺激する
- □ interactive skills 対話技術

# 1-8 大阪

 008

道具屋筋、食品サンプル講習会場、黒門市場について

### In front of a food sample shop

G: Dōguyasuji is a 150-meter-long shopping arcade. There are many **specialty shops** which sell cookware, **kitchen utensils**, restaurant supplies, uniforms, shoes, shop signs, curtains, and **paper lanterns**. They developed as **wholesale stores** in the early 20th century.

T: Wow! If I open a Japanese restaurant, I can get everything here!

G: Right! Plastic food sample-making workshops are very popular with foreign tourists. They **convey** Japanese culture to other countries.

T: The food samples in shop windows last for many years, so they **are** not **replaced with** new ones so often. That's why they **came up with** the new idea of offering lessons in order to sell plastic food samples!

G: That's right! You have the potential to become an entrepreneur!

### At a cookware shop, after taking a food sample lesson and buying sushi key chains

G: This is a takoyaki grill. About 70% of Osaka households have one.

T: I'll buy one. I may run a takoyaki restaurant in the future. Nanbo desuka?

### At Kuromon Market, after buying a takoyaki grill

G: Kuromon Market developed as a wholesale market in the early 20th century. It serves as the kitchen of Osaka. There are about 150 shops. About half of them are fresh fish shops. You can buy fresh food from a shop and eat it while walking around, or eat in the eat-in area in the shop.

T: It's really lively! I want to try fresh sashimi, Kobe beef, and fruit.

G: The shop owners' motto is "High quality food, the real thing." We say "Eemon Honmamon" in Japanese.

T: "Eemon Honmamon."

G: (Laughing) Good Osaka-ben! The menus are carefully chosen based on the results of questionnaires given to foreign visitors. A variety of **skewered food** is sold so that they can eat while walking around.

G：通訳ガイド　T：観光客

## 食品サンプル店の前で

G：道具屋筋は 150 メートルのお店のアーケードです。調理器具、台所用品、飲食
店の用具やユニフォーム、靴、お店の看板やカーテン、提灯などの専門店があり
ます。20 世紀初頭にお店は卸売店として発展しました。

T：すごいです！　和食レストランを開くならここですべてが揃いますね。

G：その通りです！　プラスチックの食品サンプルのレッスンは外国人旅行者にも人
気があります。このような講習会は日本文化を外国に伝えます。

T：ディスプレイの食品サンプルは長持ちするので、頻繁に交換されることはないで
すね。だからもっと食品サンプルを売るために講習会をすることを思いついたの
だと思います！

G：いい点をついていますね！　起業家になる素質をお持ちです！

## 食品サンプルのレッスンを受け、すしキーホルダーを購入後、調理器具店で

G：これがたこ焼き器です。大阪の家庭の約 70%の家にたこ焼き器があります。

T：買います。将来、たこ焼き屋さんを経営するかもしれません。なんぼですか？

## たこ焼き器を購入後、黒門市場で

G：黒門市場は 20 世紀初期に卸売市場として発展しました。黒門市場は大阪の台所
の役割を果たします。約 150 店あり、半数は鮮魚店です。お店から新鮮な食べ
物を買って食べ歩きも楽しめますし、お店のイートインスペースでも食べられま
すよ。

T：とても活気づいていますね。新鮮な刺身、神戸牛、果物を食べたいです。

G：店主たちのモットーは「良い品質のもの（食べ物）、本当のもの」です。「ええも
ん、ほんまもん」と大阪弁で言います。

T：「ええもん、ほんまもん」。

G：大阪弁がお上手です！　食べ物は外国人訪問者によるアンケート結果に基づき選
ばれます。食べ歩きできるように多くの串刺しの食べ物が売られています。

### 単 語 の 小 箱

□ specialty shop 専門店　□ kitchen utensil 台所用品　□ paper lantern 紙の提灯
□ wholesale store 卸売店　□ convey …を伝える　□ be replaced with ... …と交換する
□ come up with ... …を思いつく　□ skewered food 串に刺した食べ物

# 1-9 大阪

### 新世界、通天閣、ビリケンさんについて

G: Here we are in Shinsekai. The **National Industrial Exhibition** was held here in 1903. It was similar to the World Exposition. Eight years later, the western part of this area became "Luna Park," which was like a western theme park. This area looked like a "New World," which is "Shinsekai" in Japanese. Please look at the Tsūtenkaku. The first Tsūtenkaku was completed in 1912 and was the highest building in the Orient. The Tsūtenkaku was modeled on the Eiffel Tower. Many people **looked up to** western countries and loved the Tsūtenkaku. Unfortunately, however, it **caught fire** in 1943 during World War II and **was torn down**. The second Tsūtenkaku was built in 1956. The present one was renovated in 2017. The Tsūtenkaku is a nostalgic symbol of Osaka.

**Looking at the Billiken on the 5th floor of the Tsūtenkaku**

G: What do you think this is?

T: It looks like a little smiling monster, but it's a cute god, right?

G: This is the god "Billiken." The Billiken appeared in a famous American artist's dream, and she believed he was a god and created a statue of him. The Billiken became popular all over the world, and was imported into Japan. It's said if you gently **stroke** the sole of his foot, you'll get good luck.

T: Why the sole of his foot?

G: Probably because he can't **scratch** it by himself.

T: That makes sense (laughing).

G: As the god of happiness, Billiken was displayed at the entrance on the first floor, but customers did not like its appearance and the number of visitors decreased. Next, the statue was moved to the second floor, but it was unpopular and was eventually moved to the observatory on the fifth floor. Since then, it has been attracting many people and bringing them good luck. The right god in the right place!

G：通訳ガイド　T：観光客

G：ここは新世界です。内国勧業博覧会が 1903 年に開催されました。それは万博の
　　ような博覧会です。8 年後、西側のこの地域はルナパークという名前のテーマパー
　　クのような公園になりました。この地域は New World、つまり「新世界」のよ
　　うに見えました。通天閣をご覧ください。最初の通天閣は 1912 年に完成し東洋
　　一の高さでした。通天閣はエッフェル塔を模して造られました。多くの人は西洋
　　に憧れ、通天閣を愛しました。しかしながら、残念なことに第二次世界大戦中の
　　1943 年に通天閣は燃え、解体されました。2 代目の通天閣は 1956 年に建てら
　　れました。現在の通天閣は 2017 年に改装されたものです。通天閣は昔を思い出
　　させる大阪のシンボルです。

### ビリケンを通天閣の 5 階で見ながら

G：これは何だと思いますか？

T：ほぼ笑む妖怪のように見えますが、かわいい神様ですよね？

G：これはビリケン神です。ビリケンさんは有名なアメリカ人アーティストの夢の中
　　に現れ、彼女はそれを神様だと信じて作ったのです。ビリケンさんは世界中で人
　　気が出て、日本に持ち込まれました。ビリケンさんの足の裏を優しくなでたら、
　　幸運が訪れると言われています。

T：なぜ、足の裏なのですか？

G：おそらく、自分自身で足の裏をかくことはできないからでしょう。

T：理にかなっていますね（笑）。

G：幸福の神として、ビリケン像は 1 階の入り口に飾られたのですが、ビジターが独
　　特の風貌が気に入らなく客足は減りました。次に 2 階に移されたのですが不評で、
　　結局 5 階の展望台に移されました。それ以来、この像は多くの人々を引きつけ、
　　幸運をもたらしています。適材適所の神様です！

## 単語の小箱

□ National Industrial Exhibition 内国勧業博覧会　□ look up to ... …に憧れる
□ catch fire 火事になる　□ be torn down 壊される　□ stroke …をなでる
□ scratch …をかく

29

# 1-10 大阪

名物串カツ、ミックスジュース、たこ焼き、お好み焼きについて

### In a kushikatsu shop

G: Kushikatsu is deep-fried food on skewers. You can choose from many kinds of **ingredients**, such as meat, onions, mushrooms, seafood, and rice cakes. You have to share the sauce for it with the person sitting next to you. Please don't dip your food in it twice. It's not **hygienic** to dip after **taking a bite**. If you want more sauce, scoop some up with the cabbage and put it on your kushikatsu.

T: OK! My mouth is watering! (laughing)

### At a shop famous for mixed juice

G: Osaka is the birthplace of mixed juice. One fruit shop owner hit upon the idea of making mixed fruit juice from **overripe** fruit. Banana-based mixed juice is the most popular.

T: Great! Osaka merchants are so clever! Overripe fruit is delicious, but can't be displayed in shops. Osaka merchants waste nothing. They seem to use everything **efficiently**.

G: That's a good point! It's said that overripe bananas are good for your health because they reduce your stress and improve **blood circulation**.

T: Wonderful! Mixed juice may have a lot to do with Japanese people's **longevity**! I'll eat a banana every day. By the way, please tell me how to make takoyaki because I bought a takoyaki grill.

G: Mix **flour**, water, and eggs in a bowl. Pour the mix into the holes on the takoyaki grill until they are full. Add octopus, red ginger, and green onion. Keep turning them over until they are round and brown all over.

T: It's delicious! How did okonomiyaki and takoyaki become popular in Osaka?

G: After World War II, rice shortages in Japan continued, so America sent large quantities of wheat flour to Japan. Osaka people are creative and came up with various kinds of dishes by using flour. Okonomiyaki and takoyaki are two examples. They have been popular because they are delicious, cheap, easy to make, and fill you up.

G：通訳ガイド　T：観光客

## 串カツ屋で

G：串カツは串揚げです。肉、玉ねぎ、シイタケ、海鮮類、おもちなどから具材を選べます。ソースは隣に座っている人と共有しなければなりません。2回つけないでくださいね。一口食べた後でつけるのは衛生上よくないです。もし、もっとソースがほしければ、キャベツですくって串カツにつけてください。

T：はい！　よだれが出そうです。

## ミックスジュースが有名なお店で

G：ミックスジュースの発祥地は大阪です。ある果物店の店主が熟しすぎた果物を使ってミックスジュースを作ることを思いつきました。バナナをベースとしたミックスジュースが一番人気があります。

T：すごいです！　大阪商人は賢いです！　熟しすぎた果物はおいしいですが、お店では陳列できません。大阪商人は何も無駄にはしません。いろんな物を有効利用しますね！

G：良い点をついていますね。熟しすぎたバナナはストレスを減らし、血行を良くするので健康に良いと言われています。

T：素晴らしいです！　ミックスジュースは日本人が長寿であることと関係があるかもしれませんね。毎日バナナを食べますよ！　ところで、たこ焼き器を買ったので、たこ焼きの作り方を教えてくれませんか？

G：ボウルの中で小麦粉と水と卵を混ぜ合わせてください。たこ焼き器の穴に混ぜ合わせたものをいっぱいになるまで入れてください。たこと赤いショウガと青ネギを加えて、丸く茶色になるまでひっくり返します。

T：おいしいですよね！　お好み焼きやたこ焼きが大阪で人気になったきっかけは？

G：第二次世界大戦後、日本では米不足が続き、アメリカが小麦粉を大量に日本に送りました。大阪人はクリエイティブで、小麦粉を使ってさまざまなアレンジ料理を作りました。お好み焼きやたこ焼きはその一例です。おいしくて安く簡単に作れて、おなかいっぱいになるので人気があります。

## 単語の小箱

□ ingredient 素材　□ hygienic 衛生的な　□ take a bite 一口かじる
□ overripe 熟しすぎた　□ efficiently 効率的に　□ blood circulation 血液の循環
□ longevity 長寿　□ flour 小麦粉

## 瞬間英作文

**1.** 大阪は水路の大きなネットワークで有名でした。

**2.** 大阪の人たちは高速道路や通りを造るために水路を埋め立てました。

**3.** 大阪の人は企業心に富んでいると言われ、大阪は多くの起業家を生み出しました。

**4.** 松下幸之助は多くの製品を発明し、自社を世界的に有名なパナソニックへと発展させました。

**5.** 松下幸之助は、織田信長のように「起業家」で、豊臣秀吉のように「事業家」で、徳川家康のように「真の経営者」でした。

**6.** 大阪の人は食べ物にお金を使いすぎて破産すると言われています。

**7.** 大阪は、たこ焼き、ミックスジュース、回転ずし、カップヌードル、レトルトカレーの発祥の地です。

**8.** カップヌードルは貧しい国々や被災地に食料援助として送られます。

**9.** 文楽人形劇は UNESCO に無形文化遺産として指定されています。

**10.** セサミストリートのプロデューサーが文楽を鑑賞したときに、マペットを作るアイデアを得たと言われています。

**11.** たくさん笑うとストレスを減らし、NK 細胞を活性化させます。

**12.** ビリケンさんの足の裏を優しくなでたら、幸運が訪れると言われています。

---

1. waterway 水路　　2. fill in ... …を埋め立てる　　3. enterprising 企業心に富んでいる
4. expand A into B A を B へ発展させる　　5. entrepreneur 起業家
6. overspend on ... …にお金を使いすぎる　　7. heat-and-eat curry レトルトカレー
8. disaster area 被災地　　9. be designated as ... …として指定される
10. get the idea for ... …のアイデアを得る　　11. activate …を活性化させる
12. stroke …をなでる

解 答 例

1. Osaka was famous for its great network of **waterways**.

2. Osaka people **filled in** the waterways to build highways and streets.

3. Osaka people are said to be **enterprising**, and Osaka has produced many entrepreneurs.

4. Kōnosuke Matsushita invented many products and **expanded** his company **into** the world-famous Panasonic.

5. Kōnosuke Matsushita was an "**entrepreneur**," like Nobunaga Oda, a "businessperson," like Hideyoshi Tokugawa, and a "true manager," like Ieyasu Tokugawa.

6. It's said that Osaka people go bankrupt by **overspending on** food.

7. Osaka is the birthplace of takoyaki (grilled octopus dumplings), mixed juice, conveyor-belt sushi, cup noodles, and **heat-and-eat curry.**

8. Cup noodles are sent to poor countries and **disaster areas** as food aid.

9. Bunraku puppet theater has **been designated as** an Intangible Cultural Heritage by UNESCO.

10. It is said that the producer of Sesame Street **got the idea for** the Muppets when he saw a Bunraku puppet show.

11. Laughing a lot will decrease your stress and **activate** your NK cells.

12. It's said if you gently **stroke** the sole of Billiken's foot, you'll get good luck.

# 玉虫の宝庫

## 1 エネルギッシュな街、大阪を感じてもらおう

❶ 水の都だった大阪、水路を開拓し拡大した大阪の街、フロンティアスピリットを説明。

❷ 起業家、大阪発祥の物を通してフロンティアスピリットを説明。

❸ 道頓堀は文楽およびお笑い劇の発祥の地で、劇場が集まり歌舞伎や文楽が演じられ、日本のブロードウェイと呼ばれていたことを説明。

## 2 通訳ガイドからのアドバイス

### アドバイス1　お客様の祖国との共通点を準備すると話が弾む！

イギリスのお客様なら、関西国際空港がロンドンの高層ビル The Shard と同じ建築家 Renzo Piano によってデザインされたことを話します。The Shard is an 87-story building and is the highest in Europe.（87 階建ての西ヨーロッパで一番高いビルだ）と話が弾みますよ。

### アドバイス2　大阪弁や日本語をリズミカルに伝授！

このダイアローグでは、「もうかりまっか（Are you making money?）」、「ボチボチでんな（So-so）」、「おおきに（Thanks）」、「なんぼでっか（How much?）」を例に挙げましたが、その他、「アカン（No way または No good）」などを教えてあげると喜ばれますよ。また、日本語の簡単な挨拶、（こんにちは、ありがとう）なども明るく教えてあげると楽しい雰囲気を作れます。

### アドバイス3　チャレンジ精神旺盛な大阪・松下幸之助氏

海に近く川が多い大阪に運河や橋を造り、"Water Metropolis" を生み出した大阪の人々。Osaka people are willing to take on challenges!（大阪の人々は進んで挑戦します）の精神を伝えましょう。大阪ゆかりの人を紹介し、カップヌードルはカップヌードルミュージアムで、江崎グリコは通天閣に行く前に予習しましょう。話のネタとしても覚えましょう。また、パナソニックを世界企業へと発展させた松下幸之助氏は、次の項で紹介する織田信長の「企業家」、豊臣秀吉の「事業家」、徳川家康の「真の経営者」の三役を成し遂げた人です。

**アドバイス4** テーマパークのように明るく楽しく！

人形浄瑠璃は、国立文化劇場で時間があればぜひ観劇していただきたいもの。セサミストリートのプロデューサーが文楽を鑑賞し、マペットを作るアイデアを得ました（p. 20参照）。看板の遊園地とも呼ばれているので、テーマパーク感覚で楽しんでもらいましょう。

**アドバイス5** 世界で初めて作られたものが多い大阪！　ターミナルデパートも世界初！

Ichizō Kobayashi, the founder of the Hankyū Railway Corporation, opened the world's first railway terminal department store, Hankyū Department Store. Mr. Kobayashi also founded the all-female Takarazuka Revue in Takarazuka, on the Hankyū Line. He succeeded in increasing the number of passengers. Conveyor-belt sushi, cup noodles, and heat-and-eat curry were created in Osaka.

阪急電鉄の創始者の小林一三氏は世界初の阪急ターミナルデパートを設立しました。小林氏は、阪急沿線の宝塚に女性だけの宝塚歌劇団も設立しました。彼は乗客数を増加させることに成功しました。回転ずし、カップヌードル、レトルトカレーも大阪で作られました。

## 3 通訳ガイド体験日記

◎ **アメリカ人ゲストから教えてもらったこと。**

安藤百福氏が48歳でインスタントラーメンを開発したことを伝えたら、Colonel Sanders founded Kentucky Fried Chicken at the age of 65.（カーネル・サンダースは65歳でケンタッキー・フライド・チキンを創業しました）とのこと。不屈の精神で困難に立ち向かい、成功した話を聞いて共感しました。

## 4 通訳ガイドお役立ち英語表現

◎ **I see what you mean. は相手を否定しない大切な表現。**

p. 20で大阪を下調べしてきたゲストが天下の台所（the kitchen of Japan）の意味をレストランが多いからだと少し間違えて解釈していますが、通訳ガイドは I see what you mean. と天下の台所の本当の意味を説明しています。

# 2-1 大阪城

### 農民出身の豊臣秀吉が大阪城を築いた時代背景について

**G**: Today, we're visiting **Osaka Castle**, which is one of the three most beautiful castles in Japan. Before we get to Osaka Castle, let me tell you something about its history. Hideyoshi Toyotomi completed the original castle tower in 1585, as a base from which to unify Japan.

**T**: Was Hideyoshi the emperor of Japan?

**G**: No, he was a powerful **warlord**. From 1192 to 1867, the samurai, or **warrior class**, controlled the country. The emperor was respected as a god, but was a ruler in name only. Anyway, I'll tell you more about Hideyoshi, who is one of the **three unifiers** of that era. Hideyoshi unified Japan in 1590. He was a poor farmer's son.

**T**: Poor farmer's son? I'm curious to know how Hideyoshi **made his way up in the world** from a lowly position and came to rule over the whole country.

**G**: In the middle of the 16th century, Japan suffered a long series of **civil wars**. It was the "**Age of the Warring States**." Feudal lords who wanted to unify Japan fought against each other. This was a period when just a few lower-class people **overthrew** high-ranking people.

**T**: "The tail wagging the dog" might be a good way to say that.

**G**: Thank you for teaching me an interesting expression! Hideyoshi was a farmer's son in Nobunaga Oda's region. Nobunaga Oda was another of the three unifiers of that era. He **laid the foundation** for the unification of Japan. Hideyoshi started serving Nobunaga as a sandal-bearer. It is said that Hideyoshi warmed Nobunaga's sandals against his chest during a cold winter. Hideyoshi contributed a lot to Nobunaga's victories in battle, so Hideyoshi was greatly trusted by Nobunaga.

**T**: Wow! Hideyoshi was a really loyal retainer of Nobunaga's!

**G**: Hideyoshi was a very good **tactician**, so he led many soldiers and defeated many enemies after Nobunaga's death. Hideyoshi is called the "Napoleon of the Orient."

**T**: I see. Napoleon worked his way up from an **artilleryman** to an emperor who ruled over most of Europe. I'm curious to know what kind of policies Hideyoshi used to unify Japan.

G：通訳ガイド　T：観光客

G：今日は日本三大名城の一つ、大阪城をご案内しますね。大阪城に到着する前に、その歴史についてご説明します。1585 年、豊臣秀吉が天下統一の本拠地として初代天守閣を築きました。

T：秀吉は日本の天皇だったのですか？

G：いいえ、秀吉は権力のある武将でした。1192 年から 1867 年まで、侍階級、つまり、武士階級が日本を支配していました。当時の天皇は神様として尊敬されていましたが、名目上の統治者にすぎなかったのです。戦国の三英傑の一人である秀吉について、もっとお話ししますね。秀吉は 1590 年に天下統一を成し遂げました。秀吉は貧しい農家の息子でした。

T：貧しい農家の息子ですか？　彼が低い地位から、どのように天下統一を成し遂げるようになったかにとても興味があります。

G：16 世紀半ば、日本は長い内戦に見舞われていました。「戦国時代」だったのです。日本を統一したい大名たちが戦っていました。この時代は、ほんの少しの人ですが、下の者が上の者を打ち倒した時代でした。

T：「下剋上」が最もふさわしいかもしれません。

G：面白い表現を教えてくださりありがとうございます！　秀吉は信長の地域に住む農民の息子でした。信長も戦国の三英傑の一人です。信長は日本統一の土台を築いた武将です。秀吉は、「草履取り」から信長への奉公を始めました。寒い冬の間、秀吉は信長の草履を懐に入れて温めたと言われています。秀吉は戦で信長の勝利に大きな貢献をしたので、信長に厚い信頼を置かれていました。

T：すごいですね！　秀吉は信長の忠実な家来だったのですね！

G：秀吉は卓越した戦術家で、信長の死後、多くの兵士を率いましたし、多くの敵を負かしました。秀吉は東洋のナポレオンと呼ばれています。

T：なるほど。ナポレオンは砲兵の身分から、ついにヨーロッパのほとんどを支配する皇帝の座まで上り詰めましたね。私は秀吉が日本を統一するためにどのような政策を用いたかに興味があります。

## 単語の小箱

□ Osaka Castle 大坂城（明治期までは「大坂城」、明治以降は「大阪城」という表記が一般的）
□ warlord 武将　□ warrior class 武士階級　□ three unifiers 三英傑
□ make *one's* way up in the world 出世する　□ civil war 内戦
□ Age of the Warring States 戦国時代　□ overthrow …をひっくり返す、屈服させる
□ lay the foundation 基礎を築く　□ tactician 戦術家　□ artilleryman 砲兵

# 2-2 大阪城

### 太閤検地、刀狩令、お茶会、朝鮮出兵について

G: In the 17th century, farmers **accounted for** about 85% of the total population of Japan. As I explained, Hideyoshi was the son of a farmer, and he understood the strength of farmers when they unite, so he **took** two **measures**. One was a **Land Survey**. Hideyoshi **dispatched** government officials to farming villages to investigate the land area, crop yields, and cultivators of the farms. He also gave farmers the right to own **arable land**. This policy motivated farmers to work hard, and they increased their **yields**.

T: Hideyoshi was a good leader!

G: That's right. On the other hand, farmers had to pay taxes in the form of rice, so they were not able to leave the land.

T: It's a good policy to collect taxes in the form of rice, right?

G: That's absolutely right! The other was the "**Sword Hunt**." Under this policy, farmers had their weapons **confiscated**. Can you guess the purpose of the Sword Hunt?

T: Let me see. To **maintain public peace**?

G: That's right! Firstly, to prevent farmers from **banding together** and **raising rebellions**. Secondly, to prevent farmers from becoming samurai warriors.

T: Hideyoshi didn't want farmers to become warriors, right?

G: That's right. Hideyoshi wanted farmers to engage in agriculture, and he wanted to make a peaceful country. Actually, the Land Survey and Sword Hunt policies promoted a separation between warriors and farmers.

T: Was Hideyoshi popular among farmers?

G: Yes. Hideyoshi liked the tea ceremony very much. He became popular among farmers by inviting not only aristocrats and feudal lords but also farmers to **magnificent** tea ceremonies.

T: I'm surprised to hear Hideyoshi liked the tea ceremony!

G: Hideyoshi was ambitious, and he sent troops to the Korean Peninsula twice, but he died of an illness in 1598 at the age of 62, so the soldiers were called back from Korea.

G：通訳ガイド　T：観光客

G：17世紀、農民は日本の全人口の85%を占めていました。説明した通り、秀吉は農民の息子でした。農民の力が団結すると強いことを知っていたので、2つの方策を実行しました。その一つは検地でした。秀吉は役人たちを農村に派遣し、土地の広さ、生産高、耕作者について調査をさせました。また秀吉は、農民に耕作可能な土地を所有する権利を与えました。この政策は農民に一生懸命に働く意欲を起こさせ、穀物の生産が増加しました。

T：秀吉は素晴らしいリーダーですね！

G：その通りです。一方で農民は、米の年貢負担を義務付けられたので、土地を離れられなくなりました。

T：米の年貢（税）を徴収する良い政策ですね。

G：その通りです！　もう一つの政策は、「刀狩」でした。この政策下では、農民は武器を没収されました。刀狩の目的が何かわかりますか？

T：そうですね。治安を維持するためですか？

G：正解です！　まず、農民がグループを作り一揆を起こすのを防ぐこと。二つ目は、農民が武士になるのを防ぐことです。

T：秀吉は、農民に武士になってほしくなかったのですね。

G：その通りです。秀吉は農民には農業に従事してもらい、平和な国をつくりたかったのです。実際、検地と刀狩の政策は兵農分離につながりました。

T：秀吉は農民に人気がありましたか？

G：はい。秀吉は茶道を好みました。秀吉は盛大なお茶会に、貴族や大名だけでなく農民たちも招待して人気を得ました。

T：秀吉が茶道を好きだったとは驚きました。

G：秀吉は野心家で、朝鮮半島に兵を二度送りました。が、1598年に62歳で病死したため、兵は朝鮮から引き上げてきました。

## 単語の小箱

□ account for ... …を占める　□ take measures 対策を講じる　□ Land Survey 検地
□ dispatch …を派遣する　□ arable land 耕作可能な土地　□ yield 産出高
□ Sword Hunt 刀狩　□ confiscate …を没収する　□ maintain public peace 治安を維持する
□ band together 団結する　□ raise a rebellion 反乱を起こす　□ magnificent 素晴らしい

## 2-3 大阪城

徳川の日本統一、三英傑の表現、秀頼と千姫の結婚、豊臣家の崩壊について

T: I'm interested in the history of Japan after Hideyoshi's death.
G: Hideyoshi's son, Hideyori, was still six years old. Ieyasu Tokugawa, who was Hideyoshi's chief **vassal**, **governed on** Hideyori's **behalf**. Ieyasu Tokugawa wanted to control Japan. Hideyoshi's vassals **split up into** the Eastern Army and the Western Army. There was a battle between the Eastern Army and Western Army called the Battle of Sekigahara. Ieyasu Tokugawa was the leader of the Eastern Army. The Eastern Army won the **decisive battle** in 1600. Ieyasu **was appointed** shogun by the emperor and established the shogunate government in Edo, present-day Tokyo, in 1603.
T: Did that mean Ieyasu Tokugawa controlled Japan?
G: Yes. Let me tell you some famous sayings that describe the characters of the **three unifiers during the Age of the Warring States**. Nobunaga said, "If the cuckoo doesn't sing, I'll kill it." Hideyoshi said, "If the cuckoo doesn't sing, I'll make it sing." And Ieyasu said, "If the cuckoo doesn't sing, I'll wait until it sings."
T: This saying, which shows Hideyoshi's character, reminds me of Napoleon's **words of wisdom**: "Take time to **deliberate**, but when the time for action comes, stop thinking and go in." I'd like to know about the relationship between the Toyotomi and Tokugawa clans after that decisive battle.
G: Ieyasu Tokugawa was still afraid of the Toyotomi clan's power, so he married his 7-year-old granddaughter, Princess Sen, to Hideyoshi's 12-year-old son, Hideyori Toyotomi.
T: A **political marriage** between a 7-year-old girl and a 12-year-old boy?
G: Yes. However, a number of **clashes** led to the **outbreak** of the Summer War in 1615, when Hideyori was 23 years old. The Tokugawa clan defeated the Toyotomi clan and completely destroyed Osaka Castle, the symbol of Toyotomi power.

G：通訳ガイド　T：観光客

T：秀吉の死後の歴史に興味があります。

G：秀吉の息子、秀頼はまだ6歳でした。秀吉の家臣だった徳川家康は、秀頼に代わって政治を行いました。徳川家康は日本を支配したいと思っていました。秀吉の家臣は東軍と西軍に分裂しました。東軍と西軍の間に、関ケ原の戦いと呼ばれる合戦が起こりました。徳川家康は東軍のリーダーで、1600年に天下分け目の戦いで勝利を得ました。家康は天皇から将軍に任命され、1603年に江戸、現在の東京に幕府を設立しました。

T：それは徳川家康が日本を支配したことを意味しましたか？

G：はい。日本の戦国三英傑の性格を表現する言い回しを紹介させてください。信長は「泣かぬなら　殺してしまおう　ホトトギス」と、秀吉は「泣かぬなら　泣かせてみよう　ホトトギス」と言いました。そして、家康は「泣かぬなら　泣くまで待とう　ホトトギス」と言ったのです。

T：秀吉の性格を表したフレーズは、ナポレオンの「じっくり考えなさい。しかし行動する時が来たら考えるのをやめて、進みなさい」という名言を思い出させてくれます。天下分け目の戦い後の豊臣家と徳川家の関係について知りたいです。

G：徳川家康はなおも豊臣家の勢力を恐れていたので、彼の7歳の孫娘である千姫と、12歳になる秀吉の息子、豊臣秀頼を結婚させました。

T：7歳の女の子と12歳の男の子の政略結婚？

G：そうです。しかしながら、いくつかの衝突が原因で、秀頼が23歳の1615年に夏の陣が起こりました。徳川家は豊臣家を負かし、豊臣家の権力の象徴である大坂城を完全に破壊しました。

## 単語の小箱

- □ vassal 家臣　□ govern …を統治する　□ on *one's* behalf …の代わりに
- □ split up into ... …に分かれる　□ decisive battle 天下分け目の戦い
- □ be appointed 任命される
- □ three unifiers during the Age of the Warring Staes 戦国三英傑
- □ words of wisdom 名言　□ deliberate じっくり考える
- □ political marriage 政略結婚　□ clash 衝突　□ outbreak 勃発

# 2-4　大阪城

### 大手門、お濠、石垣、千貫櫓について

T: When was the present Osaka Castle Tower built?
G: Actually, the present Osaka Castle Tower is the third one. The Tokugawa shogunate rebuilt the castle in 1629 as a symbol of their **prestige**. However, the Castle Tower was burned down by lightning in 1665. In 1931, the third Osaka Castle Tower was constructed with the donations of Osaka citizens.

**On their way to the Ōtemon Gate**

G: We are heading to the Ōtemon Gate, the front entrance of Osaka Castle. Before reaching the Ōtemon Gate, please look at the big **moats** and the stone walls. They symbolize the strong defenses of the Tokugawa-built Osaka Castle.
T: Osaka Castle is surrounded by a moat filled with water, so it's difficult for enemies to attack and get inside. Rivers are regarded as natural defenses, right?
G: Absolutely right! The total length of the stone walls is 12 kilometers. Please compare the stone walls on the left of the Ōtemon Gate with those on the right. The stones on the left **were laid** first, and then, 8 years later, the stones on the right were laid **in a** more **orderly fashion**.
T: It shows that the **workmanship** improved a lot.
G: That's absolutely right! The walls are made up of 500,000 to 1,000,000 **granite stones**. The granite stones were carried from **quarries** more than 100 kilometers away.
T: Wow! Amazing!
G: Look at the Sengan-yagura Turret on the left-hand side over there. There are **loopholes** in the turret for shooting at enemies with guns. The Sengan-yagura Turret was built to defend the Ōtemon Gate from the north. The Japanese word "Sengan" means a large amount of money. The turret was a very important **military site**, so it was named Sengan Turret.

G：通訳ガイド　T：観光客

T：現在の大阪城天守閣はいつ建てられたのですか？

G：実は、現在の大阪城天守閣は3代目なのです。徳川幕府は1629年に名声の象徴として城を建て直しました。しかしながら、その天守は1665年に雷で焼け落ちました。1931年、3代目となる大阪城天守閣は市民の寄付金によって再建されました。

## 大手門に向かいながら

G：大阪城の表門である、大手門に向かっています。大手門に着く前に大きなお堀と石垣をご覧ください。徳川が建立した大阪城の防御の強さを象徴しています。

T：大阪城の周りは水で満たされたお堀で囲われていて、敵にとっては攻撃したり、侵入するのが難しいですね。川は自然の防御と見なせますね？

G：まったくその通りです！　石垣の全長は12キロです。大手門の左側にある石垣と右側のものを比べてください。左側の石が先に積まれました。それから、8年後に右側の石垣がより整然と積まれました。

T：施工技術が飛躍的に向上したことを証明していますね！

G：まったくその通りです！　石垣は50万個から100万個の御影石でできています。御影石は100キロメートル以上離れた石切り場から運ばれてきました。

T：わー！　すごいですね！

G：左手向こうの千貫櫓をご覧ください。櫓には敵を鉄砲で撃つための小窓があります。千貫櫓は大手門を北から防ぐために造られました。千貫は日本語で大金を意味します。櫓は非常に重要な軍事施設だったので、千貫櫓と名付けられています。

## 単語の小箱

□ prestige 名声　□ moat 堀　□ be laid 積まれる　□ in an orderly fashion 整然として
□ workmanship 施工技術　□ granite stone 御影石　□ quarry 石切り場
□ loophole 小窓　□ military site 軍事施設

# 2-5 大阪城

家紋、大手門前、大手口枡形の巨石について

### In front of the Ōtemon Gate

G: Here we are at the Ōtemon Gate, which is the main gate to Osaka Castle. Please look at the "**triple hollyhock crest**." This means that the castle was built as a **stronghold** of the Tokugawa government.

T: What is this triple hollyhock crest?

G: Each family has a **family crest**. The emblems for family crests are things like flowers, trees, and insects. The family crest of the Tokugawa is the hollyhock.

### In Ōtemon Square

G: Let me explain the layout of Ōte-guchi Masugata Square. "Masugata" means a square shape in English. Suppose the enemy managed to **get through** the first gate, how would they feel?

T: They would **feel trapped**.

G: If they are attacked from the front, they will find it difficult to advance through the second gate due to this layout. Please look at the Tamon-yagura Turret, which stands on the stone walls. It **was equipped with** a secret **device** to drop **spears** right on to any enemy trying to invade the castle through the gate.

T: I see. This layout prevents the enemy from moving forward.

G: Please look at the three big stones in the wall. The stone in the center is named "Ōte-Mitsuke Ishi." This is the fourth largest stone in the Osaka Castle grounds. On the left-hand side you can find the fifth largest stone, and on the right-hand side you can find the eighth largest.

T: They're so big! I want to see the biggest one.

G: I'll show you that one later as well.

G：通訳ガイド　T：観光客

## 大手門前にて

G： 大阪城の正門である大手門に到着しました。「三つ葉葵の紋」をご覧ください。これはお城が徳川幕府の要塞として建てられたことを意味します。

T： この三つ葉葵の紋とは何ですか？

G： それぞれの家系は家紋を持っています。家紋の模様は、花、木、昆虫などです。徳川家の家紋は葵なのです。

## 大手門枡形にて

G： 大手口枡形の配置について説明させてください。枡形は英語で言うと四角を意味します。敵が最初の門をどうにか通り抜けたとしましょう。彼らはどのように感じるでしょうか？

T： 彼らは罠にはまったと感じるでしょう。

G： 正面攻撃を受けたら、彼らはこの配置のために2番目の門に進むのが難しいと感じるでしょう。石垣の上の多門櫓を見てください。櫓には、門を通って城に侵入しようとする敵をめがけてやりを落とす、秘密の装置を備えていました。

T： なるほど。この配置は敵が前進するのを防ぎますね。

G： 壁の3つの大きな石を見てください。真ん中の石は「大手見付石」と呼ばれています。これは城内で4番目に大きな石です。左側の石は5番目に大きく、右側の石は8番目に大きいです。

T： とても大きいですね！　一番の巨石を見たいです。

G： それも後でご案内しますね。

## 単語の小箱

□ triple hollyhock crest 三つ葉葵の紋　□ stronghold 要塞　□ family crest 家紋
□ get through ... …を通り抜ける　□ feel trapped 罠にはまったと感じる
□ be equipped with ... …が備え付けられている　□ device 装置　□ spear やり

# 2-6 大阪城

西の丸庭園、豊國神社、パワースポット、遠足について

 016

### In front of Nishi-no-maru Garden

G: Nishi-no-maru Garden is known as the second most popular and beautiful place for cherry blossom viewing in Osaka. It is said that Hideyoshi's legal wife, Nene, also known as "Kita-no-mandokoro" lived there. It's no exaggeration to say that Hideyoshi's great success was due to his **devoted wife**, Nene. She is famous for keeping Hideyoshi motivated.

### In front of Hōkoku Shrine

G: Please look at this statue of Hideyoshi Toyotomi. This is Hōkoku Shrine, where Hideyoshi **is enshrined**. This shrine was completed by order of the Meiji Emperor, because Hideyoshi contributed so much to the nation. You can pray at this shrine to get a promotion.

### After purification, going through the Torii, and praying

G: This place is called a "power spot." Power spots are very popular now.
T: What's a power spot?
G: Power spots are places where you can get magical and special powers. Some power spots are close to a river or a waterfall with plenty of clean water. Some old trees and stones have magical powers. Some power spots **are associated with historical figures**. Here Hideyoshi gives us a magical power. I want to get a promotion, so I have a lucky charm in the shape of a **gourd**, which will bring me success.
T: It's cute! Does the gourd have a meaning?
G: Hideyoshi's emblem on the **battlefield** was a gourd. Gourds bring you good luck.
T: I want the same kind of lucky gourd charm. By the way, who are the children wearing yellow caps?
G: They're elementary school children on an excursion. They have **school excursions** in spring and autumn.

G：通訳ガイド　T：観光客

## 西の丸庭園の前で

G：西の丸庭園は、大阪でお花見をする場所として2番目に人気があるきれいな場所です。秀吉の正妻の北政所として知られる寧々が住んでいたと言われています。秀吉が成功を成し遂げたのは、献身的な妻・寧々のおかげだと言っても過言ではありません。彼女は秀吉のやる気を上げ続けたことで有名です。

## 豊國神社の前で

G：この豊臣秀吉の像をご覧ください。ここが、秀吉が祀られている豊國神社です。秀吉が国家に大きく貢献したため、明治天皇の勅令で完成させました。昇進したいならこの神社でお祈りしたらいいですよ。

## お清めをして、鳥居を通り抜けて、お祈りをしてから

G：この場所は「パワースポット」と呼ばれています。今、パワースポットはとても人気があります。

T：パワースポットとは何ですか？

G：パワースポットは不思議で特別なパワーをいただける場所です。パワースポットには、きれいな水の豊富な川や滝に近いところもあります。古い樹木や石には不思議な力があります。 歴史上の人物に関連するパワースポットもあります。ここでは秀吉が不思議な力を与えてくださいます。 私は昇進したいので、成功を運んでくれるヒョウタンの形のお守りを持っています。

T：かわいい！　ヒョウタンには意味があるんですか？

G：戦場での秀吉の印がヒョウタンだったのです。ヒョウタンはあなたに幸運を運んでくれますよ。

T：私もヒョウタンのお守りが欲しいです。ところで、黄色の帽子をかぶった子供たちは誰ですか？

G：遠足の小学生たちです。彼らは春と秋に遠足があります。

## 単語の小箱

□ **devoted wife** 献身的な妻　□ **be enshrined** 祀られる
□ **be associated with ...** …を関連付けられる　□ **historical figure** 歴史上の人物
□ **gourd** ヒョウタン　□ **battlefield** 戦場　□ **school excursion** 遠足

# 2-7　大阪城

桜門、竜虎石、空堀、蛸石、巨石の運び方について

### In front of the Sakura-mon Gate

G: The Sakura-mon Gate is the main gate to the **inner bailey**, called "Honmaru." Sakura means cherry in English. The name Sakura-mon came from a line of cherry trees near this gate during the Toyotomi era. Look at the big stones on both sides of the gate. They are called "Ryūko-ishi," which literally means "Dragon and Tiger Stone." According to **legend**, when it rained, an image of a dragon appeared on the right, and that of a tiger appeared on the left.

T: Does it have any meaning?

G: According to **Feng Shui**, the blue dragon **protects** the east and the white tiger protects the west.

T: I see. I've been wondering why this moat is dry.

G: The reason for this is unclear, but some say the ground was too hard to **dig** down to the groundwater.

### After entering the Sakura-mon Gate

G: Please take a look at this stone, the largest stone in Osaka Castle. It's called the "Octopus Stone" because the pattern on the surface looks like an octopus. It weighs 108 tons! It **is equivalent to** the weight of 90 average-sized cars. Next, please look at the third largest stone, called the "Furisode-ishi," which looks like the long **flowing sleeves** of a kimono. Here's a picture of a Furisode.

T: Very big! By the way, I'm curious to know how the big stones were carried here.

G: They are mainly from islands in the Seto Inland Sea. The transportation of such large stones required many laborers. First, they **quarried** the **massive stone blocks**. Most of them **were** carried to the port, **loaded on to** ships and transported by sea. They were unloaded at the port and transported by special sleds to the construction site. At each stage of the process, special techniques must have been used.

T: Great work!

G：通訳ガイド　T：観光客

## 桜門の前で

G：桜門は本丸への正門です。桜は英語で Cherry を意味します。「桜門」の名前は豊臣時代に門のそばに植えられた桜の列に由来しています。門の両側の大きな石をご覧ください。竜虎石と呼ばれていて、直訳すると「Dragon and Tiger Stone」です。伝説によれば、雨が降る日は右側から竜が、左側から虎が出現したと言われています。

T：それには何か意味があるのですか？

G：風水によれば、青龍は東を守り、白い虎は西を守ります。

T：なるほど。なぜこの堀が空堀なのか不思議なのですが。

G：理由は明らかではないのですが、地面が固すぎて地下水まで掘れなかったと言う人がいます。

## 桜門に入ってから

G：この石をご覧ください。大阪城で最も大きな石です。表面の模様がタコに似ているので、「蛸石」と呼ばれています。重さは 108 トンあります。平均的な車、90台分の重さに相当します。次に 3 番目に大きな石で、着物の長く垂れ下がった袖のように見える「振袖石」をご覧ください。こちらが振袖の写真です。

T：とても大きいですね！　ところで、私は巨石がどのようにしてここに運ばれて来たかに興味があります。

G：石の多くは瀬戸内海の島から運ばれています。このような大きな石の運搬には多くの労働を要しました。最初に、大きな石を切り出します。ほとんどの石は港に運ばれ、船に積まれ、海路で輸送されました。それらは港で降ろされ、特別なそりで建設現場まで運ばれました。各過程で特別なテクニックが使われたに違いありません。

T：すごいですね！

## 単語の小箱

□ inner bailey 本丸　□ legend 伝説　□ Feng Shui 風水　□ protect …を守る
□ dig 彫る　□ be equivalent to … …に等しい　□ flowing sleeves 垂れ下がった袖
□ quarry …を採石場から切り出す　□ massive stone block 大きな石の塊
□ be loaded on to … …へ積み込まれる

## 2-8 大阪城

日本庭園、MIRAIZA、タイム・カプセル EXPO '70 について

### In front of the Japanese garden

G: This Japanese-style garden was created in 1931, when the third Osaka Castle Tower was constructed. Shall I take your picture?

T: Please do! The reflection of Osaka Castle on the pond is beautiful!

### In front of "MIRAIZA OSAKA-JO"

G: This building was constructed in 1931 with donations from the citizens as the headquarters of the 4th Division of the Imperial Japanese Army. After the war, it was used as the Osaka Prefectural Police building, and then renovated and used until recently as the much-loved Osaka City Museum. It was renovated as a **complex** for gift shops, cafes, and restaurants in 2017.

### In front of "Time Capsule Expo'70"

G: **In commemoration of** Expo'70, Panasonic and the Mainichi Newspaper made two **identical** capsules and **buried** them 15 meters beneath this monument. Not only Japanese people but people from all over the world selected 2,098 items, and they **were stored** in a special metal container. The upper capsule is opened at the beginning of every century and the lower one will be opened in 6970, which means 5,000 years after Expo'70.

T: In the year 6970! I hope our Mother Earth will **prosper** and children will be living in peace.

G: That's the hope! The upper capsule was opened in 2000.

T: I'm curious to know what was in the capsule.

G: Various kinds of objects, such as a plutonium atomic clock, a world map, a "Scientific Report for the Future," short essays and paintings by elementary and junior high school students, electrical appliances, etc. The electrical appliances worked fine.

T: It shows the high quality of the time capsule and electrical appliances!

G: That's right. 2,098 items were buried in the hope of **eternal** world peace and prosperity.

G：通訳ガイド　T：観光客

### 日本庭園の前で

G：この日本式の庭園は、1931 年に３代目の大阪城天守閣が建設されたときに造られました。写真を撮りましょうか？

T：お願いします。池に映る大阪城がきれいです！

### ミライザ大阪城の前で

G：この建物は、日本陸軍第四司令部庁舎として市民の寄付を使い、1931 年に建設されました。戦後は大阪府警として使われ、その後に改装され、最近まで大阪市立博物館として親しまれていました。2017 年にギフトショップや喫茶店、レストランなどの複合施設として改装されました。

### タイム・カプセル EXPO'70 の前で

G：1970 年の万博を記念して、パナソニックと毎日新聞社が同じ内容のカプセルを２個作成し、この記念碑の地下 15 メートルに埋めました。日本人だけでなく、世界中の人々が 2,098 個のアイテムを選び、それらは特殊な金属の容器に保管されました。上のカプセルは毎世紀初めに、下のカプセルは、1970 年の万博から 5,000 年後となる 6970 年に開封されます。

T：6970 年にですか？　私は母なる大地が栄え、子孫が平和に暮らしていることを望みます。

G：それが希望なのですよ！　上のカプセルは 2000 年に開封されました。

T：何がカプセルの中に何が入っていたかを知りたいです。

G：プルトニウム原子時計、世界地図、「未来の科学レポート」、小学生や中学生の作文と絵画、電化製品など、さまざまなものです。電化製品は動きましたよ。

T：それはタイム・カプセルと電化製品の高い品質を証明しますね！

G：その通りです。2,098 のアイテムが、永遠の世界平和と繁栄を希望して埋められたのです。

## 単語の小箱

□ complex 複合施設　□ in commemoration of ... …を記念して　□ identical 同じ
□ bury …を埋める　□ be stored 保管される　□ prosper 栄える　□ eternal 永遠の

# 2-9 大阪城

 019

天守閣、鯱(しゃちほこ)、金蔵、金明水、大砲について

### In front of the Osaka Castle Tower

G: Here we are at the Osaka Castle Tower. As I explained, this third Osaka Castle Tower was built with the donations of Osaka people in 1931. It shows that Osaka people loved Osaka Castle and Hideyoshi. This Castle Tower is modeled after Hideyoshi's Castle Tower.

T: Why did Hideyoshi choose Osaka as a place to build a castle?

G: Osaka **faces** the sea and was the gateway to Japan. It's near Kyoto and Sakai, which was **thriving** as a merchant town.

T: He believed that Osaka was an important **stronghold**.

G: Yes. The Castle Tower looks like a five-story structure; however, it has eight stories. The interior has been designed as a history museum. Please look at the upside-down golden creatures on either side of the roof. They have the head of a tiger and the body of a fish. They are called "Shachihoko" in Japanese. It is believed that they protect the building from fire.

T: I see. What's this white building?

G: It's a treasure house. During the Edo era, gold and silver were kept here. The entrance has a triple door, and iron bars were used in the windows so that burglars couldn't break in.

### After passing through the ticket office

T: What are those people looking at?

G: They're looking at the "Kinmeisui" well. There was a legend that Hideyoshi **sank** a large amount of gold in it to **purify** the water, but an **investigation** showed that this well was not made by Hideyoshi, but by the Tokugawa government.

T: What's this big gun for?

G: It was used to **signal noon** in the Meiji era. This gun was very popular among the citizens, and it was nicknamed "The noon Don." The **blank shots** sounded like "Don" to Japanese people (laughing).

T: I'm **relieved** to hear that. The gun looks **scary**.

G：通訳ガイド　T：観光客

## 大阪城天守閣前で

G：大阪城天守閣の前にいます。すでにご説明したように、この3代目となる大阪城天守閣は、大阪の人の寄付で1931年に建設されました。このことは、人々が大阪城と秀吉を愛していたことを意味します。この天守閣は秀吉の天守閣をモデルに造られています。

T：秀吉はなぜお城を建てる場所として大阪を選んだのですか？

G：大阪は海に面し、日本の玄関口でした。京都と、商人の街として栄えた堺のそばに位置します。

T：彼は大阪は重要な拠点だと思ったのですね。

G：はい。大阪城天守閣は5階建てのように見えますが、実は8階建てです。内装は歴史博物館として作られています。屋根の両側にある逆さまの金の生き物を見てください。虎の頭と魚の体を持っています。日本では「鯱」と呼ばれています。城を火事から守ってくれると信じられています。

T：なるほど。この白い建物は何ですか？

G：金蔵です。江戸時代、金と銀がここに保存されました。入口は三重の扉で、鉄格子が窓にはめられているので、泥棒が入り込めません。

## 入場口を通り抜けてから

T：みんなは何を見ているのですか？

G：人々は「金明水」井戸を見ています。水を浄化させるために、秀吉が大量の金を沈めたという伝説がありましたが、調査の結果、この井戸は秀吉によって作られたのではなく、徳川幕府によって作られたことが判明しました。

T：この大砲は何のためにあるのですか？

G：明治時代に、お昼を知らせるために使われました。この大砲は市民にとても人気があり、「お昼のドン」と愛称がつけられました。空砲は日本人には「ドン」と聞こえるのです（笑）。

T：それを聞いて安心しました。大砲は怖く見えましたから。

### 単語の小箱

□ face …に面する　□ thrive 栄える　□ stronghold 重要な拠点
□ sink …を沈める　□ purify …を浄化させる　□ investigation 調査
□ signal noon 昼を合図する　□ blank shot 空砲　□ be relieved 安心する　□ scary 怖い

# 2-10　大阪城

展望台、からくり秀吉、夏の陣、黄金の茶室について

G: Let's take the elevator up to the 5th floor and take the stairs up to the observation deck on the 8th floor.

**On the 7th floor, after enjoying a panoramic view on the observation deck**

G: This diorama contains 19 scenes from Hideyoshi's life. It takes about 20 minutes to watch all the scenes. It's interesting to see Hideyoshi moving around in the miniature scenes.

**After watching the scenes**

T: I'm impressed with Hideyoshi's leadership. No matter who **took on** the repair work for Nobunaga's residence, they made slow progress. But he completed it in a few days by making teams and **allocating** an area **to** each team. He made them compete with each other. He understood the importance of cooperation and competition.

**On the 5th floor**

G: The folding screens showing the "Summer War of Osaka" were made by a Tokugawa supporter. Over here, the main panoramic scenes are shown on the digital screen.

T: What an **intense battle**! You can see how the samurai warriors fought each other. It's sad to see the common people running away.

**On the 3rd floor**

G: This is a full-scale reconstruction of the Golden Tea Room. A typical Japanese-style tea room **is characterized by** its simplicity. This gorgeously decorated tea room expresses Hideyoshi's character.

T: Wow! It's dazzling.

**On the 2nd floor**

G: Please look at the full-size replicas of the golden Shachihoko, crouching tiger, and chrysanthemum crest used on the Castle Tower.

G：通訳ガイド　T：観光客

G：5階までエレベーターを使って上がり、8階の展望台までは階段を使いましょう。

**展望台で全景を楽しんだ後に7階で**

G：このジオラマで秀吉の人生の19の場面を見ることができます。全シーンを見るには約20分かかります。ミニアチュアの風景の中を秀吉が動くのを見るのは面白いです。

**シーンを見た後に**

T：私は秀吉の指導力に感動しました。信長の住居の修理を誰が着手してもなかなか進まなかった。だけど秀吉がチームを作り、各チームに分担した持ち場を割り当てたことで、数日で完了したのですね。秀吉はチームを競争させた。彼は協力と競争の大切さを理解していたことがわかりました。

**5階で**

G：大坂夏の陣図屏風は徳川側の人物によって作られました。こちらで、主なパノラマシーンがデジタルスクリーンで見られます。

T：激しい戦ですね！　武士たちがどのように戦っていたかを見られますね。庶民が逃げている姿を見て悲しいです。

**3階で**

G：これは実物大で復元された黄金の茶室です。典型的な日本の茶室は質素であることを特徴としています。この豪華に装飾された茶室は、秀吉の性格を表しています。

T：わあ、なんてまばゆい！

**2階**

G：大阪城天守閣で使われている、金の鯱と伏虎と菊の紋の原寸大レプリカをご覧ください。

## 単語の小箱

□ take on ... …に着手する　□ allocate A to B　A を B に割り当てる
□ intense battle　激戦　□ be characterized by ...　…を特色とする

## 2-11 大阪城

残念石、刻印石広場、山里、極楽橋について

G: Look at this stone, called "Zannen-ishi," which means "Unfortunate Stone." There are many Zannen-ishi. Stones which **fell down** on the **quarry site** or on their way to the castle were regarded as unlucky, so they weren't used.

T: This stone looks beautiful.

G: Zannen-ishi have cracks, stains, or dents. Only the very best stones were used to construct the Tokugawa-era Osaka Castle. Feudal lords competed to make their laborers carry stones here to show their power. Now, Zannen-ishi are used as art objects in many places in Osaka.

T: We should respect the efforts of laborers!

G: We're in the "Kokuinseki-hiroba," meaning "marked stone square" in the Yamazato-maru. There are about 80 stones, including Zannen-ishi. Some of them **are marked with** the family crests of feudal lords, patterns, or symbols. These marked stones show the **boundaries** of the places to which feudal lords were allocated. If you look closely at the stone walls, you can find them. Also, research on the marked stones shows that they only date from the Tokugawa period. This means the walls were laid from the base up by the Tokugawa government.

T: The stones are silent, but they can tell us about history!

G: Nice! Hideyoshi enjoyed the tea ceremony as well as cherry blossom viewing here. This is a monument to Hideyori Toyotomi and his mother Yodo-dono, who **committed suicide** in this area after the fall of Osaka Castle. They preferred to die rather than be put to shame. Hideyori was the husband of Princess Sen, Ieyasu's granddaughter. Princess Sen was rescued by order of Ieyasu Tokugawa.

T: That's a sad story.

G: Let's cross the "Gokurakubashi," which means Paradise Bridge. The original of this bridge was constructed by Hideyoshi Toyotomi to welcome **envoys** from **Ming China**. It's said that the **European missionaries admired** its beauty, saying, "This is the most luxurious bridge in the world, shining brilliantly." The present one was constructed in 1961.

G：通訳ガイド　T：観光客

G：「不運な石」を意味する「残念石」を見てください。多くの残念石があります。石切り現場で、またはお城に来る途中に落ちた石は不吉だと見なされ、使われませんでした。

T：この石はきれいに見えます。

G：「残念石」はひび割れやしみ、へこみがあったりします。最高級の石だけが、徳川時代の大阪城を築くために使われました。大名たちは権力を誇示するために、競って労働者たちに石をここへ運ばせました。現在、残念石は大阪市内のいろいろな場所でオブジェとして使われています。

T：労働者の努力をリスペクトしなければね！

G：今、私たちは山里丸の「刻印石広場」にいます。残念石を含む、約80個の石があります。いくつかのものには、大名の家紋や文様、記号が刻まれています。これらの刻印石は、大名が割り当てられた場所の境界を示します。注意深く石垣を見ると、刻印石が見つけられますよ。また、刻印石の調査では、徳川時代の石だけが存在していたことが判明しました。これは石垣が基礎から徳川幕府によって築かれたことを意味します。

T：石は黙っているけれども、歴史を語ってくれますね。

G：いいですね！　秀吉はお茶会だけでなく、お花見もここで楽しみました。これは、大阪落城後にこの場所（山里丸）で自害した豊臣秀頼と母の淀殿の記念碑です。2人は辱められるよりも死ぬことを選びました。秀頼は家康の孫娘、千姫の夫でした。千姫は徳川家康の命によって救出されました。

T：悲しいお話です。

G：Paradise Bridge を意味する「極楽橋」を渡りましょう。この橋の初代は、明朝からの使節を迎えるために豊臣秀吉によって建設されました。ヨーロッパの伝道者たちが「鮮やかに輝く世界で一番豪華な橋だ」と言って美しさを褒めたと言われています。現在の橋は、1961年に造られました。

### 単語の小箱

□ fall down 落ちる　□ quarry site 石切り場　□ be marked with ... …の印がついている
□ boundary 境界　□ commit suicide 自殺する　□ envoy 使者　□ Ming China 中国の明
□ European missionary ヨーロッパの伝道者　□ admire …を称賛する

# 2 - 12　大阪城

　022

### 青屋門、鬼門、忍者、アクアライナー、造幣局について

G: This Aoya-mon Gate is located in the northeast of Osaka Castle. According to Feng Shui beliefs, the northeast was considered to be the "Demon Gate." In the old days, this gate was always closed. It was built for defensive purposes.

T: Why was the northeast considered the Demon Gate?

G: It's dark and damp in the northeast, so it was believed that demons might enter from that direction. We don't believe that now, but we try to make the northeast direction clean and beautiful.

T: I see. By the way, I want to know about ninja. I've heard ninja were able to walk on the water.

G: Ninja used a special tool for walking on water, such as moats or rivers. Some people from other countries think ninja still exist, but they don't. Ninja were active during the wars from the middle of the 15th century to the beginning of the 17th century.

T: They **disguised themselves** in black kimono outfits with hoods, right?

G: Right! Ninja **sneaked into** castles in black, hooded kimono outfits. A ninja was a kind of spy who was employed by warriors. The main roles of ninja were **investigating** the enemy's strategies and **assassinating** their leaders. Ninja fought by throwing special knives called "shuriken," shaped like crosses or stars. If you like, I'll take you somewhere where you can play **virtual reality games**.

T: I'd love to. I want to disguise myself as a ninja and play VR games.

### In the "Aqua-Liner"

G: Look at the **Japan Mint**. It is the most popular place for cherry blossom viewing in Osaka. Fifty percent of all Japanese coins are made here. What's the most popular **specialty** of Osaka?

T: (laughing) It's takoyaki!

G: (laughing) It's coins! And Osaka merchants like "**coining money**"!

G：通訳ガイド　T：観光客

G：この青屋門は、大阪城の北東に位置しています。風水によると北東は「鬼門」と見なされていました。昔はこの門はいつも閉ざされていました。防御目的で造られたのです。

T：なぜ、北東は鬼門と見なされたのですか？

G：北東は暗くて湿っているので、鬼がその方向から入ってくるかもしれないと信じられていました。私たちは、今はそのようなことは信じていませんが、北東の方向を清潔で美しくするよう心がけています。

T：なるほど。ところで、私は忍者について知りたいです。忍者は水の上を歩けると聞いたことがあります。

G：忍者は堀や川を渡るときには特別な道具を使っていました。海外から来た方々の中には、忍者がまだ存在すると思っている人もいらっしゃいますが、存在しません。忍者は 15 世紀半ばから 17 世紀初頭の戦いで活動していました。

T：黒いフード付きの着物を身に着け、変装しましたよね。

G：その通り！　忍者は黒いフード付き着物をまとい、お城に忍び込んだのです。忍者はスパイの一種で武将に雇われていました。忍者の主な役割は、敵の戦術を調査したり、敵のリーダーを暗殺することでした。忍者は十字架や星のような形の手裏剣と呼ばれる特別なナイフを投げて戦いました。興味があるなら仮想現実ゲームを楽しめる場所にお連れしますよ。

T：ぜひ、お願いします。忍者に変装して VR ゲームをしたいです。

### アクアライナーの中で

G：造幣局をご覧ください。大阪の造幣局は大阪で一番、お花見で人気があります。日本の硬貨の 50％がここで造られています。大阪で一番人気のある特産品は何ですか？

T：（笑って）たこ焼き！

G：（笑って）コインです！　大阪商人は「お金もうけ」が好きですよ！

## 単語の小箱

□ disguise *oneself* 変装する　□ sneak into ... …へ忍び込む　□ investigate …を調査する
□ assassinate …を暗殺する　□ virtual reality game VR ゲーム　□ Japan Mint 造幣局
□ specialty 特産品　□ coin money 金もうけをする

## 瞬間英作文

1. 初代・大阪城天守閣は、そこから天下を治める本拠地として、1585 年に豊臣秀吉によって築かれました。

2. 貧しい農民の子だった豊臣秀吉は武将となり、1590 年に日本を統一しました。

3. 秀吉は戦術家で、多くの兵士を率い、多くの敵を負かしました。

4. 秀吉の死後、徳川家は豊臣家を打ち破り、豊臣家の権力の象徴としての大阪城を完全に破壊しました。

5. 徳川幕府は 1629 年に名声の象徴として、天守閣を建て直しました。

6. 徳川幕府が建てた大阪城天守閣は、1665 年に雷で焼け落ちました。

7. 大きなお堀と石垣は、徳川が建設した大阪城の防御の強さを象徴しています。

8. 敵陣が大手門の最初の門を突破したとしましょう、敵陣はこの枡形（四角形）の配置のために罠にはまったと感じるでしょう。

9. 多聞櫓には、敵をめがけてやりを落とす装置が備えられていました。

10. 秀吉が国家に大きな貢献をしたので、明治天皇の勅令で豊國神社は完成しました。

---

1. from which ... …から　　2. warlord 武将　　3. tactician 戦術家
4. defeat …を負かす　　5. prestige 名声　　6. be burned down 焼け落ちる
7. moat お堀　　8. get through ... …を通り抜ける
9. be equipped with ... …を備えている　　10. contribute to ... …に貢献する

# 解答例

1. Hideyoshi Toyotomi completed the original Castle Tower in 1585, as a base **from which** to unify Japan.

2. Hideyoshi Toyotomi, a poor farmer's son, became a **warlord** and unified Japan in 1590.

3. Hideyoshi was a **tactician** who led many soldiers and defeated many enemies.

4. After Hideyoshi's death, the Tokugawa clan **defeated** the Toyotomi clan and completely destroyed Osaka Castle, the symbol of Toyotomi power.

5. The Tokugawa shogunate rebuilt the Osaka Castle Tower in 1629 as a symbol of their **prestige**.

6. The Tokugawa-built Osaka Castle Tower **was burned down** by lightning in 1665.

7. The big **moats** and stone walls symbolize the strong defenses of the Tokugawa-built Osaka Castle.

8. Supposing the enemy managed to **get through** the first gate into Ōtemon Masugata Square, they would feel trapped due to this square layout.

9. The Tamon-yagura Turret **was equipped with** a device to drop spears on to the enemy.

10. Hōkoku Shrine was completed by order of the Meiji Emperor because Hideyoshi **contributed** so much **to** the nation.

## 瞬間英作文

**11.** 出世を願うなら、豊國神社でお祈りするといいでしょう。

**12.** 桜門は本丸へ入る正門です。

**13.** 一番大きな石は、表面のしみがタコに似ているので「蛸石」と呼ばれています。

**14.** ミライザ大阪城は、ギフトショップと喫茶店、レストランの複合施設です。

**15.** ３代目大阪城天守閣は、市民の寄付金によって 1931 年に建設されました。

**16.** 大阪人は秀吉を愛し、大阪城は秀吉のものだと信じています。

**17.** 鯱は、虎の頭と魚の体を持ち、建物を火事から守ると信じられています。

**18.** 大阪歴史博物館が、大阪城公園の南西方向にあります。

**19.** 大阪城天守閣は 1997 年に改修されました。

**20.** 2 平方キロメートルに及ぶ大阪城公園をご覧ください。

**21.** 大きなスポーツイベントや大規模なコンサートが開催される多目的ホール、大阪城ホールをご覧ください。

**22.** 秀吉は明朝からの使節を迎えるために、初代・極楽橋を建造しました。

**23.** 大阪城公園では、2 月上旬から 3 月中旬まで約 1,300 本の梅の花が楽しめます。

---

11. rise in society 立身出世する　　12. inner bailey 本丸（内郭）　　13. stain しみ
14. complex 複合施設　　15. donation 寄付　　16. belong to ... …に属する
17. protect A from B　A を B から守る　　18. to the southwest of ... …の南西に
19. be renovated 改修される
20. two square kilometers in size 広さ 2 平方キロメートル　　21. multi-purpose 多目的の
22. envoy from the Ming Dynasty 明朝からの使節　　23. blossom 花

解答例

**11.** You can pray at Hōkoku Shrine if you want to **rise in society**.

**12.** The Sakura-mon Gate is the main gate to the **inner bailey**.

**13.** The largest stone is called the "Octopus Stone" because the **stain** on the surface looks like an octopus.

**14.** MIRAIZA is a **complex** for gift shops, cafes, and restaurants.

**15.** The third Osaka Castle Tower was constructed with the **donations** of Osaka citizens in 1931.

**16.** Osaka people love Hideyoshi, and they still believe Osaka Castle **belongs to** Hideyoshi.

**17.** Shachihoko have the head of a tiger and the body of a fish, and they are believed to **protect** the building **from** fire.

**18.** Osaka History Museum is located **to the southwest of** Osaka Castle Park.

**19.** Osaka Castle Tower **was renovated** in 1997.

**20.** Please look at Osaka Castle Park, which is **two square kilometers in size**.

**21.** Please look at the **multi-purpose** Osaka Castle Hall, where big sporting events and major concerts are held.

**22.** Hideyoshi built the original "Gokurakubashi" to welcome **envoys from the Ming Dynasty**.

**23.** You can enjoy the **blossoms** of about 1,300 plum trees in Osaka Castle Park from the beginning of February till the middle of March.

# 玉虫の宝庫

## *1* 栄華とロマンの大阪城（豊臣秀吉から徳川家康の時代）へ

大阪人にとって、「大阪城」と言えば「太閤さん」つまり、豊臣秀吉です。しかし、大阪城のお堀や見事な石垣は、徳川時代のものです。

❶ **大手門（大阪城の正面玄関）に向かう道**　お堀、石垣、千貫櫓の説明をしましょう。

❷ **大手口枡形**　敵の侵入を防ぐ役割を担います。大手見付け石があります。

❸ **多聞櫓**　土塁や石垣に建てられた長い櫓で、やりを落とす装置を備えます。

❹ **西の丸庭園**　春には桜のお花見で有名。秀吉の正室の寧々（北政所）の話をしましょう。

❺ **豊國神社**　秀吉が祀られていてパワースポットとしても有名で、出世を祈願できます。秀吉の死後、京都に建立され、1961 年に大阪城内に移転されました。

❻ **桜門**　一番大きな石の「蛸石」や、3 番目に大きな石の「振袖石」の説明をします。

❼ **日本庭園**　1931 年の第 3 代大阪城築城の際に造られた写真スポットです。

❽ **ミライザ大阪城**　ヨーロッパ調のビルには興味を持たれる人が多く説明が必要な場合もありますが、レストラン、お土産屋さんの複合施設の説明だけでも OK。

❾ **タイム・カプセル EXPO'70**　興味を持つ人が多いので、カプセルの中に入っている物などを覚えましょう。

❿ **大阪城天守閣前**　3 代目大阪城天守閣は外見は 5 階建てで、内部は 8 階建ての歴史博物館であること、お城を火事から守る「鯱」について説明しましょう。

⓫ **金蔵**　江戸時代金と銀が貯蔵された金庫。興味を持つ人は少ないです。

⓬ **金明水**　大阪城天守閣に入る前に目につくので、のぞきこむ人も多いです。

⓭ **大砲**　「ドン」というニックネームの説明をすると楽しんでもらえます。

**大阪城天守閣内で歴史を楽しもう**

⓮ 8 階までエレベーターで上がって景色を楽しみ、下に降りる。

⓯ 7 階で秀吉の人生の 19 シーンを約 20 分で見る。

⓰ 5 階の「大坂夏の陣図屏風」のスクリーンは、外国人観光客に人気があります。

⓱ 3 階の黄金の茶室で、秀吉の性格を説明するのもよいでしょう。

⓲ 2 階で You can try on a helmet, battle surcoat, or a "komon" kimono and have your picture taken for a fee.（兜、陣羽織、小紋の着物などを着用し、有料で写真撮影してもらえますよ）と写真撮影を勧めると、喜ぶお客様も多いです。

**大阪城天守閣前の残念石を説明し、山里丸の刻印石広場で**

⓳ 残念石が使われなかった理由と有効利用について説明しましょう。

### 山里丸の刻印石広場を見学し、アクアライナーに乗船

⑳ 山里丸の刻印石広場で刻印石の説明をし、徳川時代の石だけが存在し、石垣は基礎から徳川幕府によって築かれたことがわかったことを説明しましょう。
㉑ 秀吉が山里丸でお茶会を楽しんだ話や、歴史に興味がある人なら秀頼と千姫の話、大阪落城後に自害した秀頼と母の記念碑の話、自害が美徳の時代について説明しましょう。
㉒ 秀吉が明朝からの使節団を迎えるために造った極楽橋について説明しましょう。極楽橋は大阪城天守閣を撮影する絶好のスポットです。
㉓ 青屋門と鬼門の位置の関係について説明しましょう。
㉔ アクアライナーに乗船し、造幣局本局の説明などをします。

## 2 通訳ガイドからのアドバイス

### アドバイス1　旅の思い出は楽しく
歴史的人物の話、巨大石や堀の話など、話題たっぷりの大阪城ですが、景色を楽しみに来ている人も多いですし、遠足の生徒を喜ぶ人、豊國神社の前での花嫁姿に感動する人などさまざまです。臨機応変に応対しましょう。

### アドバイス2　豊臣秀吉は東洋のナポレオン
Napoleon worked his way up from an artilleryman to an emperor who ruled over most of Europe.（ナポレオンは砲兵の身分から、ついにヨーロッパのほとんどを支配する皇帝の座まで上り詰めましたね）と世界的な歴史上人物と比べることで一層興味を引きます。

### アドバイス3　織田信長、豊臣秀吉、徳川家康の三英傑について説明できるように

#### ●織田信長　楽市楽座・鉄砲とキリスト教の伝来
織田信長は**日本の統一の基礎**を作った**歴史的な人物**です。信長は1534年に貧しい大名の子供として生まれました。しかし、多くの戦に勝利し、近隣を支配し、室町幕府を倒して英雄となりました。**彼は何事も行動に起こすのが早かったのです。**彼は新しい考えや政治機構を取り入れました。例えば、**自由市場政策**を採用しました。この制度のおかげで商業が発達しました。**彼はシーザーとよく比較されます。**
信長の時代の歴史的背景について説明させてください。**1543年、ポルトガル人が日本に鉄砲**を伝えました。**フランシスコ・ザビエルは1549年にキリスト教を伝えました。**信長は生まれながらに戦略力を持っていました。彼は戦で鉄砲を巧みに使い、

敵を次から次へと負かしました。彼はキリスト教を保護したので、新しい文化が伝来しました。また、ポルトガルとスペインとの貿易も発展しました。

### 英訳

Nobunaga Oda was a **historical figure who laid the foundation** for the unification of Japan. Nobunaga was born in 1534, the son of a poor feudal lord. However, Nobunaga became a hero by winning many battles, dominating the neighboring provinces, and defeating the Muromachi shogunate. **He was quick to take action in everything.** He introduced new ideas and political structures. For example, he introduced a **free market policy**. Thanks to this policy, commerce developed. **He is often compared to Julius Caesar.**

Let me explain the historical background to Nobunaga Oda's age. **The Portuguese introduced guns to Japan in 1543. Francis Xavier introduced Christianity to Japan in 1549.** Nobunaga was gifted with strategic ability. He made good tactical use of guns in his battles and defeated his rivals. As Nobunaga protected Christianity, a new culture was introduced. Also, trade with Portugal and Spain developed.

### ●徳川家康公　260年にわたる平和な時代を築く

徳川家康は1603年に将軍の称号を受け、江戸に幕府を開きました。幼少の頃より家康は**人質**として苦労を経験していたので、戦争の怖さを知っていました。試練を乗り越えたその生き方は、何世紀のもの間、人々を感動させています。家康は忍耐の人だったので、**多くのビジネスリーダーは彼を尊敬しています**。家康は豊臣の重臣でしたが、豊臣家を滅ぼし、1615年に日本を統一しました。

家康の支配下で「武家諸法度」が制定され、それは平和な時代を築く助けとなりました。家康は多くの忠実な家臣に恵まれていました。このことは、彼が大成功を収めた理由の一つです。彼の大きな業績は、260年にわたる平和な時代を築いたことでした。世界遺産に指定されている日光東照宮は、徳川家康を祀っています。

### 英訳

Ieyasu Tokugawa received the title of shogun in 1603 and established his government in Edo. Ieyasu had spent his childhood as a **hostage**, experienced hardships, and knew the terror of war. The way he survived his trials has impressed Japanese people for centuries. Ieyasu was a man of endurance, so **many business leaders respect him**. Though Ieyasu was a chief vassal of Toyotomi, he defeated the Toyotomi clan and unified Japan in 1615.

Under Ieyasu's rule, "Samurai Laws" were enacted, and this helped to establish a new era of peace. Ieyasu had many loyal retainers, which is one of the reasons he was so successful. His main accomplishment was a 260-year-long age of peace. Nikkō Tōshōgū Shrine, which is designated as a World Heritage Site, is dedicated to Ieyasu Tokugawa.

## アドバイス4　将軍とは？　「秀吉公は将軍ではなかった」にゲストは驚く

"Shogun" was originally a title given by the emperor to the supreme commander of an expeditionary army. Hideyoshi Toyotomi was not a shogun, but a chief advisor to the emperor.（将軍とは、元は天皇が遠征軍の総司令官に与える称号でした。豊臣秀吉は将軍ではなく、関白でした）と説明しましょう。さらに、In the Edo era, it became an official title given by the emperor to the top administrator of the country. This shogunate system lasted until 1867.（江戸時代には、天皇が国の首席行政官に与える正式な称号になりました。将軍制度は1867年まで続きました）も説明しましょう。

## アドバイス5　柔道や空手を見学できる！

豊國神社のそばに修道館があります。A Shūdō-kan is a hall where people practice martial arts, such as Judo and Kendo.（修道館で人々は柔道や剣道の武芸の練習をしています）と紹介しましょう。外からでも見ることができます。

## アドバイス6　豊臣秀吉時代の石垣公開施設は、大阪人が秀吉を愛している証明！

豊臣家の大坂城は、徳川幕府がその上に城を再建したときに地下深く埋められてしまいました。残念なことに、豊臣時代の石垣も見ることができません。栄華を誇った豊臣時代の大坂城の石垣は掘り起こされ、展示される予定です。この施設では、大阪城の本物の歴史と文化を体感できます。

Hideyoshi Toyotomi's Osaka Castle was buried deep underground when the Tokugawa shogunate rebuilt the castle on top of it. Unfortunately, not even the stone walls of the Toyotomi-era castle remained visible. So, these walls from the prosperous Toyotomi period were excavated and are going to be exhibited. At this facility, visitors can experience the real history of Osaka Castle.

## アドバイス7　ジョークも入れて楽しく！

アクアライナーに乗船すると必ず造幣局（Japan Mint）の前を通ります。The most popular specialty of Osaka is coins!（大阪の特産品は硬貨です）の説明は、大阪が商人の街であることを説明するフレーズでもあります。

# 3 通訳ガイド体験日記

## ◎武士が発生した理由がうまく答えられなかった。

諸説ありますので、次のように説明しましょう。

①都は貴族に支配されていました。一方、10世紀から11世紀にかけて、律令体制が崩壊しました。地方では、有力な農民たちがさらに多くの土地を所有し、力を持つようになりました。治安は悪くなり、犯罪も増加したので、有力な農民たちは自分たちの土地を守るために武装しました。これが武士の始まりです。

The capital was controlled by aristocrats; on the other hand, from the 10th to the 11th century, the Ritsuryō (law and order) system declined. Influential farmers became more powerful by getting more land in the provinces. Public order worsened, and the number of crimes increased. Major farmers armed themselves to protect their own land. This is the origin of the samurai.

②都には、武道に従事して、朝廷や貴族に仕える下級貴族たちがいました。武力に優れた人は、都から地方に派遣されました。派遣された後、彼らは独自の勢力を築き、武士になることもありました。

In the capital, there were low-ranking nobles who were engaged in the martial arts and served the imperial court and the nobility. People with superior military abilities were dispatched from the capital to the provinces. After they were dispatched, they sometimes built up their own power and became samurai warriors.

## ◎大阪城天守閣の外壁の桐のレリーフと菊紋について、曖昧な答えをした。

いつも鯱の説明しかしないのですが、お客様から桐のレリーフについて聞かれたので、豊臣家（秀吉）の紋だと答えました。菊紋については、天皇家の家紋と答えました。今では次のようにお伝えしています。

The chrysanthemum and paulownia family crests were originally emblems of the imperial family. Both the chrysanthemum and paulownia crests were given to Hideyoshi by the imperial court. This means that Hideyoshi was greatly trusted by the emperor. Until the Edo era at the beginning of the 17th century, distinguished people were sometimes given two family crests.

菊と桐の家紋は、元は天皇家の紋章です。これらの紋は、朝廷から秀吉に与えられたものです。これは秀吉が天皇から厚い信頼を得ていたことを意味します。江戸時代の17世紀初頭まで、名士には家紋が2つ与えられることがありました。

### 参考 1
大阪城の正門大手門には、徳川家の家紋の葵の紋があります。見えにくいですが、お客様には説明しています。

### 参考 2
家紋については、次のように説明しましょう。
Each family has a family crest. Japanese people worship nature, so the signs used in family crests are usually flowers, trees and insects. By looking at a family crest, you can tell what someone's origins are.
それぞれの家系には家紋があります。日本人は自然を崇拝しているので、家紋には主に花、木、昆虫などが使われます。家紋を見ると、その人の家系がわかるのです。

◎「なぜ大阪城天守閣の外壁に虎のレリーフがあるの？」と聞かれ、西を守るからとしか答えらえなかった。

秀吉は虎をたいへん好きだったと言われています。虎は強じんな生命力を持っており、「一日にして千里を行き、千里を帰る」と言われます。厄を払い、家運隆盛を導くとも言われ、魔よけの意味合いで描かれます。秀吉は長生きするために、虎の脳みそを食べていたという人もいます。

It is said that Hideyoshi loved tigers. Tigers have a strong life force, so it is said that they "go a thousand miles and return a thousand miles in one day." Also, the tiger is said to ward off evil and bring prosperity to the family. It is depicted as a protection against evil. Some say that Hideyoshi liked to eat tiger brains for longevity.

◎天守閣5階で夏の陣の模型を見た際、ミニチュアの兵士が担ぐ大きな袋（母衣）について質問されたが答えられなかった。

Why are some warriors wearing red balloons on their backs?（なぜ兵士たちは赤い風船を背負っているのですか？）のという質問に対しては、The warriors are wearing balloons, called "Horo," to protect themselves from attacks by archers.（侍たちは弓兵による攻撃から身を守るために、母衣と呼ばれる赤い風船を着用しています）と答えましょう。

## 4 通訳ガイドお役立ち英語表現

Let me get back to my story. には注意が必要です。相手が話題を変えて質問してきたときに何度も使ったことがありますが、少し横柄に聞こえることもあるので気をつけましょう。

# 3-1 住吉大社

### 神道、住吉大社の歴史、海の神様、遣唐使について

**G**: Before we arrive at Sumiyoshi Taisha, let me explain about Shinto. Shinto is Japan's native religion, and there is no founder. Shinto doesn't have any **scriptures**, either. It is believed that **deities** live in many **objects**, such as mountains, rocks, **gorges**, seas, ponds, rivers, and trees. There are myriads of Shinto deities. These deities **are worshipped** at shrines.

**T**: I see. So it's nature worship, right?

**G**: Yes. Let me explain about Sumiyoshi Taisha. It is said that **Empress** Jingū **founded** Sumiyoshi Taisha in 211 to **enshrine** three sea deities to give thanks for their help.

**T**: Sea deities?

**G**: Yes. The three sea deities are believed to have appeared from the ocean and helped Empress Jingū to **conquer** a part of Korea, so Sumiyoshi Taisha **is revered** as a miraculous shrine among voyagers and fishermen. They are also called "the deities of safety at sea." People used to pray in Sumiyoshi Taisha for the safety of their voyages on **missions to Tang Dynasty China**.

**T**: I see. So the sea deities protected people who traveled to Tang Dynasty China by ship?

**G**: Exactly. Sumiyoshi Taisha is the most popular shrine in Osaka. At the beginning of every year, more than two million **worshippers** visit Sumiyoshi Taisha to **pray for health and prosperity**. Osaka people **affectionately** call it "Sumiyoshi-san." Japanese people put "san" at the end of the name when we **address** someone.

**T**: Please call me Betty-san!

**G**: OK, Betty-san.

### In front of a Torii

**G**: Here we are in front of a shrine gate, called a "Torii." Sumiyoshi Taisha faces west, because the sea deities are enshrined here and Osaka Bay is to the west of Sumiyoshi Taisha.

G：通訳ガイド　T：観光客

G：住吉大社に到着する前に、神道について説明させてください。神道は日本固有の宗教ですが、創始者がいません。神道には経典もありません。神様が山、岩、渓谷、海、池、川、木など、多くのものに住んでいると信じられています。八百万（やおよろず）の神様がいらっしゃいます。神様は神社にお祀りされています。

T：なるほど。自然崇拝ですね。

G：そうです。住吉大社について説明させてください。211年、神功皇后（じんぐう）がその加護に感謝するために、3柱の海の神様をお祀りして創建されたという言い伝えがあります。

T：海の神様ですか？

G：はい。海の神様3神が海から出現し、神功皇后が朝鮮の一部を征服するのを加護したと信じられていますので、住吉大社は航海者や漁師の間で霊験あらたかな神社として崇敬されています。海の神様は「航海の安全の神様」とも呼ばれています。遣唐使としての航海の安全を、住吉大社にご祈願したものでした。

T：なるほど。海の神様は唐に航海した人々を守ってくださったのですね？

G：その通りです。住吉大社は大阪で一番人気のある神社です。毎年、年始めには200万人の参拝者が、健康と繁栄をお祈りするために住吉大社を訪れます。大阪の人は、親しみを込めて「住吉さん」と呼びます。日本人は人の名前を呼ぶとき、名前の最後に「さん」を付けます。

T：Betty さんと呼んでくださいね。

G：OK、Betty さん。

**鳥居の前で**

G：今、私たちは「鳥居」と呼ばれる神社の門の前にいます。住吉大社は西を向いています。というのも、ここには海の神様が祀られていて、大阪湾は住吉大社の西にあるからです。

## 単語の小箱

□ scripture 経典　□ deity 神　□ object 物　□ gorge 渓谷　□ be worshipped 祀られる
□ empress 皇后　□ found …を創建する　□ enshrine …を祀る　□ conquer …を征服する
□ be revered 崇敬される　□ mission to Tang Dynasty China 遣唐使
□ worshipper 参拝者　□ pray for health and prosperity 健康と繁栄を祈る
□ affectionately 親しみを込めて　□ address …に呼びかける

# 3-2 住吉大社

鳥居、こま犬、太鼓橋、お月見（観月祭）について

### In front of a Torii

G: Let me explain about the Torii. The Torii separates the **ordinary world** from the **sacred world**. I'll give you some advice about **going through** the Torii. You are expected to bow in front of a Torii to pay respect to the deity like this. It's polite not to go through the center of the Torii, because the deities go through the center.

T: OK. By the way, what are these two animals? I'm not sure if they are lions or dogs.

G: They are a pair of imaginary animals called Komainu, which guard shrines.

### In front of Taikobashi (Soribashi)

G: This arched bridge is called "Taikobashi," which literally means "Drum Bridge." You can see the reflection of the bridge, which looks like a drum on the water, from over there. It is said that this bridge was made to connect Sumiyoshi Taisha with an **inlet** in Osaka Bay.

T: This shrine was so close to the sea!

G: Yes! It's said that you are purified by crossing over this bridge in Sumiyoshi Taisha. This bridge **is** also **compared to** a rainbow between heaven and earth.

T: How romantic! A rainbow is considered to be a **good omen** in our country, too.

G: On a **full moon** night around the 15th of September, a festival is held on this bridge. "Tanka," Japanese poems, are read, and traditional dances and music are performed. Even today, many Japanese celebrate the full moon by offering **Japanese pampas grass**, newly **harvested vegetables** and **rice dumplings**.

T: We don't have a moon festival back in England. I'd like to experience it.

G: Farmers worked until late at night around the 15th of September because this is the **harvest season**. Farmers appreciated the light of the full moon. This festival began to be held to give thanks for the **blessings of the moon**.

G：通訳ガイド　T：観光客

## 鳥居の前で

G：鳥居について説明させてください。鳥居は俗世界と神聖な世界を分けています。鳥居を通り抜けることのアドバイスをしますね。鳥居の前では、神様に敬意を払うために、このようにお辞儀をしなければなりません。鳥居の真ん中を通らないようにするのが正しい作法です。なぜなら、神様が鳥居の真ん中をお通りになるからです。

T：わかりました。この2頭の動物は何ですか？　ライオンか犬なのかわかりません。

G：神社を守る、一対のこま犬と呼ばれる想像上の動物です。

## 太鼓橋の前で

G：このアーチ型の橋は「太鼓橋」と呼ばれていて、Drum Bridge を意味しています。向こうから、水に浮かぶ太鼓のように見える、水面に映し出されている橋が見えます。この橋は、住吉大社と大阪湾の入り江を結ぶためにつくられたと言われています。

T：この神社はとても海に近かったのですね。

G：はい！　住吉大社にあるこの橋を渡ることで、お清めされると言われています。この橋は天国と地球の間の虹にもたとえられています。

T：なんてロマンチックなのでしょう！　虹は私の国でも吉兆とされています。

G：9月15日頃の満月の夜、この橋の上でお祭りが行われます。短歌という日本の詩が詠まれ、伝統的な舞や音楽が披露されます。今日でも多くの日本人は、ススキと収穫したばかりの野菜、お団子を満月にお供えしてお祝いします。

T：イングランドには満月のお祭りはないのです。一度見てみたいです。

G：この時期は収穫期だったので、その昔、農民たちは9月15日頃は遅くまで働いていました。農民たちは、満月の光に感謝しました。そして、このお祭りが月の恵みに感謝するために行われるようになりました。

## 単語の小箱

□ ordinary world 俗界　□ sacred world 神聖な世界　□ go through ... …を通り抜ける
□ inlet 入り江　□ be compared to ... …に例えられる　□ good omen 良い前兆
□ full moon 満月　□ Japanese pampas grass ススキ
□ harvested vegetables 収穫された野菜　□ rice dumpling 団子
□ harvest season 収穫期　□ blessings of the moon 月の恵み

# 3-3 住吉大社

手水舎、神の使いのウサギ、イースターとクリスマスについて

### In front of the Temizusha

G: Here we are at the purification place, which is called "Temizusha" in Japanese. We have to purify ourselves here before praying. Please copy what I do. First, hold the **ladle** with your right hand, and **scoop up** a ladle of water and wash your left hand. Then do the same thing with your left hand. Secondly, hold the ladle with your right hand and **pour** some water into the **cup of your left hand**, and rinse your mouth with it. You must be careful not to **gargle** or drink it.

T: Oops! I was just going to drink it!

G: Then rinse your left hand again by pouring some water over it. Lastly, you should clean the handle of the ladle with all the **remaining water** by holding the cup upwards and the handle downwards. Then, please **put** it **back** where it was.

T: So it's polite to clean the handle of the ladle! It's a little bit complicated, but it's interesting. By the way, this rabbit **spouting water** is really cute.

G: Yes! The rabbit is a messenger of the deity of Sumiyoshi Taisha. Sumiyoshi Taisha was built in the Year of the Rabbit. Rabbits can jump forward, which means they can live positively and bring good luck. The rabbit is also a symbol of fertility and rich harvests because it has many babies.

T: In my country, too. Do you know Easter, when we celebrate Jesus Christ's **resurrection**? Rabbits and eggs are symbols of Easter. An egg is also a symbol of life and **revival**, so we celebrate Easter by making colorful eggs. We have Easter games, special dishes, candies, and so on, to celebrate Easter.

G: Most Japanese celebrate Christmas because we like festivals. Some celebrate Christmas for commercial reasons. The **polytheistic** nature of Shintoism **allows** us **to** celebrate other religions' festivals. I think we will start to celebrate Easter, just like we celebrate Christmas and Valentine's Day.

G：通訳ガイド　T：観光客

## 手水舎の前で

**G：**「手水舎」という名のお清めの場所にいます。お祈りする前にお清めをしなければなりません。私のまねをしてください。まず、柄杓を右手で持ち、柄杓いっぱいの水をすくい取って左手を洗ってください。そして、左手でも同じことをしてください。次に右手で柄杓を持ち、あなたの左手のくぼみに水を入れて、口をすすいでください。飲んだりうがいをしないように、気をつけなければなりません。

**T：**おっと！　飲んでしまうところでした。

**G：**それから、左手に水をかけてもう一度すすぎます。最後に、柄杓のカップを上に柄を下にして持ち、残りの水をすべて使って柄杓の柄を洗わなければいけません。そして、元あった場所に戻しておいてください。

**T：**柄杓の柄を洗うなんて礼儀正しいですね。ちょっと複雑ですが、興味深いです。水を出しているこのウサギはかわいいですね。

**G：**はい！　ウサギは住吉大社の神様のお使いなのです。住吉大社は卯年に創建されました。ウサギは前向きにジャンプすることができ、それはウサギたちが前向きに生き、幸運を運ぶことを意味します。ウサギは赤ちゃんをたくさん産むので、多産や豊穣のシンボルでもあります。

**T：**わたしの国でも同じです。イエス・キリストの復活をお祝するイースターをご存じですか？　ウサギと卵はイースターのシンボルです。それから、卵は生命と復活の象徴でもあります。だから、私たちはカラフルな卵を作り、イースターをお祝いします。イースターを祝うためのイースターゲーム、メニュー、キャンディーなどがあります。

**G：**私たちはお祭りが好きなので、ほとんどの日本人はクリスマスをお祝いします。商業上の理由でクリスマスをお祝いする人もいます。神道の多神教の性格が、私たちがほかの宗教のお祭りを楽しむことも許してくれるのです。クリスマスやバレンタインデーをお祝いするように、イースターも祝うようになると思います。

## 単語の小箱

- ☐ ladle 柄杓　☐ scoop up ... …をすくいあげる　☐ pour …を注ぐ
- ☐ cup of *one's* left hand …の左手のくぼみに　☐ gargle うがいをする
- ☐ remaining water 残りの水　☐ put A back Aを返却する　☐ spout water 水を出す
- ☐ resurrection 復活　☐ revival 復活　☐ polytheistic 多神教の
- ☐ allow A to *do* Aが…することを可能にする

# 3-4 　住吉大社

本殿の形、お祈りの方法、巫女について

### In front of the main shrine

G: The first, second, and third main sanctuaries **lie in a straight line**, but the fourth main sanctuary lies next to the third. Seen from the sky, it looks like a group of ships. The three sea deities and Empress Jingū **are enshrined** in each sanctuary. The current main shrine was built in 1810. This **architectural style dates back to** the 5th century.

### In front of the first main hall

T: I like the vermilion color. Vermilion is the color of happiness!

G: Yes, it also **dispels evil spirits**. I'll show you how to pray at a Shinto shrine. Bow slightly and **toss money into the offertory box**. Bow deeply twice, **clap your hands** twice, and **make a wish**. Bow deeply once again. This **signifies** the end of the prayer.

T: How much money should I toss in?

G: It's up to you. How about "Goen," five yen? "Goen" sounds the same as the word for "good relationships." In olden times, rice wrapped in paper was offered to a shrine instead.

### After praying

T: Who are the women over there in their white costumes?

G: They are "Miko," **shrine maidens**. They assist the priests in **conducting ceremonies**.

T: I'm interested in those hairpins they wear.

G: The hairpins are in the shape of pine trees with **egrets** on them. Sumiyoshi Taisha is famous for its pine trees. The egret has been regarded as a messenger of a deity. According to legend, when Empress Jingū was looking for a place to enshrine the sea deities, she found three egrets on a pine tree, so she decided to build Sumiyoshi Taisha here. Next, I'll take you to the sacred place where that sacred pine tree used to be.

G：通訳ガイド　T：観光客

## 本殿の前で

G：第一本宮と第二本宮、第三本宮は直線上にありますが、第四本宮は第三本宮の隣に並んでいます。空から見ると、船団のように見えます。3柱の海の神様と神功皇后が、それぞれの本宮に祀られています。現在の本殿は1810年に建てられました。この建築様式は5世紀にさかのぼります。

## 第一本宮の前で

T：朱色が好きです。朱色は幸福の色です！

G：そうです。それに悪霊を払いますよ。神道の神社でのお祈りの方法を教えましょう。軽くお辞儀をして、お金をさい銭箱に投げ入れます。深く二度お辞儀し、手を2回打って、お願い事をしてください。もう一度深くお辞儀をしてください。これはお祈りの終わりを意味します。

T：お金はいくら入れればいいですか？

G：あなた次第です。「五円」はいかがですか？「五円」は「良縁」を意味する言葉と同じに聞こえます。昔は、紙に包んだ米をお供えしました。

## お祈りした後で

T：白い衣装をまとった、あそこにいる女性たちは誰ですか？

G：巫女さんです。巫女は、神主さんが儀式を行うお手伝いをします。

T：彼女たちが身に着けている髪飾りに興味があります。

G：髪飾りは、シラサギが止まっている松の木の形をしています。住吉大社は松の木で有名です。シラサギは神様のお使いと見なされています。伝説によれば、神功皇后が海の神様をお祀りするための場所を探していたときに、3羽のシラサギが松の木に止まっているのを見つけたので、住吉大社をこの地に創建することに決めました。次に、その神木の松の木があった神聖な場所にお連れしましょう。

### 単語の小箱

□ lie in a straight line 一直線に並ぶ　□ be enshrined 祀られている
□ architectural style 建築様式　□ date back to ... …に起源がさかのぼる
□ dispel evil spirits 悪霊を払う
□ toss money into the offertory box お金をさい銭箱に入れる
□ clap one's hands 手をたたく　□ make a wish お願いごとをする　□ signify …を意味する
□ shrine maiden 巫女　□ conduct a ceremony 儀式を行う　□ egret シラサギ

77

# 3-5 住吉大社

 027

パワースポット五所御前の五大力、楠珺社(なんくんしゃ)の招き猫、しめ縄

### In front of Goshogozen, where the history of Sumiyoshi Taisha began

G: This is the place where the **sacred pine tree** was. It's said that if you collect a set of three stones with the characters "五 (go)," "大 (dai)," and "力 (riki)" inside the "tamagaki," the surrounding fence, and keep them as charms, your **prayers** will be answered. Look at these Chinese characters. "五 (go)" means five, "大 (dai)" means big, and "力 (riki)" means power. It is also said that you will get five powers.

T: What are the five powers?

G: They are the power of life, good fortune, physical power, **intellectual power**, and **financial power**. You can put the stones in a bag and **keep** them **as a lucky charm**. You can buy a bag at the **amulet office** later. Look at mine.

T: Amazing! I've found them! How lucky!

G: Great! If your prayer is answered, you have to return them and place a set of stones here with the letters "五 (go)," "大 (dai)," and "力 (riki)" on them as a token of gratitude.

### In front of Nankun-sha, after praying at a 1,000-year-old sacred camphor tree

G: Here we are in front of Nankun-sha. Please look at the **beckoning cats**. Their left hands are inviting people and prosperity; their right hands are inviting money and success.

T: Great! I want to invite all of them! I want this cat too!

G: You can get a beckoning cat at Nankun-sha.

### In front of the Couple Camphor Tree, after praying at Nankun-sha

T: What's that straw rope with white cut paper around the tree?

G: You mean the "Shime-nawa" around the sacred Couple **Camphor Tree**? A Shime-nawa **indicates** the presence of deities. The Shime-nawa is a symbol of a sacred place or thing.

G：通訳ガイド　T：観光客

## 住吉大社の歴史が始まった五所御前前にて

G：ここが神聖な松の木のあった場所です。周囲を囲む玉垣内の「五」、「大」、「力」とある3つの石を集めてお守りとして持つと、願い事がかなうと言われています。この漢字をご覧ください。「五」は five、「大」は big、「力」は power を意味します。5つの力が手に入るとも言われています。

T：5つの力とは何ですか？

G：寿（命）力、幸運、体力、知力、財力です。袋に入れてお守りとして持つことができます。後で袋をお守り授与所で購入できますよ。私のをご覧ください。

T：驚いたわ！　見つけられた！　なんてラッキーなんでしょう。

G：すごいです。願いがかなったら返却して、「五」、「大」、「力」と書かれた1セットの石を感謝の印として、ここに置いてください。

## 千年神木楠にお祈りした後、楠珺社の前で

G：楠珺社の前です。招き猫を見てください。猫の左手は人と繁栄を招き、右手はお金と成功を招いています。

T：素晴らしい！　私はそれらすべてを招きたいです。この猫もほしいです！

G：招き猫は楠珺社で手に入りますよ。

## 楠珺社でお参りした後、夫婦楠の前で

T：木の周りの、切られた白い紙がついたあの縄は何ですか？

G：神木の夫婦楠についている「しめ縄」のことですね。しめ縄は神様の存在を示します。神聖な場所や物である印です。

## 単語の小箱

□ sacred pine tree 神聖な松の木　□ prayer 祈り　□ intellectual power 知力
□ financial power 財力　□ keep A as B A を B として持つ　□ lucky charm お守り
□ amulet office お守り授与所　□ beckoning cat 招き猫　□ camphor tree 楠（クスノキ）
□ indicate …を示す

# 3-6 住吉大社

種貸社、一寸法師について

 028

### In front of a big soup bowl

G: You can **pray for the birth of a baby** as well as a good harvest at Tanekashi-sha. I'll tell you a story about a boy called "Issun-bōshi." Once upon a time, there was an old couple who prayed for the birth of a baby at this shrine. A baby boy, who was the size of the woman's little finger, was born.

T: Little finger? How cute!

G: The old couple named the baby "Issun-bōshi," and brought him up in a loving way. Issun-bōshi was very kind. One day, he said, "I want to travel to the **capital** to improve myself." Issun-bōshi used a bowl as a boat and a chopstick as a **paddle**, and **rowed** to the capital. He carried a needle with him as a sword.

T: Wow! How creative! Issun-bōshi was small enough to use a bowl as a boat!

G: Upon arriving at the capital, Issun-bōshi visited a minister's house and said to the minister, "Please make me your **retainer**." The minister was impressed by his politeness and employed him as his retainer. Issun-bōshi worked so hard that he was loved by everybody.

T: So Issun-bōshi was kind, polite, and hard-working!

G: One day, Issun-bōshi and the other retainers accompanied a princess on her visit to a temple. Suddenly, two demons appeared and said, "Leave the princess here." The other retainers ran away. Issun-bōshi fought alone against the demons, but he **was swallowed by** a demon.

T: Did Issun-bōshi die?

G: No. Issun-bōshi **pricked** the demon's **belly with** his needle. The demon screamed, **spat** him **out**, and ran away.

T: Was Issun-bōshi severely injured?

G: No, he was OK. The princess found a **magic mallet** on the ground. She shook it, saying, "Please grow up." He grew bigger, married the princess, and invited his elderly parents to the capital, and they lived happily ever after.

T: I like this success story. It means our efforts will **be rewarded**!

G：通訳ガイド　T：観光客

## 大きなお椀の前で

G：種貸社（たねかし）では、豊作だけでなく赤ちゃんの誕生をお祈りできます。「一寸法師」の物語をお話ししますね。昔々、この神社で赤ちゃんの誕生をお祈りした老夫婦がいました。女性の小指の大きさほどの小さな男の子が生まれました。

T：小指の大きさ？　かわいいですね！

G：老夫婦は赤ちゃんを「一寸法師」と名付け、愛情いっぱいに育てました。一寸法師はとてもやさしかったです。ある日、一寸法師は「自分を高めるために都に行きたい」と言いました。一寸法師子はお椀を舟に、お箸をオールにして都へとこぎ出しました。彼は、針を刀の代わりに身に着けていました。

T：すごい！　クリエイティブですね！　一寸法師はお椀を舟に使えるほどに小さかったのですね。

G：都に着くと一寸法師は大臣の家を訪問し、大臣に「どうか私をあなたの家来にしてください」と言いました。大臣は一寸法師の礼儀正しさに感銘を受け、家来にしました。一寸法師は一生懸命に働き、みんなに愛されました。

T：一寸法師は優しく、礼儀正しく、働き者なのですね！

G：ある日、一寸法師とほかの家来たちは、姫のお寺の参拝にお供しました。突然、2匹の鬼が現れて「姫をここに置いていけ」と言いました。ほかの家来は逃げました。一寸法師だけが鬼と戦いましたが、鬼に飲み込まれてしまいました。

T：一寸法師は死んでしまったのですか？

G：いいえ。一寸法師は鬼のおなかを針で突き刺しました。鬼は叫び声を上げて彼を吐き出し、逃亡しました。

T：一寸法師は大けがをしたのですか？

G：いえ、彼は大丈夫でしたよ。姫は魔法の木槌が落ちているのを見つけました。「大きくな〜れ」と言いながら、打ち出の小槌を振りました。一寸法師は大きくなって姫と結婚し、年老いた両親を都に呼び寄せ、幸せに暮らしました。

T：私はこのサクセスストーリーが好きです。努力は必ず報われることを意味しますね！

## 単語の小箱

- □ pray for the birth of a baby 赤ん坊の誕生を祈る　□ capital 都　□ paddle オール
- □ row こぐ　□ retainer 家来　□ be swallowed by ... …に飲み込まれる
- □ prick *one's* belly with A　A でB のおなかを刺す　□ spit A out　A を吐き出す
- □ magic mallet 魔法の木槌　□ be rewarded 報われる

1

大阪

81

# 3-7　住吉大社

大阪で立身出世、一粒万倍、田植え、水田で米作する理由、茅の輪くぐりについて

G: The story of Issun-bōshi shows that the weak can overcome the strong. **Rising in society** is very important in this merchant city of Osaka. Hideyoshi Toyotomi rose from farmer's son to warlord and unified Japan. He has always been respected in Osaka.

T: By the way, what is written on the paper lantern?

G: It's "Ichiryū-manbai." The phrase means that even one seed can **eventually** produce a great harvest. Sumiyoshi Taisha is a shrine of agriculture, commerce, and industry, too.

### At the rice field, after visiting Ōtoshi-sha

G: I'll explain a little bit about the two main festivals of Sumiyoshi Taisha. One is the biggest rice transplanting ritual in Japan, on June 14. It has been carried out since ancient times. **Rice seedlings** handed down from the deities are carefully planted. Sacred Shinto music and dances are performed.

T: Rice seedlings are from the deities? Now I'm gradually starting to understand Shinto.

G: Farmers begin planting the rice seedlings in May. In the countryside, you can see farmers **transplanting rice seedlings** from their **nurseries** into the **paddy fields** in the middle of June, in the rainy season. We should be grateful for the blessing of water!

T: By the way, why do you grow rice in paddy fields?

G: Paddy fields prevent the rice plants from being blown down, even in strong winds. They protect rice plants from **weeds** and pests. Also, water lowers the temperature of the ground. They protect the rice plants from typhoons and hot summers.

T: That makes sense! I'd love to see the rice transplanting festival.

G: The other festival is the summer festival. Sumiyoshi Taisha is a shrine of purification. Please look at this picture of the "Chinowa-kuguri." You can purify yourself by going through a **hoop** made of kaya grass. Kaya grass looks like a weed, but has the same power as a **sacred sword** to drive away evil spirits.

G：通訳ガイド　T：観光客

G： 一寸法師のお話は、弱い者が強い者に勝てることを示しています。商人の街・大
阪では立身出世が大切です。豊臣秀吉が農民の息子から武将になり、日本を統一
しました。大阪では秀吉はずっと尊敬され続けています。

T： ところで、提灯には何が書かれていますか？

G： 「一粒万倍」です。このフレーズは、「一粒の種も、最後には大きな収穫となる」
ことを意味します。住吉大社は農業、商業、工業の神社でもあります。

### 大歳社を参拝した後、御田で

G： 住吉大社の2つの主なお祭りについて少し説明しますね。一つは日本で一番大き
な田植えの儀式で、6月14日に行われます。それは古代から行われています。
神様から伝えられたお米の苗は丁寧に植えられます。神聖な神道の音楽が演奏さ
れ、舞が披露されます。

T： 神様から米の苗ですか？　神道について次第にわかり始めてきました。

G： お百姓さんは、5月に米の苗を植え始めます。田舎の方では、雨季の6月の半ばに、
お百姓さんが稲の苗を苗床から水田に植え替えるのを見ることができます。水の
恵みに感謝しなければ！

T： なぜお米を水田で栽培するのですか？

G： 水田は、強い風の中であっても、稲が倒れるのを防ぎます。雑草や害虫からも守っ
てくれます。それから、水は地面の温度を下げてくれます。稲を台風や暑い夏か
ら守ってくれます。

T： 理にかなっていますね！　ぜひ田植えのお祭りが見たいです。

G： もう一つのお祭りは夏祭りです。住吉大社は禊の神様です。この「茅の輪くぐり」
の写真をご覧ください。カヤでできた輪をくぐることで、お清めができるのです。
カヤは雑草のように見えますが、神聖なる刀と同じ力を持ち、悪霊を追い払って
くれます。

## 単 語 の 小 箱

☐ rise in society 立身出世する　☐ eventually ついには
☐ rice seedling 米の苗　☐ transplanting rice seedlings 米の苗を植え替えること
☐ nursery 苗床　☐ paddy field 水田　☐ weed 雑草　☐ hoop 輪
☐ sacred sword 神聖なる刀

# 3-8 住吉大社

石燈籠、七五三、朱印、路面電車について

 030

### On the way to the amulet office, after taking pictures of the "Drum Bridge"

G: Look at these **stone lanterns**. There are about 600 stone lanterns. Half of them were donated by marine and river **transport companies**. Sumiyoshi Taisha is a shrine of marine safety. **Marine transport** began to **prosper** in the 17th century, and people started praying for safety at sea. The oldest stone lantern is from the late 17th century.

T: I see. By the way, who are the children in kimono over there?

G: November 15 is "Shichi-go-san" day. Seven-year-old girls, five-year-old boys, and three-year-old boys and girls are taken to shrines to celebrate their healthy growth. They give thanks and pray for divine blessings. The children are carrying paper bags of candies. There are pictures of cranes, turtles, and pine trees on the paper bags. They are symbols of **longevity**.

T: They're cute! By the way, what's that long line for?

G: They're standing in a line to get a "Shuin," or **red ink stamp**. Many temple or shrine visitors collect stamps in their notebooks. Priests put a red ink stamp in your book and write the name of the temple or shrine in calligraphy. Some visitors from abroad are very interested in Shuin. If you receive a stamp after praying, you will earn even more merit.

### On a tram, after getting an amulet bag for the three stones

G: We're going to Tennōji by tram. It's the only tram in Osaka.

T: It feels kind of nostalgic.

G: Trams have **been in service** for more than 110 years. This tram has been called the "Chin-chin Train." This is probably because the bell that the conductor used to signal the driver sounded like "Chin-chin." (laughing)

G：通訳ガイド　T：観光客

## 太鼓橋の写真撮影をしてから、お守り授与所に行く途中で

G：この石燈籠をご覧ください。約 600 基の石燈籠があります。半分は海運、および河川の輸送会社から奉納されたものです。住吉大社は海上安全の神社です。海上輸送が 17 世紀に栄え始め、人々が海上の安全をお祈りし始めました。一番古い石燈籠は 17 世紀後半の物です。

T：なるほど。向こうにいる着物姿の子供たちは誰ですか？

G：11 月 15 日は「七五三」です。7 歳の女の子、5 歳の男の子、3 歳の男の子と女の子が、健康な成長を祝うために神社に連れて来られます。子供たちは神様に感謝し、ご加護をお祈りします。子供たちは飴の紙袋を持っています。紙袋には、鶴と亀、松の木の絵があります。それらは長寿のシンボルです。

T：かわいいですね！　ところで、あの長い列は何ですか？

G：「朱印」というスタンプをもらうために並んでいるのです。お寺や神社の参拝者の多くは、帳面にスタンプを集めています。神職が帳面に赤い色のスタンプを押し、寺社仏閣の名前を毛筆で書きます。海外からの参拝者にも、朱印に興味がある人がいます。参拝後にご朱印を拝受するとさらに功徳があります。

## 五大力のお守り袋をいただいた後、路面電車で

G：路面列車で天王寺へ行きます。大阪ではこの路線のみ路面電車が運行しています。

T：懐かしさを感じますね。

G：路面電車には 110 年以上の歴史があります。この電車はチンチン電車と呼ばれてきました。車掌から運転手への合図のベルが「チンチン」だったからだと言われています（笑）。

## 単語の小箱

□ stone lantern 石燈籠　□ transport company 運送会社　□ marine transport 海上輸送
□ prosper 栄える　□ longevity 長寿　□ red ink stamp 朱印　□ be in service 運行する

## 瞬間英作文

**1.** 鳥居は俗世界と神聖な世界を分けます。

**2.** 私たちは自然の恵みに感謝すべきです。

**3.** 住吉大社は、神功皇后が3柱の海の神様の加護に感謝をするために、211年に創建したと言われています。

**4.** 人々は、遣唐使の航海の安全を住吉大社にご祈願していました。

**5.** 向こうから、水面で太鼓のように見えるアーチ型の橋の反射が見えます。

**6.** 十二支のシンボルは子、丑、寅、卯、辰、巳、午、未、申、酉、戌、亥です。

**7.** 豊穣のシンボルであるウサギは、住吉大社の神様のお使いです。

**8.** 周囲を囲む壁の中にある「五」、「大」、「力」とある3つの石のセットを集めてお守りとして持つと、願い事がかなうと言われています。

**9.** 招き猫は左手で人と繁栄を招き、右手でお金と成功を招きます。

**10.** 一寸法師のお話は、弱き者が強い者に勝てることを示しています。

**11.** 田植えの儀式は「日本の重要無形民俗文化財」として登録されています。

**12.** カヤでできた輪をくぐることで、お清めができます。

**13.** 参拝記念に神社の御朱印をいただけます。

---

1. sacred world 神聖な世界　　2. blessings of nature 自然の恵み
3. enshrine …をお祀りする　　4. mission to Tang Dynasty China 遣唐使
5. arched bridge そり橋（太鼓橋）　　6. the Chinese Zodiac 十二支
7. rich harvest 豊穣　　8. be answered 応えられる（かなう）　　9. beckoning cat 招き猫
10. the weak 弱き者　　11. rice transplanting 田植え　　12. hoop 輪
13. red ink stamp 朱印

解答例

1. The Torii separates the ordinary world from the **sacred world**.

2. We should be grateful for the **blessings of nature**.

3. It is said that Empress Jingū founded Sumiyoshi Taisha in 211 to **enshrine** three sea deities to give thanks for their help.

4. People used to pray at Sumiyoshi Taisha for the safety of their voyages on **missions to Tang Dynasty China**.

5. You can see the reflection of the **arched bridge**, which looks like a drum on the water, from over there.

6. The symbols of **the Chinese Zodiac** are the mouse, ox, tiger, hare, dragon, serpent, horse, sheep, monkey, cock, dog, and boar.

7. The rabbit, a symbol of **rich harvests**, is the messenger of the god of Sumiyoshi Taisha.

8. It's said that if you collect a set of three stones with the characters "五 (go)," "大 (dai)," and "力 (riki)" on them inside the surrounding fence and keep them as charms, your prayers will **be answered**.

9. **Beckoning cats** are inviting people and prosperity with their left hands and inviting money and success with their right hands.

10. The story of Issun-bōshi shows that **the weak** can overcome the strong.

11. The **rice transplanting** ritual is registered as an "Important Intangible Folk Cultural Property of Japan."

12. You can purify yourself by going through a **hoop** made of kaya grass.

13. You can receive a shrine's **red ink stamp** to commemorate your visit.

# 玉虫の宝庫

## 1 航海安全の神様・住吉大社で、自然崇拝する神道を感じてもらいましょう

**❶ 鳥居**　神道と鳥居の説明と、神功皇后が海の神の住吉大社を創建された理由、位置と遣唐使の航海安全の御祈願を説明しましょう。こま犬の説明もしましょう。

**❷ そり橋**　住吉大社と大阪湾の入り江をつなぐために造られた虹の橋にも例えられていて、「太鼓橋」とも言われています。お月見とお祭りについて話しましょう。

**❸ 手水舎**　お清めの方法の説明と、住吉大社の神のお使いのウサギについて説明。

**❹ 本殿**　第一本宮から参拝しましょう。空から眺めると船団の形をしています。第一本宮から第四本宮の説明と、巫女さんの役割とシラサギが止まっている松の髪飾りについて説明。

**❺ 五所御前**　パワースポットで五大力を見つけましょう！

**❻ 楠珺社**　招き猫の解説をし、楠珺社前の夫婦木でしめ縄の説明をしましょう。

**❼ 種貸社**　一寸法師の話は楽しく。「一粒万倍」の説明もしましょう。

**❽ 大歳社**　おもかる石は、持ち上げて軽ければ願いがかなう、重ければしばらく待つ、という啓示です。

**❾ 御田**　海外のゲストで田植えの話を喜ばれる方も多いです。

## 2 通訳ガイドからのアドバイス

**アドバイス1　文化の違いを理解しながら、満月の日にお祭りをする理由を話す**

西洋人も満月を美しいと感じますが、オオカミや犯罪、不眠などを連想する人もいます。農民たちが夜遅くまで田んぼで働き、月に照らしてもらったことに感謝するために始まったのがお月見だと知ってもらいましょう。自然の恵みに感謝する神道を説明する良い機会でもあります。

**アドバイス2　相手の国の文化を大切にイースターなどの話をできるように**

住吉大社の神様の使い（divine messenger）がウサギであることから、イースターに会話が広がっています。ほかの宗教のお祭りも話せるようになりましょう。神道が多神教的な性格（polytheistic nature）を持つことを説明する良い機会です。

**アドバイス3　一寸法師の話は明るくビジュアルを使って！　写真撮影も**

老夫婦が子宝を授かるように祈願をしたこと（prayed for the birth of a baby）や、勇敢で心優しき一寸法師が立身出世し（rise in society）、幸せに暮らした話は楽しく絵本を見せて説明しています。お椀の中に入っての写真撮影も喜ばれますよ。

### アドバイス 4　七五三を祝う理由を話す

三歳　Children begin to speak at the age of three.
五歳　Children begin to learn at the age of five.
七歳　Children start to grow their adult teeth at the age of seven.

### アドバイス 5　お礼をする日本文化

五所御前で五大力の石をゲストが見つけた場合、If you keep this as a good luck talisman, your wish will surely be granted, so please come to Japan again.（これをお守りとして持てば願いがかなうので、また日本に来てね）、別に 1 セットの五大力を奉納する理由は、Japanese people give something as a token of their gratitude when they receive a present.（日本人はプレゼントをもらったら何かお返しをする）と、日本文化の説明をするのもよいでしょう。

## 3 通訳ガイド体験日記

◎「鶴は千年、亀は万年」の説明をしたが、本当の寿命が答えられなかった。
The average life span of cranes is said to be from 20 to 30 years, and that of turtles is said to be from 70 to 80 years.（鶴の平均寿命は 20 年から 30 年だと言われています。亀は 70 年か 80 年ぐらいです）と答えています。

## 4 通訳ガイドお役立ち英語表現

◎朱色は vermilion ですが、orange と言うゲストもいます。
表現が異なる場合には、ゲストに合わせましょう。

◎ 遣唐使は Missions to Tang Dynasty China です。その他の中国の王朝名は以下の通り。

隋：Sui Dynasty China　　唐：Tang Dynasty China
宋：Song Dynasty China　元：Yuan Dynasty China
明：Ming Dynasty China　清：Qing Dynasty China

## 4-1　四天王寺

聖徳太子、仏教の伝来、十七条の憲法、冠位十二階について

G: Today, we're visiting Shitennōji Temple. Shitennōji was the first state temple in Japan. Shitennōji **was** founded in 593 by Prince Shōtoku and **dedicated to** the **Four Heavenly Kings**. First, let me tell you about Buddhism and Prince Shōtoku. Buddhism was introduced into Japan in 538. There was a **conflict** between the **pro-Buddhist** and anti-Buddhist **factions**. Prince Shōtoku was pro-Buddhist and made small, portable-sized statues of the Four Heavenly Kings to pray for peace and victory. The pro-Buddhist faction won. Prince Shōtoku greatly contributed to the **rise** of Buddhism. Prince Shōtoku believed in Japan's **indigenous** Shintoism, too.

T: So, Prince Shōtoku believed in both Buddhism and Shintoism?

G: Yes. Prince Shōtoku thought that Japan needed a doctrine. Shintoism doesn't have any scriptures, so he thought Buddhism was suited to Japan's needs. Prince Shōtoku based his government on Buddhism. Prince Shōtoku is called the "Father of Japanese Buddhism."

T: Was Prince Shōtoku a politician?

G: Prince Shōtoku was a politician and **regent to** Empress Suiko in the 6th century. He decided to establish a **centralized government**. **Under his supervision**, the "**Seventeen-Article Constitution**" and the "**Twelve Level Cap and Rank System**" were introduced.

T: What's in the Seventeen-Article Constitution?

G: The importance of harmony was emphasized in the Seventeen-Article Constitution. For example, it is important to reach decisions through group discussions. Prince Shōtoku is respected as the politician who said, "Harmony is the greatest of virtues."

T: I see. What is the Twelve Level Cap and Rank System?

G: Under the Twelve Level Cap and Rank System, capable people could be promoted as officials regardless of their origins. Prince Shōtoku was also said to have eight ears. This means that he was able to listen to many people's opinions seriously and impartially. This shows the depth of his humanity. His first project was the construction of Shitennōji Temple.

G：通訳ガイド　T：観光客

**G**：今日は、四天王寺をご案内しましょう。四天王寺は日本初の官寺でした。聖徳太子によって 593 年に創建され、四天王がお祀りされています。まず初めに仏教と聖徳太子についてお話しさせてください。仏教は 538 年に伝来しました。崇仏派と排仏派の間に衝突が起こりました。聖徳太子は崇仏派で、小さな携帯できるサイズの四天王像を作り、平和と勝利を祈願されました。崇仏派が勝利を収めました。聖徳太子は仏教の興隆に大きく貢献された方です。聖徳太子は日本古来の神道も信じてらっしゃいました。

**T**：聖徳太子は神道も仏教も信じてらっしゃったのですね

**G**：そうです。聖徳太子は日本には理論が必要だと考えました。神道には経典がないので、聖徳太子は仏教が日本が必要としているものにふさわしいと考えられたのです。聖徳太子は仏教を基本とした政治を行いました。聖徳太子は「日本仏教の父」と呼ばれています。

**T**：聖徳太子は政治家でしたか？

**G**：6 世紀に聖徳太子は政治家で、推古天皇の摂政でもあられました。聖徳太子は中央集権国家をつくることを決意しました。彼の指導の下で十七条の憲法や冠位十二階が制定されました。

**T**：十七条の憲法には何が書かれていますか？

**G**：十七条の憲法では、和の重要性が強調されています。例えば、集団の中では話し合って結論を出すことが大切です。彼は「和をもって貴しとなす」という言葉を発した政治家として尊敬されています。

**T**：なるほど。冠位十二階とは何ですか？

**G**：冠位十二階の下で、有能な人々は身分に関係なく役人に昇進できたのです。聖徳太子は 8 つの耳を持っていると言われていました。それは聖徳太子が、多くの人の意見を熱心に公平に聞かれたことを意味します。彼の人間的な奥深さを意味するのです。聖徳太子が最初になされたのは四天王寺の建立でした

### 単語の小箱

☐ be dedicated to ... …が祀られている　☐ Four Heavenly Kings 四天王　☐ conflict 衝突
☐ pro-Buddhist faction 崇仏派　☐ rise 興隆　☐ indigenous 固有の
☐ regent to ... …の摂政　☐ centralized government 中央集権国家
☐ under *one's* supervision …の管理下　☐ Seventeen-Article Constitution 十七条の憲法
☐ Twelve Level Cap and Rank System 冠位十二階

# 4-2 四天王寺

### 遣隋使、西門（鳥居）、夕日、彼岸、箕形の扁額について

G: Prince Shotoku founded Shitennōji Temple to save everyone in the world. Osaka was the gateway to Japan from China and Korea in the 6th century. Prince Shōtoku also **contributed to** the establishment of good relations between Japan and China by sending **missions to Sui Dynasty China**. Buddhist monks and scholars were dispatched to China and they brought back many things, such as technology and medicine.

### At the West Gate (Stone Torii gate)

G: Here we are in front of the Torii gate of Shitennōji Temple. It separates the sacred place from the ordinary world. Torii gates are usually found in shrines. However, Shitennōji is a temple. This means that we can worship both Buddha and the Shinto deities. This Torii gate is also the West Gate of Shitennōji. This West Gate was close to the sea in ancient times. It was believed that the "**Buddhist Paradise**" was located over the sea. People worshipped the sunset over the gate. The name of this district is "Yūhigaoka," which means "Sunset Hill." The most beautiful sunsets can be seen around the vernal and autumnal equinoxes, called "Higan." Higan is the Buddhist Paradise, where our ancestors live. **Vernal Equinox Day** is around March 20. Autumnal Equinox Day is around September 23. During these weeks, we **visit our ancestors' graves** to pay our respects.

T: In my country, we have the same days, but we don't do anything.

G: I see. Please look at the shape of the **tablet** on the gate. What does it look like?

T: It's a **dustpan**! Why is the tablet in the shape of a dustpan?

G: No, it's in the shape of a **winnowing basket**, which was used for separating the rice from the **chaff**. Just as a winnowing basket scoops up rice, it also scoops up your wishes. This means all your wishes will come true.

T: I'm lucky to be here! By the way, what's written on this tablet?

G: It says this is where Buddha came to **preach**.

G：通訳ガイド　T：観光客

G：聖徳太子はこの世のすべての人を救うために四天王寺を建立されたのです。6世紀には、大阪は中国と朝鮮にとって日本の玄関でした。聖徳太子は遣隋使派遣で中国と日本の友好関係の樹立にも貢献されました。仏僧や学者が派遣され、技術や薬など多くの物が伝わりました。

### 西門で（石の鳥居）

G：鳥居の前にいます。鳥居は神聖な世界と俗界を分けます。鳥居は通常は神社で見られます。しかしながら、四天王寺はお寺です。このことは、私たちは四天王寺では仏様と神道の神様の両方にお祈りできることを意味します。この鳥居は四天王寺の西門でもあります。古代では、この西門は海に近かったのです。当時は極楽浄土が海の向こうに存在すると考えられていました。人々は西門にかかる日没を拝みました。この地域の名前は英語では Sunset Hill を意味する「夕陽丘」です。最も美しい夕日が「彼岸」と呼ばれる春分と秋分の日あたりに見られます。彼岸とは「極楽浄土」を意味し、ご先祖様が住んでいらっしゃいます。春分は3月20日で、秋分は9月23日です。この週に私たちはご先祖様を敬うためにお墓参りをします。

T：私たちの国にも春分の日と秋分の日がありますが、特別なことは何もしません。

G：なるほど。門の上にある扁額を見てください。何に見えますか？

T：ちり取りです！　なぜ、扁額はちり取りの形をしているのですか？

G：いいえ、箕の形をしています。箕はお米ともみ殻をふるい分けるために使われました。箕がお米をすくい取るように、あなたの望みもすくいとってくれます。あなたの望みが実現することを意味するのですよ。

T：ここに来ることができて幸運です。ところで、扁額には何が書かれているのですか？

G：釈迦如来がお越しになられて説法された場所だと書かれています。

## 単語の小箱

□ contribute to ... …に貢献する　□ mission to Sui Dynasty China 遣隋使
□ Buddhist Paradise 極楽浄土　□ Vernal Equinox Day 春分の日
□ visit *one's* ancestor's grave 墓参りをする　□ tablet 扁額（飾り板）　□ dustpan ちり取り
□ winnowing basket 箕　□ chaff もみ殻（くず）　□ preach 説法する

# 4-3 四天王寺

西大門（極楽の門）、転法輪、香炉、四天王寺式伽藍、仁王について

### In front of the Great West Gate (Saidaimon)

**G**: This is the Great West Gate, also called the Gate of the Buddhist Paradise. The area around the West Gate and the Great West Gate attracts people who want to be reborn in the Buddhist Paradise. Please **spin** this **Dharma Wheel** and say, "Teach me the Buddha's law."

**T**: I'll try. Experiencing different cultures is very interesting.

**G**: Come this way. This is an **incense burner**. Smoke is considered to be the **breath of the Buddha.** You can **waft** the smoke on to any part of your body that may need **healing**.

**T**: Oh, it's holy smoke! I'm forgetful (laughing), so I'll waft the smoke on to my head. This temple **compound** looks very orderly and sacred.

**G**: Over the centuries, the temple buildings in these grounds have been destroyed repeatedly by various disasters and World War II. However, thanks to the **devotion** of the citizens, Shitennōji Temple was rebuilt several times. The latest reconstruction took place in 1963.

**T**: You mean, the people's devotion has made this temple sacred?

**G**: Yes. Also, the layout of the Inner Precinct of Shitennōji makes this compound look more sacred. The Inner Gate, the five-storied pagoda, the Golden Hall, and the Lecture Hall **are in a line** from south to north, and a **cloister** surrounds the whole complex. This is one of the oldest styles in Japan. It was rebuilt in the Asuka-period style of the 6th century.

### In front of the Deva Kings at the Central Gate

**G**: This pair of Deva Kings is one of the largest in Japan. They're guarding the temple. Look at the Deva King on the right. His mouth is open. He seems to be uttering "Ah." Look at the Deva King on the left. His mouth is closed. He seems to be uttering "Un." They are the first sound and the last sound of the Sanskrit phonetic system. They represent the whole of Buddha's teaching and the entire life span of human beings.

G：通訳ガイド　T：観光客

## 西大門の前で

G：これは西大門で極楽の門とも言われています。西門と西大門の辺りは、極楽で生まれ変わりたい人々を魅了しています。転法輪を回し「仏の法を教えてください」と言ってください。

T：やってみるわ！　異なる文化を体験することはとても面白いです。

G：こちらに来てください。これは香炉です。煙は仏様の息と見なされています。治療が必要な部分にふんわりとかぶってください。

T：まあ、なんて神聖な煙なんでしょう！　私は記憶力が悪いので（笑）、煙を頭にかぶります。このお寺の境内はとても整然としていて神聖ですね。

G：何世紀にもわたり、境内にあるお寺の建物はさまざまな災害や第二次世界大戦によって、たびたび破壊されました。それでも人々の強い信仰心のおかげで、四天王寺は何回も再建されたのです。最後の再建は 1963 年に行われました。

T：つまり、強い信仰心がこのお寺を神聖にしているということ？

G：そうです。また四天王寺の伽藍の配置がこの境内をもっと神聖に見せます。中門、五重塔、金堂、講堂は南から北に一列に並び、回廊がそれを囲む形式です。これは、日本で一番古い形式の一つです。6 世紀の飛鳥時代の様式で再建されました。

## 中門の仁王の前で

G：日本で最大級の仁王様です。お寺を守っています。右側の仁王を見てください。口を開けていますね。「あ」の音を発しているようです。左側の仁王を見てください。口を閉じていますね。「うん」の音を発しているようです。これは、サンスクリット語の音声システムの始まりと終わりです。仏の教えすべてと人間の生涯を表しています。

単　語　の　小　箱

□ spin …を回す　□ Dharma Wheel 転法輪　□ incense burner 香炉
□ breath of the Buddha 仏様の息　□ waft …をかぶる　□ healing 治療
□ compound 境内　□ devotion 強い信仰心　□ be in a line 一列に並ぶ　□ cloister 回廊

大阪

# 4-4 四天王寺

金堂、如来、菩薩、救世観音菩薩、四天王、邪鬼、合掌について

G: Here we are in the Golden Hall. I'll give you a mini-lesson about the difference between Buddhas and Bodhisattvas. Buddhas have **reached the state of enlightenment**. Bodhisattvas are practicing to reach the state of enlightenment. Bodhisattvas are deepening their training by saving people. Please look at Guze Kannon Bodhisattva. Prince Shōtoku is said to have been a **reincarnation** of Guze Kannon Bodhisattva. It's believed that Prince Shōtoku appeared in this world to save human beings, even though he **was qualified** to be a Buddha.

T: So, Prince Shōtoku is a **savior**, like Christ?

G: Right! I have a quiz for you. Can you guess why Guze Kannon **sits with one leg crossed**?

T: Guze Kannon seems to be relaxed and preaching the importance of harmony.

G: Good guess, but it's incorrect. Guze Kannon can stand up quickly from this **posture**. Guze Kannon is always ready to save people who are in trouble or suffering.

T: Great! Guze Kannon is really **merciful**.

G: Right! Next, please look at the Four Heavenly Kings. They are four guardian gods. Jikoku-ten protects the east and supports the country. Zōchō-ten protects the south and brings a **bountiful harvest**. Kōmoku-ten protects the west and has eyes that see far and wide. Tamon-ten protects the north and listens to the teachings of Buddha. The Four Heavenly Kings are stamping on demons to punish them for their wrongdoing.

T: I see, but the demons look cute, probably because I see myself in them.

G: You have a point. When I look at the demons, I feel I need to correct my behavior. This may be one of the reasons why they are secretly popular.

T: Demons can teach us many things. By the way, why do people place both hands together when they pray at temples?

G: The right hand is considered pure. The left hand is considered impure. Placing both hands together symbolizes your true self. It indicates **obedience** to the Buddha.

G：通訳ガイド　T：観光客

G：今、金堂にいます。如来と菩薩のついてのミニレッスンをさせてください。如来は仏の悟りの境地に達した者です。菩薩は悟りの境地を目指し、修行している者です。菩薩は人々を救済することで修業を深めます。救世観音菩薩をご覧ください。聖徳太子は救世観音菩薩の生まれ変わりと言われています。聖徳太子は如来になる資格があるにもかかわらず、人々を助けるためにこの世に現れたと信じられています。

T：聖徳太子はキリストのように救世主であられるのですね。

G：その通りです！　クイズがあります。救世観音はなぜ片足を組まれているのでしょうか？

T：救世観音はゆったりと落ち着かれて、「和」の大切さを説法されているようです。

G：いい推測ですが、ハズレです。救世観音はこの姿勢を取ることで、早く立ち上がれるのです。いつも困っている人、苦しんでいる人々を助ける準備ができています。

T：偉大ですね。救世観音は本当に慈悲深いですね。

G：その通りです！　次に四天王をご覧ください。4守護神です。持国天は東を守り、国を支えます。増長天は南を守り、五穀豊穣をもたらします。広目天は西を守り、広く見通せる目を持っています。多聞天は北を守り、仏の教えを聞きます。四天王は邪鬼の悪行を罰するために、彼らを踏みつけています。

T：なるほど、邪鬼の中に自分自身を見るからか、私には邪鬼がかわいく見えます。

G：いい点を突いていますね。邪鬼を見ると、私は自分の行動を正さなければならないと思います。これは、邪鬼が密かに人気のある理由の一つかもしれませんね。

T：邪鬼は私たちに多くのことを教えてくれますね。ところで、なぜ人々はお寺でお祈りするときに両手を合わせるのですか？

G：右手は清浄、左手は不浄と見なされています。両手を合わせることは、真実のあなた自身を表します。仏に従うことを意味します。

## 単語の小箱

☐ reach the state of enlightenment 悟りの境地に達する　☐ reincarnation 生まれ変わり
☐ be qualified 資格がある　☐ savior 救世主　☐ sit with one leg crossed 片足を組んで座る
☐ posture 姿勢　☐ merciful 慈悲深い　☐ bountiful harvest 豊作　☐ obedience 服従

# 4-5　四天王寺

講堂の十一面観音菩薩と阿弥陀如来、五重塔、亀井堂の経木流し(きょうぎ)について

### In the Lecture Hall

G: This is the Lecture Hall, where lectures about Buddhist law and **scriptures** are held. The east side of the Lecture Hall is called the "Winter Hall." An Eleven-faced Kannon Bodhisattva is enshrined here. The Eleven-faced Bodhisattva has eleven faces in different directions and saves you in every direction in this world. The west side is called the "Summer Hall," and Amitabha Buddha is enshrined here. He can lead you to paradise in the next life.

T: Wow! I can become happy in this world and in the **afterlife** by praying in this lecture hall.

### After explaining the five elements of a five-story pagoda

G: This eighth-generation, five-story pagoda was built thanks to the efforts of the citizens in 1959. The **ashes of Gautama** are on the fifth floor. It's unusual to be able to climb up to the top. Shall we try?

T: I'd love to!

### Floating wooden sutra tablets at Kameidō Hall

T: What are these people doing?

G: They are praying for their **departed loved ones**. The **wooden sutra tablet** has a dead person's name on it. This wooden sutra tablet has been prayed to by a monk. It is being floated in **holy water**, called Kamei water, in this **stone basin**. Holy water flows out from under the foundations of the Golden Hall and into the stone basin. It is believed that the floating wooden sutra tablets will **guide** the departed souls **to rebirth** in the Buddhist Paradise.

T: Great! I hope that my dead father is living happily in heaven. By the way, I like this stone basin in the shape of a turtle.

G: This stone basin is from the 7th century. This **was proved by a study** in 2019. Rituals using water may have been performed here.

T: This stone-turtle basin must have **witnessed** the whole history of Shitennōji.

G：通訳ガイド　T：観光客

## 講堂で

G：講堂は経典を講じたり法を説いたりするお堂です。東が冬堂で十一面観音菩薩がお祀りされています。十一面観音菩薩は異なる方向に十一面持ち、この世のすべての方向でお救いくださいます。西側は「夏堂」と呼ばれ、阿弥陀如来がお祀りされていて、来世は極楽にお導きくださいますよ。

T：すごい！　講堂に参拝すればこの世でも来世でも幸せになれるのですね。

## 五重塔の五元素の説明をしてから（p. 184 参照）

G：8 代目の五重塔は、人々の努力のおかげで 1959 年に再建されました。お釈迦様の遺骨が一番上に納められています。五重塔の一番上まで登れます。登りましょうか？

T：喜んで。

## 亀井堂にて経木流し

T：あの人々は何をしているのですか？

G：亡くなった、愛する人のために祈っているのです。経木には亡くなった人の名前が書かれています。この経木は僧侶によって拝んでもらっています。経木は石鉢の中で、亀井水と呼ばれる霊水に浮かべられています。霊水は金堂の地下から湧き出て、石鉢に届きます。経木流しをすると、亡くなった人が極楽往生する（極楽で生まれ変わり、幸せに暮らせる）ように導かれると信じられています。

T：素晴らしいですね。亡くなった父が天国で幸福に暮らしてくれていることを望みます。ところで、私は亀形のこの石鉢が好きです。

G：この石鉢は 7 世紀の物です。2019 年に調査の結果、判明しました。水を使った儀式が行われていたに違いありません。

T：この亀の形の鉢は、四天王寺の歴史を見てきたのでしょうね。

### 単語の小箱

□ scripture 経典　□ afterlife 来世　□ ashes of Gautama お釈迦様の遺骨
□ departed loved one 亡くなった愛する人　□ wooden sutra tablet 経木
□ holy water 霊水　□ stone basin 石鉢　□ guide A to B A を B に導く
□ rebirth 生まれ変わること　□ be proved by a study 調査によって判明する
□ witness …を目撃する

# 4-6 四天王寺

六時堂、和宗、おもかる地蔵、賓頭盧様について

### In front of Rokuji-dō

G: The present Rokuji-dō Hall was built in the 17th century and has luckily **survived** various disasters. The Yakushi Nyorai Buddha, who has the power to cure illnesses, is enshrined here. Various Buddhist rituals are performed all day long. It's said that Rokuji-dō Hall was established by Saichō, the **founder** of the Japanese Tendai Sect of Buddhism. Saichō practiced Buddhism here in Shitennōji Temple. Also, Kūkai, the founder of the Shingon Sect, and Shinran, the founder of Jōdo Shinshū, **did training** here at Shitennōji Temple. Prince Shōtoku preached the importance of harmony. Shitennōji **follows his teaching** and respects all sects. Shitennōji belongs to its own sect, "Wa-shū," which means "Harmony Sect."

T: I see. It feels very peaceful here in Shitennōji Temple.

G: This area is a popular spiritual "power spot," and it has **been on television** and **featured** in magazines.

### In front of Omokaru Jizō (Heavy or Light Jizō)

G: This **Heavy or Light Jizō** tells you whether your wish will **be granted** or not. When you lift it up, if it feels light, your wishes will be granted. If it feels heavy, it's not the time for your dreams to be realized. Pray to the Heavy or Light Jizō and chant: "On kakaka bisanmaei sowaka." It means, "I follow you so that my wish will be granted." Then lift it up with both your hands.

T: OK. "On kakaka bisanmaei sowaka." It feels light! (laughing)

### Binzuru Pindola

G: It's said that Binzuru Pindola had supernatural powers and showed them off too much, so he was ordered to do training and save people outside the hall. When you have a pain in your body, please rub the **corresponding part** of Pindola. Your pain will go away.

T: Wow! I can have my pain removed here too! I've already **had** my pain **relieved** by the incense.

G：通訳ガイド　T：観光客

## 六時堂の前で

G：現在の六時堂の建物は17紀に建造され、幸運にも災害を乗り切り（にも打ち勝ち）現存しています。六時堂では病気平癒の功徳のある薬師如来が祀られています。一日中、さまざまな儀式が行われます。六時堂は日本天台宗の最澄によって創建されたと言われています。最澄は四天王寺で修行しました。また真言宗の空海も、浄土真宗の親鸞も四天王寺で修行しました。聖徳太子は和の大切さを説かれた方です。四天王寺はその教えを守り、それぞれの宗派も尊重します。四天王寺は、「ハーモニー」を意味する独自の「和宗」に属します。

T：なるほど。ここ四天王寺では平和だな〜と感じます。

G：この辺りは人気のあるパワースポットとして、テレビで放映されたり雑誌でも紹介されたことがあります。

## おもかる地蔵の前で

G：このおもかる地蔵は、あなたの望みがかなうかどうかを教えてくれます。持ち上げたときに軽く感じたら、あなたの望みはかないます。重いと感じたら、あなたの夢は実現するときではありません。お祈りして「おんかかか・びさんまえい・そわか」と唱えてください。それは「望みがかなうようにあなたに従います」を意味します。それから両手で持ち上げてください。

T：「おんかかか・びさんまえい・そわか」。軽く感じます！（笑）

## 賓頭盧ピンドラ

G：賓頭盧ピンドラは神通力を持つのですが、使いすぎたために、お堂の外で修行し、人々を助けるように命令されたと言われています。体に痛みがあるとき、それと同じ場所をなでればあなたの痛みは消え去ります。

T：すごい！　ここでも私の痛みは取り除いてもらえるのですね。香炉の煙でも取り除いてもらいましたよ。

### 単語の小箱

□ survive …を生き残る、乗り切る　□ founder 創始者　□ do training 修行する
□ follow *one's* teaching 教えを守る　□ be on television テレビで放映される
□ be featured 取り上げられる　□ Heavy or Light Jizō おもかる地蔵　□ be granted かなう
□ corresponding part 相当する場所　□ have A relieved A を和らげる

101

# 4-7  四天王寺

石舞台、極楽浄土の庭、桜のじゅうたん、白道

### At the stone stage

G: This stone stage is from the 17th century and is one of the three largest stone stages in Japan. On April 22, a **memorial service in commemoration of** Prince Shōtoku is held here. A traditional dance called "Bugaku" is performed.

T: I see. I like this turtle pond. There are a lot of turtles sunbathing!

G: Harmony can be seen here, too.

### In Gokuraku-jōdo Garden, after praying at the Buddha's Footprints

T: Wow! The fallen cherry blossom petals are covering the ground like a beautiful pink carpet.

G: In Japan, we love cherry blossom viewing. This garden **is modeled on** the Garden of the Buddhist Paradise. One Chinese monk preached: "There are two rivers you must not fall into. One is human anger. The other is human greed. We should walk the narrow path between them, called 'Byakudō,' which means 'white road.' The white road **leads to** the Buddhist Paradise." This is the Gautama Waterfall. The stones, which symbolize a **Gautama Triad**, are welcoming you and **encouraging** you **to** go forward.

T: I see. That means we should go ahead along the right path, without hesitating.

### In the "Washōan" tearoom

G: This is the Pond of Paradise. The Amitabha Triad stones are welcoming us. You can enjoy the **azaleas**, **lotus flowers**, and autumn leaves.

T: This garden is a real urban oasis. It's also nice to see a Japanese tatami room here!

G: Sweets and tea are served here. This is a "hanging bell sweet," a **specialty** of Shitennōji.

T: The combination of the sweet bean paste bun and the bitter tea is excellent.

G：通訳ガイド　T：観光客

### 石舞台で

G：この石舞台は 17 世紀のもので、日本三大石舞台の一つです。4 月 22 日は聖徳太子をしのんで法要が行われます。「舞楽」と呼ばれる伝統舞踊が披露されます。

T：なるほど。私はこの亀池が好きです。多くの亀が日光浴を楽しんでいますね。

G：ここでもまた「和」が見られます。

### 仏足石を拝んでから極楽浄土の庭で

T：わあ！　桜の花びらが一面を覆い、まるで美しいピンクのじゅうたんのようです。

G：日本ではお花見が大好きなんですよ。この庭は極楽浄土をモデルにしています。ある中国の僧侶の言葉によると、「2 つの落ちてはいけない河があります。瞋りの河と貪りの河です。私たちはその間にある細い道 " 白道 " を歩くべきなのです。白道は極楽浄土へと続きます」。こちらが釈迦の滝です。こちらの釈迦三尊を表す石があなたを迎え、進むようにと勇気づけてくれます。

T：なるほど。迷わず正しい道へと進むべきことがわかりました。

### 和松庵で

G：こちらは極楽の池です。阿弥陀三尊像を表す石がお迎えしてくれています。ツツジ、蓮の花、紅葉をここで観賞できます。

T：このお庭は本当に都会のオアシスですね。日本の畳の部屋も見られて幸せです。

G：お茶とお菓子ですよ。この釣鐘まんじゅうは四天王寺の名物です。

T：あんこの入ったおまんじゅうと苦いお茶の組み合わせは最高です。

### 単語の小箱

□ memorial service 法要　□ in commemoration of … …を記念して
□ be modeled on … …を模している　□ lead to … …へ続く
□ Gautama Triad 釈迦三尊　□ encourage A to *do* A が…するように勇気づける
□ azalea ツツジ　□ lotus flower 蓮の花　□ specialty 名物

# 4-8 四天王寺

八角亭、英霊堂、地蔵山について

 038

### Octagonal House and abbot's quarters

G: This **Octagonal House was exhibited** at the National Industrial Exhibition in Osaka in 1903. It was similar to the World Exposition, and more than ten foreign countries, including Britain, Germany, and America participated in it. This was a time when Japanese companies were **prospering** thanks to Japan's victory in the **Sino-Japanese War**.

T: This Renaissance-style Octagonal House really matches this garden!

G: Right! You can see the spirit of harmony here, too. Look at these **abbot's quarters**, which were built in the 17th century. This structure survived several disasters.

### In front of Eirei-dō on the way back

G: The world's biggest **hanging bell** used to be hung here, in Eirei-dō Hall. During World War II, the hanging bell was taken from this hall to **be turned into** weapons. You ate those sweets in the shape of a hanging bell in the tearoom!

T: They were modeled on the hanging bell in this hall! They were delicious!

### At Jizō Mountain

G: Jizō is very popular as a **guardian deity**. Jizō leads **wandering souls** to the right path. Jizō guards babies and unborn babies with much affection, too. Parents pray to Jizō to protect their dead children. Jizō wears a red **bib** to **drive away evil spirits**. Jizō statues are often found on the roadside. Jizō is also the guardian of travelers and pregnant women. Here there are many types of Jizō: a Jizō for healing eyes, a Jizō for a long life, a Jizō for traffic safety, a Jizō for **warding off** evil, and so on.

T: I see! By the way, there are students in school uniforms walking around.

G: Yes, Shitennōji has schools, hospitals, pharmacies, and homes for elderly people. The spirit of Prince Shōtoku has **been passed down** in these educational and welfare projects.

G：通訳ガイド　T：観光客

## 八角亭と方丈

**G：** この八角亭は、1903年に大阪で開催された内国勧業博覧会に展示されていました。それは万博のようなもので、英国、ドイツ、アメリカなど10か国以上が参加しました。日本の企業が日清戦争の勝利で拡大していた時期でした。

**T：** このルネッサンス様式の八角亭がこの庭園によく合っていますね。

**G：** その通りです。ここでも和の精神が見られます。17世紀に建造された方丈をご覧ください。数々の災害に耐えてきました。

## 帰路、英霊堂の前で

**G：** この英霊堂には、世界最大の釣鐘がつるされていました。第二次世界大戦中、釣鐘はこのお堂から取り外されて武器が作られました。茶室で釣鐘の形のおまんじゅうを食べたでしょ。

**T：** このお堂の釣鐘をまねて作られたのですね！　おいしかったです！

## 地蔵山にて

**G：** お地蔵様は守護神として大変人気があります。迷える魂を正しい道へ導いてくださいます。赤ちゃんや胎児（生まれることのできなかった赤ちゃん）ですら、優しく守り導いてくださいます。幼い子供を亡くした親たちは、お地蔵様に子供の守護を願います。お地蔵様は悪霊を退治するために赤いよだれかけをしています。お地蔵様は道端にも見られます。お地蔵様は旅人や妊婦の守護神でもあります。ここには多くの種類のお地蔵様がいらっしゃいます。目の治療の地蔵、長寿の地蔵、交通安全の地蔵、厄払いの地蔵などです。

**T：** そうですか！　制服姿の生徒が歩いていますね。

**G：** はい。四天王寺には学校、病院、薬局、老人ホームなどがあります。聖徳太子の精神が教育と福祉事業に引き継がれています。

## 単語の小箱

□ Octagonal House 八角堂　□ be exhibited 展示される　□ prosper 繁栄する
□ Sino-Japanese War 日清戦争　□ abbot's quarters 方丈　□ hanging bell 釣鐘
□ be turned into ... …に変えられる　□ guardian deity 守護神
□ wandering soul さまよえる魂　□ bib よだれかけ　□ drive away ... …を追い払う
□ evil spirit 悪霊　□ ward off ... …を撃退する　□ be passed down ... …へ伝えられる

## 瞬間英作文

1. 聖徳太子は仏教の興隆に貢献し、四天王寺を 593 年に創建しました。

2. 聖徳太子は遣隋使を派遣し、中国と日本の友好関係の樹立に貢献されました。

3. 仏僧や学者が中国に派遣され、技術や薬など多くの物が伝わりました。

4. 西門は極楽の門と言われています。

5. 転法輪を回し「仏の法を教えてください」と言ってください。

6. 中門、五重塔、金堂、講堂は南から北に一列に並び、回廊がそれを囲みます。

7. 持国天は東を守り、国を支えます。

8. 増長天は南を守り、五穀豊穣をもたらします。

9. 広目天は西を守り、広く見渡させる力を持ちます。

10. 多聞天は北を守り、仏の教えを聞きます。

11. 菩薩は悟りに達する前に人類の救済に献身しています。

12. 十一面観音菩薩は異なる方向に十一面を持ち、この世のすべての方向でお救いくださいます。

13. 経木流しをすると亡くなった人が極楽で生まれ変わり、幸せに暮らせるようになると信じられています。

---

1. rise 興隆    2. mission to Sui Dynasty China 遣隋使    3. bring back ... …を持ち帰る
4. Buddhist Paradise 極楽    5. Dharma Wheel 転法輪    6. cloister 回廊
7. support …を支える    8. bountiful harvest 五穀豊穣
9. see far and wide 広く見渡す    10. teaching of Buddha 仏の教え
11. reach enlightenment 悟りに達する
12. Eleven-faced Kannon Bodhisattva 十一面観音菩薩
13. floating wooden sutra tablet 経木流し

解 答 例

1. Prince Shōtoku contributed to the **rise** of Buddhism and founded Shitennōji Temple in 593.

2. Prince Shōtoku contributed to the establishment of good relations between Japan and China by sending Japanese **missions to Sui Dynasty China**.

3. Buddhist monks and scholars were dispatched to China, and they **brought back** many things, such as technology and medicine.

4. The West Gate is called the Gate of the **Buddhist Paradise**.

5. Please spin this **Dharma Wheel** and say, "Teach me the Buddha's law."

6. The Inner Gate, the five-storied pagoda, the Golden Hall, and the Lecture Hall are in a line from south to north and a **cloister** surrounds the whole complex.

7. Jikoku-ten protects the east and **supports** the country.

8. Zōchō-ten protects the south and brings a **bountiful harvest**.

9. Kōmoku-ten protects the west and has eyes that **see far and wide**.

10. Tamon-ten protects the east and listens to the **teaching of Buddha**.

11. Boddhisattva are dedicated to saving mankind before they **reach enlightenment**.

12. An **Eleven-faced Kannon Bodhisattva** has eleven faces in different directions and saves you in every direction in this world.

13. It is believed that the **floating wooden sutra tablet** will lead departed souls to rebirth in the Buddhist Paradise.

# 玉虫の宝庫

## *1* 四天王寺で仏教の基礎も学習しましょう

❶ **西門** 「極楽の東門」と呼ばれ、春分と秋分の日に美しい夕日が見られます。

❷ **西大門** 西門から西大門は極楽浄土で生まれ変わりたい人を魅了し、西大門は「極楽の門」と呼ばれています。転法輪（Dharma Wheel）があります。

❸ **香炉** 治療が必要なところに煙（＝仏様の息）をかけてもらいましょう。

❹ **四天王寺式伽藍** 中門、五重塔、金堂、講堂が南から北に並び、それを回廊が囲む飛鳥時代の様式を戦後、発掘調査で再現。仁王像は日本で最大級です。幾度もの災害や戦で破壊された五重塔は 8 代目です。

❺ **金堂** 菩薩と如来の違いや、聖徳太子が救世観音の生まれ変わりであり、如来になる資格があるにもかかわらず、現世で人々を救済されていることを説明します。

❻ **講堂** 十一面観音菩薩は現世でお救いくださり、阿弥陀如来は来世で極楽に導いてくださいます。現世と来世でも幸福へと導いてくださいます。

❼ **太子殿** 聖徳太子がお祀りされています。年に一度だけ公開される秘蔵です。

❽ **亀井堂** 経木流しをし、旅立った人の極楽往生を祈ります。

❾ **六時堂** 17 世紀の建造物で薬師如来が祀られ、一日中儀式が行われています。

❿ **おもかる地蔵** 両手で持ち上げたお地蔵様が軽ければ願いがかない、重ければ今は実現するときではないと言われています。

⓫ **賓頭盧さん** 神通力を持ち、体の痛みのある場所をなでれば痛みが消えます。

⓬ **石舞台** 厳島神社、住吉大社に並ぶ日本三大石舞台の一つです。

⓭ **極楽浄土の庭** 二河白道（にがびゃくどう）に基づく庭園です。浄土宗などで、火の河（怒りを表す）と水の河（貪欲を表す）の間にある、極楽浄土に通じる白い道とされています。

⓮ **地蔵山** 多くの地蔵様が魂を優しく導いてくださいます。

## *2* 通訳ガイドからのアドバイス

> **アドバイス1　観光客にもアクティブに楽しく参加してもらう！**
> 手水舎でのお清め、西大門で転法輪（Dharma Wheel）を回す、西大門を通り抜け香炉で仏様の息（Buddha's breath）をいただく、おもかる地蔵を持ち上げる、賓頭盧さんをなでるなど、楽しい思い出づくりをしてもらいましょう。

> **アドバイス2　救世観音像が片足を組んでいる理由は？**
> p. 96 で Guze Kannon is always ready to help people who are in trouble or suffering. と説明しているように、救世観音は苦しんでいる人、困っている人を助ける準備

ができているのです。

### アドバイス3　四天王像と邪鬼

四天王寺の四天王像は邪鬼を踏みつけていますが、表情は優しいです。邪鬼も反省を促しているようです。四天王の覚え方は、持国天、増長天、広目天、多聞天の頭文字より「持増広多（じぞうこうた）」です。

### アドバイス4　日本で唯一の経木流し

亀の形をした7世紀からの水槽の霊水（holy water）に経木を流し、旅立った愛する人（departed loved one）の極楽往生を祈ります。

### アドバイス5　日本で唯一の舎利出し法要（毎日11時より金堂にて）

僧侶が参拝者の頭に仏舎利を乗せてくださり、参拝者は御仏のお導きを祈ります。僧侶がお経を唱えるのを聞くことができます。

A Buddhist priest places relics of the Buddha on each worshipper's head, and the worshipper prays for the guidance of Buddha. You can listen to the Buddhist priests recite sutras.

### アドバイス6　行事を楽しんでもらう！

英語で座禅修行する（practice Buddhist meditation）の日、能や落語、七夕祭り、お盆の万燈籠、盆踊りなど、多くの行事があります。毎月21日はお大師さんの命日（Kūkai Memorial Day）、毎月22日はお太子さんの命日 (Prince Shōtoku Memorial Day) で、さまざまな仏教の行事が開催されます。

## 3 通訳ガイド体験日記

◎ **How many female emperors were there in Japan?（女性天皇の人数は？）の質問に答えられなかった。**

There were ten female emperors. です。

## 4 通訳ガイドお役立ち英語表現

「修行する」は do training、「修行を積む」は deepen *one's* training と言います。

# 5-1 梅田スカイビル

### 世界初の連結超高層建築と耐震性、リフトアップ工法について

G: Today, we're visiting Umeda Sky Building, which is a landmark of Osaka. *The Times* reported in 2008 that Umeda Sky Building had been selected as one of the top 20 buildings in the world, alongside the Parthenon, Taj Mahal, and Sagrada Familia. Have you ever tried to imagine the "Hanging Gardens of Babylon"?

T: Yes, it's one of the Seven Wonders of the World!

G: Right! I think we all dream of experiencing a world we have never seen. Today, you can experience it by visiting the "Kūchū Teien," which means "Floating Garden."

### In front of Umeda Sky Building

G: Here we are at Umeda Sky Building. Umeda Sky Building was the first connected **high-rise building** in the world. It's an epoch-making building in world architectural history.

T: It looks like a modern version of the **Arc de Triomphe in Paris**!

G: Right! Umeda Sky Building has been praised as a space-age version of the Arc de Triomphe. As for its **structural design**, connected buildings have great **stability**. Suppose two standing people are holding hands in a moving train; it's more stable than standing alone. It'**s resistant to** earthquakes. Also, connections at the top and in the middle **ensure** multiple secure **evacuation routes** in case of fire.

T: This structure is excellent from the point of view of disaster prevention!

G: The "lift-up" by wire construction method was used in this building for the first time ever. The basic structure of the Floating Garden **was assembled** on the ground and hoisted to a height of 150 meters by the lift-up method and **fixed** on to the top. You can watch how it was lifted up in a video in the "Architecture" room in the 40th-floor observatory. Both the aerial escalator and aerial bridge **were hoisted** up by the lift-up method. Please look up at the building. The elevator shaft can be seen on the west tower. The two escalators form a "V" shape. Today, we'll use the elevators and the escalators.

G：通訳ガイド　T：観光客

G：今日は、大阪のランドマークである梅田スカイビルに行きます。『タイムズ』紙は 2008 年に梅田スカイビルをパルテノン神殿、タージマハル、サグラダ・ファミリアに並んで世界の建造物 TOP20 として紹介しました。「バビロンの空中庭園」を想像してみたことはありますか？

T：はい。世界七不思議の一つですね。

G：その通りです。私たちはまだ見ぬ世界を体験することを夢見ているのだと思うのです。今日、あなたは梅田スカイビルの Floating Garden を意味する「空中庭園」を訪れ、それを体験することができます。

## 梅田スカイビルの前で

G：梅田スカイビルに到着しました。梅田スカイビルは、世界初の連結超高層建築でした。世界の建築史で画期的な高層ビルなのです。

T：近代版のパリの凱旋門のようですね！

G：その通りです！　梅田スカイビルは宇宙時代の凱旋門と称賛されています。構造様式に関して言えば、連結ビルには安定感があります。2 人の人が手をつなぎ合って動く電車の中で立っている姿を思い浮かべてみましょう。1 人で立つよりも安定しています。地震に強い構造です。頂部と中間層で連結されているため、火災時などの避難経路も複数確保されています。

T：この構造は防災上の観点からも優れていますね。

G：ワイヤーによるリフトアップ工法が、世界で初めてこの高層ビルに使われました。空中庭園の基礎部分は地上で組み立てられ、150 メートルまで持ち上げられ頂上に固定されました。リフトアップ工法でどのように持ち上げられたかは、40 階展望台フロアの「ARCHITECTURE」という部屋で映像をご覧になれます。空中エスカレーターも空中ブリッジも、同じ工法で持ち上げられました。ビルを見上げてください。エレベーターのシャフトがウエストタワーにあります。2 つのエスカレーターは V の形をしています。今日は、そのエレベーターとエスカレーターを使いますよ。

## 単語の小箱

☐ high-rise building 高層ビル　☐ Arc de Triomphe in Paris パリの凱旋門
☐ structural design 構造様式　☐ stability 安定　☐ be resistant to ... …に強い
☐ ensure …を確実にする　☐ evacuation route 避難経路　☐ be assembled 組み立てられる
☐ be fixed 固定される　☐ be hoisted 持ち上げられる

# 5-2 　梅田スカイビル

空中エレベーター、エスカレーター、ハートロック、空中庭園について

G: The journey up to the 39th floor is really exciting. First, let's take the see-through elevator from the 3rd to the 35th floor. For me, it's a little bit **scary**, but then we'll take a 45-meter, tube-type, see-through escalator from the 35th floor to the 39th floor. It feels as if you're climbing up into the sky.

### On the 40th floor, after going through the ticket office

G: The concept of this floor is clouds, so the interior is a uniform white. You feel you're in the clouds. You can get a "Heart Lock" made if you make a reservation. It takes less than 10 minutes to have your name, your **sweetheart**'s name and today's date **engraved on** it. Afterwards, you can go to the lovers' area called the "Lumi Deck" on the **rooftop observatory**, where you can swear your **eternal** love by locking it on the fence called the "Fence of Vows." Or, you can keep it as a **love charm**. It's up to you. Umeda Sky Building is famous as a romantic and popular spot.

T: I wish I had a girlfriend. Next time, I'll get a Heart Lock made.

### In the Kūchū Teien (Floating Garden Observatory)

G: The Kūchū Teien has no flowers or trees, but you can enjoy 360-degree panoramic views from the open deck. Many people **gather** on the west side of the building each evening to see the sun set over the Rokkō mountain range. At night, you can enjoy spectacular views of the shining lights of the skyscrapers to the south. You can walk on the Milky Way, made of luminous stones. It's very romantic!

T: Flowers and trees are not necessary in this observatory. There's a nice fresh breeze from the heavens. It's great being in the sunlight on the open deck during the daytime.

G: Please look down through this hole. It's been compared to a spaceship **launch pad**.

T: Superb!

G：通訳ガイド　T：観光客

G：39階までの旅はとてもエキサイティングですよ。まず、3階から35階までシースルーエレベーターに乗りましょう。私はちょっと怖いのですが、それから35階から39階までは45メートルのチューブタイプのシースルーエスカレーターに乗ります。エレベーターでは空に登っていくように感じると思いますよ。

### 受付ブースを通り抜けて40階で

G：このフロアのコンセプトは雲なので、内装は白色で統一されています。雲の上にいるように感じますよね。予約をすれば、「Heart Lock」を作ってもらうことができます。10分以内で、あなたの名前と恋人の名前、今日の日付を彫り込んでもらえます。それから、屋上展望台「ルミデッキ」という恋人たちの場所に行き、「誓いのフェンス」と呼ばれるフェンスにそれをロック（つる）して、永遠の愛を誓うことができます。愛のお守りとして持っていてもいいですよ。あなたの好きなようにできます。梅田スカイビルはロマンチックで人気のあるスポットとして知られています。

T：ガールフレンドがいればなあと思います。次回は「Heart Lock」を作ってもらいますね。

### 空中庭園展望台で

G：空中庭園には花も木もありませんが、オープンデッキから360度の全景を楽しめます。毎夕、多くの人が六甲山の連なりに沈む夕日を見に西側に集まります。夜には南側で高層ビルのきらびやかなライトを楽しめます。またルミナスストーン（発光する石）で作られた天の川を歩けるのですよ。とてもロマンチックです。

T：ここの展望台には花も木も必要ないですね。天からのさわやかなそよ風が吹いています。昼間、オープンデッキで輝く太陽の下にいられることは素晴らしいです。

G：この穴（開口部）をどうぞご覧ください。これは宇宙船が飛び立った発射台に例えられています。

T：すてきです！

## 単 語 の 小 箱

□ scary 怖い　□ sweetheart 恋人　□ engrave A on B AをBに彫る
□ rooftop observatory 屋上展望台　□ eternal 永遠の　□ love charm 愛のお守り
□ gather 集まる　□ launch pad 発射台

大阪

113

# 5-3 梅田スカイビル

昭和レトロの残る滝見小路、ペットブーム、交番について

### While walking along the "Takimi Kōji" in the basement

G: Here you can enjoy the nostalgic atmosphere of the Shōwa Era, during the "Era of High Economic Growth."

T: It's a time slip! We can see the "Space-age Arc de Triomphe," the Floating Garden in the sky, and nostalgic Japan! What's this dog?

G: The painting by a British painter called "His Master's Voice" is very popular. "Little Nipper" was the model for this painting. Little Nipper always listened to his master's voice from a **phonograph** after his death. Nipper-kun has been used as a trademark by a music company.

T: Great! I love animals. I've heard that Japanese dogs **are loyal to** their masters.

G: Yes. In front of Shibuya Station in Tokyo, you can see a **statue of a dog** called "Hachi." All his life, Hachi came to meet his master at Shibuya Station, and even after his master's death.

T: Wow! Hachi was also a loyal dog. I've heard that there are cat cafes in Japan.

G: Yes. You can play with cats in cat cafes. People who don't have pets at home probably visit cat cafes to relax. Japan is experiencing an ever-growing pet boom. I think this comes from the **aging society** and the **declining birthrate**.

T: You mean, both lonely senior citizens and children need friends?

G: Yes. Cats and dogs are taken good care of as family members.

T: What's this small, box-like house?

G: It's a small neighborhood **police box** called a "Kōban." Police boxes these days are bigger than this one. You can find Kōban everywhere in Japan. It's said that Japan has been a safe country thanks to Kōban. Kōban **are staffed** 24 hours a day in shifts **by** police officers in uniform.

G：通訳ガイド　T：観光客

## 地階の滝見小路を歩きながら

**G：** ここでは、昭和期の高度経済成長期時代のノスタルジックな雰囲気をお楽しみいただけます。

**T：** タイムスリップ！　宇宙時代の凱旋門、空中庭園、そして、ノスタルジックな日本も見られるのですね！　この犬は何ですか？

**G：** 英国の画家によって描かれた「飼い主の声」の絵は人気があります。「リトルニッパー」がこの絵のモデルです。ニッパー君は飼い主の死後も、蓄音機からいつも飼い主の声を聞いていました。ニッパー君は音楽会社の商標として使われています。

**T：** すごいです！　私は動物が大好きです。日本犬は飼い主に忠実だと聞いたことがあります。

**G：** はい。東京の渋谷駅前には、「ハチ」という犬の像があります。ハチはずっと渋谷駅に飼い主を迎えに行っていたのです。飼い主が亡くなった後でさえもです。

**T：** すごいですね。ハチも忠犬だったのですね。日本には猫カフェがあると聞きました。

**G：** はい。猫カフェでは猫と遊べます。おそらく家でペットを飼っていない人たちが、猫カフェに来てくつろぐのだと思います。日本はとめどなく続くペットブームなのです。これは高齢化社会と少子化によるものだと思います。

**T：** つまり、孤独な高齢者や子供たちが友達を必要としているということですか？

**G：** はい。犬も猫も家族として大切にされています。

**T：** この小さな箱のような家は何ですか？

**G：** これは「交番」と呼ばれる、近隣にある（身近な）警官派出所です。現在の警官派出所はこれよりは大きいです。交番はあちこちで見つけられますよ。日本は交番のおかげで安全な国だと言われています。交番では制服を着用した警察官が、24時間交代で勤務しています。

---

### 単語の小箱

□ **phonograph** 蓄音機　□ **be loyal to ...** …に忠実である　□ **statue of a dog** 犬の像
□ **aging society** 高齢化社会　□ **declining birthrate** 少子化　□ **police box** 交番
□ **be staffed by ...** …が配置されている

115

# 5-4 梅田スカイビル

### 世界に認められた梅田スカイビル、新里山について

### Having an okonomiyaki lunch in a restaurant in Takimi Kōji

**T**: I'm very impressed with Umeda Sky Building. I'd like to know about the history of it.

**G**: It was completed in 1993. It's one of the most popular tourist spots in Japan. Actually, it has experienced ups and downs. The number of visitors dropped around 2003, probably because Japan was in the middle of a **recession**, so I think Japanese people lost interest in bright, shining, **state-of-the-art** skyscrapers. However, it's becoming more and more popular, and this building is always on tourist **itineraries**. The day may come when it's one of the landmarks of Japan.

**T**: When did Umeda Sky Building become so popular?

**G**: Since it was selected as one of the top 20 buildings in the world in 2008, the number of visitors has been **skyrocketing** (laughing). Also, the world-famous travel guide book *Lonely Planet* recommended this building to travelers from abroad. Good creations are always **recognized** by professionals around the world.

**T**: I'm encouraged to hear that. I hope I'll be recognized as a musician.

**G**: I'm sure you'll be. The first presentation proposed a skyscraper of three connected towers, but this was changed to two. If three connected towers had been built, it wouldn't now be nicknamed the "Space-age Arc de Triomphe."

**T**: That's destiny! Interesting!

### In Shin-Satoyama, next to Umeda Sky Building

**G**: There's a rural Japanese landscape here called Shin-Satoyama, right in the middle of the city. This garden was created to attract wild birds and butterflies back to this area. There are rice paddy fields, too.

**T**: Great! By the way, I feel like going up to the rooftop observatory again. I especially loved the tube-type, see-through escalator. It felt like an exciting trip to space!

G：通訳ガイド　T：観光客

## 滝見小路のレストランでお好み焼きを食べながら

T：梅田スカイビルにとても感動しています。梅田スカイビルの歴史について知りたいです。

G：1993 年に完成しました。日本で最も人気のある観光地の一つです。実は、良い時代も悪い時代も経験しているのです。訪問者数は 2003 年頃に大幅に落ち込みました。日本が不景気の真っただ中にあったので、おそらく人々は最新鋭のキラキラ輝く高層ビルに興味をなくしたのだと思います。ですが、梅田スカイビルは年々ますます人気が出て、旅程表には必ず入っていますよ。日本のランドマークの一つになる日が来るかもしれません。

T：梅田スカイビルはいつこんなにも有名になったのですか？

G：2008 年に世界の建造物 TOP20 の一つに選ばれてから、訪問者数はうなぎ上りですよ（笑）。また、世界的に有名な旅行ガイドブック『ロンリープラネット』もこのビルを海外からのお客様に紹介しています。良いものは必ず世界のプロに認められるのです。

T：そのお話を聞いて元気が出ました。僕もミュージシャンとして認められたいです。

G：必ず認められると思いますよ！　最初のプレゼンでは三連の高層ビルが提案されたのですが、2 つに変更になりました。三連結高層ビルなら「宇宙時代の凱旋門」というニックネームで呼ばれてはいないでしょうね。

T：運命ですね。とても興味深いお話です！

## 梅田スカイビルに隣接する新里山で

G：新里山と呼ばれる田舎の風景が、都会のど真ん中にあります。この庭は野生の鳥や蝶々が戻ってくるようにデザインされています。田んぼもあります。

T：すごいですね！　ところで、空中庭園にもう一度登りたいです。特にチューブタイプのシースルーエスカレーターが好きですよ。心ときめく宇宙への旅行のように感じます。

## 単 語 の 小 箱

□ recession 不景気　□ state-of-the-art 最新鋭の　□ itinerary 旅程表
□ skyrocket 急激に伸びる　□ recognize …を認める

# 5-5 海遊館

天保山ハーバービレッジ、海遊館の8階、日本の森から世界の海について

### In front of the Kaiyūkan

G: Tempōzan Harbor Village consists of two parts: the "Kaiyūkan" Aquarium and Tempōzan Marketplace. The Kaiyūkan Aquarium was opened in 1990. It's one of the largest aquariums in the world. There are 620 **species** and 30,000 creatures. Fish, **mammals**, birds, **reptiles**, and **amphibians** are living together and **interacting** here. The most dynamic **feature** of the Kaiyūkan is the Pacific tank, which is a **recreation** of the Pacific Ocean. The Kaiyūkan has done everything possible to recreate the natural environment. I hope you enjoy it!

### On the 3rd floor

G: Here we are at the "Aqua Gate."
T: Beautiful! A tunnel in the sea! I feel like I'm walking under the sea.
G: It's exciting, isn't it? We'll take the elevator up to the 8th floor. On the 8th floor, you can experience the Japanese forest and walk down the spiral slope. You can enjoy observing the life of marine animals and fish on each floor. You can **peep inside** the lives of creatures from all over the world. The highlight of this aquarium is the **whale shark**, which can be seen from the 4th to the 6th floor. The whale shark is the biggest fish in the world.
T: I can't wait to see it.

### On the 8th floor

G: This is the "Japan Forest." Our trip to the seas of the world begins here!
T: I can't wait!
G: The **rainfall** in the forests creates small **streams** and they **flow into** the rivers, which **ultimately** flow into the sea.
T: So, forests are the source of water!

G：通訳ガイド　T：観光客

### 海遊館の前で

**G：**天保山ハーバービレッジは海遊館と天保山マーケットプレースの２つのセクショ
ンからできています。海遊館は1990年にオープンしました。世界最大級の水族
館です。620種類3万点の生き物がいます。魚類、哺乳類、鳥類、爬虫類、両
生類がお互いに関わり合いながら、一緒に暮らしています。海遊館の最もダイナ
ミックな特色は、太平洋を再現した太平洋水槽です。海遊館は最大限に自然環境
を再現しています。ご期待ください。

### 3階にて

**G：**「アクアゲート」に到着！

**T：**きれいですね！　海のトンネルですね！　海中を歩いているように感じます。

**G：**ワクワクしますよね！　エレベーターで8階に登ります。8階では日本の森を体
験できます。それから降りてきましょう。各フロアで海洋動物や魚の生活の見学
が楽しめますよ。世界中の生き物の生活をのぞくことができます。この水族館の
ハイライトは4階から6階にわたって見られるジンベエザメです。世界で一番大
きな魚です。

**T：**早く見たいです。

### 海遊館の8階にて

**G：**こちらは「日本の森」です。私たちの世界中の海への旅がここから始まります。

**T：**楽しみです！

**G：**森に降った雨は小さな流れとなり、やがて川へと流れ込み、最終的には海へと流
れ込みます。

**T：**森林は水の源ですね。

### 単語の小箱

□ **species** 種類　□ **mammal** 哺乳類　□ **reptile** 爬虫類　□ **amphibian** 両生類
□ **interact** 相互に作用する　□ **feature** 特色　□ **recreation** 再現、再生
□ **peep inside ...** …をのぞき込む　□ **whale shark** ジンベエザメ　□ **rainfall** 雨降り
□ **stream** 小川　□ **flow into ...** …へ流れ込む　□ **ultimately** 最終的に、ついに

# 5-6 海遊館

謎の多いジンベエザメ、神秘的なクラゲについて

### On the 6th floor

G: This is the Pacific Ocean area! A whale shark is coming towards us!

T: It's huge! The whale shark is big and calm, like a whale, just as the name suggests. I've seen several movies with man-eating sharks in them.

G: Whale sharks belong to the shark family, but they're not **violent** at all. They have 8,000 small, weak teeth. They **live on** plankton.

T: By the way, how much do they eat a day?

G: I've heard that one whale shark **is fed** from 6 to 8 kilograms of plankton a day, depending on its physical condition from day to day. There are two whale sharks in this aquarium: the male one is 0.7 tons, and the female one is 1.8 tons.

T: I've heard that there are many mysteries about the whale shark. Could you give an example?

G: When a whale shark **was captured** in Taiwan in 1995, 300 babies were found in its body, but this is only one example. Their **migratory paths** and **breeding patterns** are still a mystery.

T: Amazing! It's relaxing to watch this whale shark swimming around peacefully. I could stay here for hours.

### In the jellyfish area on the 3rd floor

G: This is the jellyfish area. It's dark. It looks like a galaxy of jellyfish!

T: I like the movements of the jellyfish. The shiny transparent jellyfish are floating in space. It looks really mysterious!

G：通訳ガイド　T：観光客

## 6階で

G：こちらが太平洋エリアです。ジンベエザメがこっちに来ますよ。

T：すごく大きいですね。ジンベエザメは名前（whale shark）が示している通り、クジラのように大きく穏やかですね。人食いザメが登場する映画を何本か見たことがあるのですが。

G：ジンベエザメはサメ科に属しますが、ちっとも狂暴ではないです。退化した小さな 8,000 本の歯を持っています。プランクトンを食べて生きています。

T：1日にどれくらいの量を食べるのですか？

G：日々の体調によりますが、1匹当たり6キロから8キロくらいの餌を与えられていると聞いています。この水族館には2匹のジンベエザメがいます。オスは 0.7 トン、メスは 1.8 トンです。

T：ジンベエザメは謎の多い動物だと聞いています。何か例を挙げてくれますか？

G：1995 年にジンベエザメが台湾で捕獲されたときには、300 匹もの胎児が体内から見つかりました。ですがこれは一例です。彼らの回遊経路や繁殖形態はいまだ謎なのです

T：すごい！　ジンベエザメが穏やかに泳いでいるのを見てリラックスできます。ここにずっといたいです。

## 3階の海月銀河で

G：こちらがクラゲのエリアです。暗いです。クラゲの銀河みたいですよね！

T：クラゲの動きが好きです。キラキラ輝く透明のクラゲが空間を浮遊していますね。ほんとうに神秘的ですね！

【 単 語 の 小 箱 】

□ violent 狂暴な　□ live on ... …を主食とする　□ be fed 餌を与えられる
□ be captured 捕獲される　□ migratory path 回遊経路　□ breeding pattern 繁殖形態

# 5-7 万博記念公園

 045

高度経済成長期と1970年大阪万博、太陽の塔①について

G: Today, we're visiting the Expo'70 **Commemorative** Park, which was developed on the site of the Japan World Exposition of 1970 in Osaka. Before we arrive, let me tell you about it. The Osaka World Exposition of 1970 was the first Expo to be held in Asia. This was the biggest Expo ever in the world at the time.

T: How many countries participated in it?

G: Seventy-seven countries participated in it. It was open for 183 days. The number of visitors was 64 million. It was a great success! There were 116 pavilions.

T: I'd like to know why Osaka was chosen as the site of Expo'70.

G: It was a time when Japan was in the middle of the "**Era of High Economic Growth**." It's said that at this time Japan became the second largest **economic power** after the U.S. Transportation systems were developed, and many shops opened to welcome people from all over the world to Expo'70.

### In front of the Tower of the Sun

G: Please look at the Tower of the Sun, the symbol of Expo'70.

T: It looks like the Tower of the Sun is welcoming us with both hands.

G: Right! It has three faces. The Golden Mask **represents** the future. The front face shows the present. The black sun on the back represents the past. The Tower of the Sun represents the source of life. The theme of Expo'70 was "Progress and Harmony for Mankind." I think this means many things. The progress of technology has brought us many **benefits** in our lives. On the other hand, it causes many problems. We should **achieve** a harmonious kind of progress.

T: Right! That's our challenge!

G: The Tower of the Sun was opened to the public in 2018 after a restoration project, so we can go inside. People had to wait for a few hours to enter it during Expo'70. I like the "Tree of Life" inside. At the bottom of the tree, we can see amoeba, and then fish, **dinosaurs**, and humans as we go up. You can see the **evolution** process of life.

G：通訳ガイド　T：観光客

G： 今日は 1970 年の大阪万博の会場跡地を整備した、万博記念公園を訪問します。
これについて、到着前にお話しさせてください。1970 年の大阪万博はアジアで
開催された最初の万博でした。これは当時、世界で一番大きな博覧会でした。

T： 何か国が参加したのですか？

G： 77 か国が参加しました。183 日間開催されました。入場者数は 6,400 万人でした。
大成功でした！　116 の展示館がありました。

T： なぜ大阪が 1970 年の万博の開催地として選ばれたのか知りたいです。

G： 日本は「高度経済成長期」の真っただ中でした。日本がアメリカに次ぐ経済大国
になった時だと言われています。大阪万博に来る世界の人々を歓迎するために、
交通機関は開発され、多くのお店がオープンしました。

### 太陽の塔の前で

G： 大阪万博のシンボルである太陽の塔を見てください。

T： 太陽の塔は両手を広げて歓迎してくれているみたいですね。

G： そうですね！　顔が 3 つあります。黄金色の顔は未来を表しています。正面の顔
は現在です。背面の黒い太陽は過去を表現しています。太陽の塔は生命の源を表
しています。大阪万博のテーマは「人類の進歩と調和」でした。私はこれが多く
のことを意味すると思います。技術の進歩は私たちの生活にたくさんの恩恵をも
たらしてくれています。その一方で、多くの問題ももたらしています。私たちは、
調和の取れた進歩を実現させなければならないのだと思います。

T： その通りです。これは私たちの課題ですね！

G： 太陽の塔は 2018 年に再生事業を経て一般公開されましたので、内部に入れます。
大阪万博開催中は、中に入るのに何時間もかかったのですよ。私は塔の内部にあ
る「生命の樹」が好きです。樹の一番下はアメーバで、そこから上がるにつれ、魚、
恐竜、人類に至るまでの進化の過程を見ることができます。

## 単 語 の 小 箱

☐ commemorative 記念の　☐ Era of High Economic Growth 高度経済成長期
☐ economic power 経済大国　☐ represent …を表す　☐ benefit 恩恵
☐ achieve …を達成する　☐ dinosaur 恐竜　☐ evolution 進化

# 5-8 万博記念公園

太陽の塔②、4つの時代の日本庭園、万博の時代について

### After leaving the Tower of the Sun

G: How did you like the inside of the tower?
T: I was impressed by the Tree of Life, which represents the evolutionary process of life. I felt as if I was part of the process of evolution.
G: Great! When I was seven years old, I went inside. I felt I was in space. And talking of space, the U.S. Pavilion displayed a moon rock brought back by Apollo 12. The U.S. Pavilion was very popular.

### Walking around the Japanese landscape gardens

G: Let's go along the stream from west to east. The special feature of these gardens is that you can enjoy gardens from four different periods: the Heian period from the 8th to the 12th century, the Kamakura and Muromachi periods from the 12th to the 16th century, the Edo period from the 17th to the 19th century, and the modern era.
T: It's fantastic! We can enjoy only one style of garden in a temple or shrine. Wow! The **azaleas** are in full bloom.
G: During the Edo period, there was a **horticulture boom**, and **plant breeding** was popular, so you can enjoy various types of azaleas here. You can enjoy different types of flowers in different seasons. Expo'70 is a calendar of flowers!

### After enjoying the National Museum of Ethnology, the Japan Folk Crafts Museum, and the Osaka Expo'70 Pavilion

T: The park is really huge. I enjoyed it a lot.
G: I'm happy to hear that. Electric bicycles, wireless telephones, and **videophones** were exhibited at Expo'70. Now we use them every day. People's dreams have come true. This was also the time when the first Kentucky Fried Chicken and McDonald's were opened in Japan. The number of visitors from overseas in 2019 was about 29 million. In 1970, it was under one million. Japanese people were very glad to see guests from abroad. Expo'70 helped them to **broaden their horizons**.

G：通訳ガイド　T：観光客

## 太陽の塔を出てから

G：塔の中はどうでしたか？

T：生命の進化の過程を表した生命の樹を見て、感銘を受けました。進化の過程に自分自身がいるような気持ちになりました。

G：素晴らしいです！　私は7歳のときに入館したことがあります。宇宙にいるかのように感じました。宇宙と言えば、アメリカのパビリオンがアポロ12号が持ち帰った月の石を展示していました。アメリカのパビリオンはとても人気でした。

## 日本庭園周辺を歩きながら

G：小川に沿って西から東に歩きましょう。この庭園の特色は、4つの時代の異なった庭を見られることです。8世紀から12世紀までの平安時代、12世紀から16世紀までの鎌倉・室町時代、17世紀から19世紀までの江戸時代、そして現代です。

T：素晴らしい！　お寺や神社では1つの時代の庭園しか見ることができないですよね。すごい！　ツツジが満開です。

G：江戸時代は園芸ブームで、品種改良も人気でしたので、多くの種類のツツジを見られます。異なる季節に異なるお花を楽しめます。大阪万博はお花のカレンダーなのですよ！

## 国立民族学博物館、日本民芸館、EXPO'70 パビリオンを訪問したのちに

T：万博記念公園は本当に大きいですね。とても楽しかったです。

G：それを聞いてうれしいです。大阪万博では電気自転車、ワイヤレステレホン、テレビ電話が展示されていました。今は普通に使っていますね。人々の夢が実現したのです。また、当時は日本にケンタッキーフライドチキンやマクドナルドの1号店が開店した時代です。2019年の来日外国人の数は2,900万人でした。1970年には100万人にも届きませんでした。日本人は海外からのお客様に会えてとても喜んだのです。大阪万博のおかげで、人々は視野を広げることができたのです。

### 単語の小箱

□ azalea ツツジ　□ horticulture boom 園芸ブーム　□ plant breeding 品種改良
□ videophone テレビ電話　□ broaden *one's* horizons 視野を広める

## 瞬間英作文

1. 梅田スカイビルは世界初の連結超高層建築です。

2. ワイヤーによる「リフトアップ」工法が、世界で初めてこの連結超高層ビルに使われました。

3. 海遊館のハイライトは、4階から6階にいるジンベエザメです。

4. あるジンベエザメが台湾で捕獲されたときは、300匹の胎児が体内から見つかりました。

5. 1970年の大阪万国博覧会はアジアで初めて開かれた、当時世界で一番大きな博覧会でした。


### 解答例

1. Umeda Sky Building was the first **connected high-rise building** in the world.

2. The **"lift-up" by wire construction method** was used in this connected high-rise building for the first time ever.

3. The highlight of the Kaiyūkan aquarium is the **whale shark**, from the 4th to the 6th floor.

4. When a whale shark **was captured** in Taiwan, 300 babies were found in its body.

5. The Japan World Exposition of 1970 in Osaka was the first Expo to **be held** in Asia and was the biggest Expo ever in the world at the time.

---

1. connected high-rise building　高層連結ビル
2. lift-up by wire construction method　ワイヤーによるリフトアップ工法
3. whale shark　ジンベエザメ　　4. be captured　捕獲される　　5. be held　開催される

瞬間英作文 ❖ 玉虫の宝庫

## 玉虫の宝庫

# 1 梅田スカイビル、天保山・海遊館、万博記念公園のポイント

❶ **梅田スカイビル** 世界の建造物 TOP 20 にランクインした、未来の凱旋門とも呼ばれる連結超高層建築ビル。地階は昭和レトロ商店街。

❷ **天保山・海遊館** マーケットプレースは昭和レトロ。海遊館はジンベエザメが人気の、世界有数の規模を誇る水族館です。

❸ **万博記念公園** 平安、鎌倉・室町、江戸、現代と各時代の日本庭園を楽しめて、パビリオンでは昭和レトロを堪能することができます。隣の EXPOCITY にある、生きているミュージアム「ニフレル」も人気があります。

# 2 通訳ガイドからのアドバイス

**アドバイス 1　難しい耐震性の話はわかりやすく！**
連結超高層ビルの梅田スカイビルでは「動く電車の中を 1 人で立つより、2 人で手をつなぐ方が安定感がある」と説明しましょう（p. 110 参照）。

**アドバイス 2　日本事象も入れて楽しく！**
梅田スカイビルの昭和レトロ商店街で交番（police box）の紹介やペットブームの話から、少子高齢化社会の話も盛り上がります。

# 3 通訳ガイド体験日記

海遊館ではゲストの撮影係に徹していました。When a whale shark was captured, 300 babies were found in its body. は台湾のゲストから聞き、それ以来この話をしています。

# 4 通訳ガイドお役立ち英語表現

①②③のエリアでは、You can enjoy the nostalgic atmosphere of the Shōwa Era during the years of high economic growth from 1955 to 1973.（あなたは 1955 年から 1973 年までの高度成長期の昭和の雰囲気を味わえます）と紹介しましょう。1970 年の万博をきっかけに Bigger is better.（大きいことはいいことだ）という表現が流行しました。

# その他の名所めぐり

## ❶ 中之島

### 中之島公園　バラの咲き乱れる都会のオアシス

Nakanoshima Park was established in 1891 as **Osaka's first city park**. It is a waterfront park sandwiched between the Dōjima and Tosabori rivers. The city's first beer garden was incorporated into this park. This park is famous as a rose garden, featuring about 310 rose species and 3,700 rose bushes. Tourists like to walk around this park, and office workers enjoy their break times here. This park is beautifully illuminated at night at the end of the year.

＊　＊　＊

　中之島公園は、1891年に**大阪市で初めて誕生した公園**です。堂島川と土佐掘川に挟まれた水辺公園で、大阪市初のビアガーデンが公園内に取り入れられました。この公園は約310種、約3,700株からなるバラ園でも知られています。観光客は公園の散策を好み、オフィスワーカーも休憩時間を楽しんでいます。年末には美しくライトアップされます。

### 大阪市立中央公会堂　大阪商人の魂が生きるネオルネサンス様式の建物

This is Osaka City Central Public Hall, built of red brick in the Neo-Renaissance style. Osaka City Central Public Hall has played a very important role in cultural, artistic, and social activities since it was completed in 1918. For example, a lecture was held here by the social activist **Helen Keller**. **Yuri Gagarin**, who was the first man in space, gave a lecture here, too. The construction costs were covered by a donation of one million yen from Einosuke Iwamoto, who was a stockbroker. **One million yen at that time** is equivalent to **about 50 billion yen today**. **Mr. Iwamoto**, who went to America on an inspection tour, was impressed by the **charity work** and endowments there, and, having learned the importance of building public facilities, **donated one million yen to Osaka City**. It's also said that he was impressed by Carnegie Hall. Unfortunately, after that, his stock market investments failed. People around him advised him to ask for at least part of the donation back, but he refused to do so, saying that it would be shameful for an Osaka merchant. Sadly, he committed suicide before the completion of the hall. If he saw it today, he would be pleased. Many important events are held here, and it is loved by many people as **one of the symbols of Osaka**. Osaka City Central Public Hall was designated as an Important Cultural Property of the nation in 2002.

＊　＊　＊

　こちらは赤れんがで造られた、ネオルネサンス様式の大阪市中央公会堂です。1918年に完成して以来、文化面、芸術面、社会活動面で大切な役割を果たしています。例えば、ここでは社会活動家の**ヘレン・ケラー**の講義が行われました。人類初の宇宙飛行士**ユーリ・ガガーリン**の講演も行われました。建設費用は株式仲買人・岩本栄之助氏の100万円の寄付で賄われました。**当時の100万円**は現在の**50億円**に相当します。岩本氏はアメリカに視察旅行に行き、**慈善事業**と寄付に感銘を受け、公共施設の建設の重要性を学んで**大阪市に100万円を寄付**しました。

カーネギーホールに感銘を受けたとも言われています。その後、不運にも彼は株式投資に失敗してしまいました。周囲の人は、大阪市への寄付金を少しでも返してもらうように勧めましたが、岩本氏は「それは大阪商人の恥」として拒否しました。残念ながら、彼はホールが完成する前に自殺してしまいました。岩本氏が今の公会堂を見たら、喜ぶことでしょう。多くの大切な行事がここで開かれ、**大阪のシンボル**の一つとして、たくさんの人に愛されています。大阪市中央公会堂は 2002 年に、国の重要文化財に指定されました。

**アドバイス** ➡ ゴルバチョフやアインシュタインも講演した公会堂で、アクアライナーからも見えます。建設費の寄付をした岩本氏の大阪商人の魂にも驚くゲストが多いです。

## 中之島図書館　レトロなネオバロック様式

The Osaka Prefectural Nakanoshima Library is in the Neo-Baroque style. Its four wide columns remind us of a **Grecian temple**. It was built in 1904. Do you know Japan's three biggest conglomerates? They are Mitsui, Mitsubishi, and Sumitomo. The 15th head of the Sumitomo family donated a large amount of money for its construction and the purchase of books. You will be surprised by its high ceilings, stained glass, and well-polished stairway handrails.

＊　＊　＊

大阪府立中之島図書館はネオバロック様式です。4 本の太い柱が**ギリシャ神殿**を思い出させます。1904 年に建設されました。日本の三大財閥をご存じですか？　三井、三菱、住友です。住友家の 15 代目当主が、図書館建設と図書購入のために多額のお金を寄付しました。高い天井、ステンドグラス、磨かれた階段の手すりを見た人は驚きます。

# ❷ 御堂筋のイチョウ並木と彫刻

The Ginkgo is a symbolic tree of Osaka. The Ginkgo tree is said to be a fossil which survived the Ice Age. The Midōsuji Avenue connects two centers of the city's activities, the Umeda central business district in the north and the Namba entertainment district in the south. **Midōsuji Avenue** is called **the "Champs-Elysées of the Orient."** Ginkgo trees line both sides of the avenue. The Ginkgo trees cast a lovely shade in summer. When the leaves turn yellowish gold in autumn, you feel as if you are walking on a carpet of golden leaves. You can enjoy the beauty of nature in an urban area. From November to January you can enjoy brilliant illuminations stretching for 4 kilometers. Different illuminations can be seen in different seasons. In 2015, Midōsuji Avenue was recognized as the street with the **"most illuminated trees" by the Guinness Book of Records**. This avenue is also called "Midōsuji Sculpture Avenue" because there are 29 sculptures by famous sculptors.

＊　＊　＊

イチョウは大阪のシンボルの木です。イチョウは氷河期を生き抜いた化石と呼ばれています。御堂筋は北のビジネスの中心地・梅田と南の娯楽街・難波を結んでいます。**御堂筋**は「**東洋のシャンゼリゼ**」と呼ばれています。通りの両側にはイチョウ並木があります。イチョウの木は

夏には美しい木陰を作ります。葉が黄色味がかった金色に色づく秋には、黄金色の葉のカーペットの上を歩いているような気分になります。都会で美しい自然を楽しめるのです。11月から1月には、色鮮やかなイルミネーションを4キロにわたって楽しめます。季節が異なると、異なるイルミネーションが見られます。御堂筋は、2015年には「**最も多く街路樹にイルミネーションを施した通り**」として、**ギネス世界記録に認定**されました。通りには有名彫刻家たちの29の作品があり、「御堂筋彫刻通り」とも呼ばれています。

## ❸ 菅原道真を祀る大阪天満宮

Michizane Sugawara, the 9th century **scholar and politician**, is enshrined in Osaka Tenmangu. He is revered as **the patron of learning**.

\* \* \*

　9世紀の**学者であり政治家**の菅原道真が、大阪天満宮にお祀りされています。道真は**学問の守護神**として尊敬されています。

## ❹ 日本三大祭りの一つ、天神祭

The Tenjin Festival in Osaka is one of the three major festivals in Japan, along with the Tokyo Kanda Festival and the Kyoto Gion Festival. The Tenjin Festival is a spectacular festival held every year on July 24 and 25. The history of the Tenjin Festival is said to date back to 951. The festival's highlights are the gorgeous procession of 3,000 people in costumes and the procession of 100 boats on the river. **The spirit of Michizane**, transferred to a **portable shrine** with a phoenix decoration, is carried down to the Ōkawa River. The spirit of Michizane is then transferred to a boat and taken up and down the river. One hundred boats go back and forth along the river. This festival represents the **"Water Metropolis Osaka."** There are two main purposes to this festival. One is to express gratitude to Michizane and show him Osaka's prosperity. The other is to pray for future prosperity. The last event of the festival is the **"Votive Fireworks Display."** Five thousand fireworks are set off and beautifully decorate the sky. These days, on the day before the festival, the portable shrine is carried by 80 young ladies who have been selected by audition. This also attracts many people.

\* \* \*

　大阪の天神祭は、東京の神田祭、京都の祇園祭と並ぶ、日本三大祭りの一つです。天神祭は華やかな祭りで、毎年7月24日と25日に開催されます。天神祭の歴史は951年にさかのぼります。祭りのハイライトは衣装を身につけた3,000人の豪華な行列と、100隻もの船渡御の列です。**菅原道真の御神霊**が鳳凰の装飾をつけた**みこし**に移され、大川まで行きます。道真の御神霊は、それから船に移され、川を下ります。100隻もの船が川を行き交います。これは「**水都大阪**」を代表する祭りで、2つの目的があります。1つは道真に感謝し、大阪の繁栄を見せること。もう1つは、これからの繁栄を祈ることです。祭りの最後のイベントは「**奉納花火**」です。約5,000発の花火が打ち上げられ、空を美しく飾ります。今日では、お祭りの前日にオーデイションで選ばれた80人の若い女性がみこしを担ぎます。これも多くの人々を魅了してい

ます。

**アドバイス** ➡ 神様の魂をみこしに乗せて感謝し、繁栄を祈るのが日本の祭りの基本です。夏祭りでは浴衣姿（light cotton kimono）を喜ぶゲストが多いです。

# ❺ 百舌鳥・古市古墳群と仁徳天皇陵
## 大仙陵古墳とも呼ばれている

The Mozu-Furuichi Kofun Group was designated as a World Heritage Site in 2019. The Mozu-Furuichi Kofun Group includes 49 burial mounds, which represent the culture of the Kofun period in Japan from the 3rd to the 6th century. The most famous one is the mausoleum of Emperor Nintoku, located in Sakai City. It was built in the 5th century. It is the largest keyhole-shaped tumulus in Japan. It's 486 meters long and 306 meters wide. The total area is 464,000 square meters. The mausoleum of Emperor Nintoku is **one of the three most famous burial mounds**, along with the Great Pyramid in Egypt and the mausoleum of the first Qing emperor of China.

＊　＊　＊

　百舌鳥・古市古墳群は、2019 年に世界文化遺産に登録されました。百舌鳥・古市古墳群は、3 世紀から 6 世紀の日本の古墳時代の 49 古墳を含んでいます。最も有名なのは、堺にある仁徳天皇陵です。5 世紀に造られました。日本で一番大きな前方後円墳です。長さは 486 メートル、幅は 306 メートル。総面積は 46 万 4,000 平方メートルです。仁徳天皇陵は、エジプトの大ピラミッド、中国の秦始皇帝陵とともに、**世界の三大墳墓の一つ**です。

# ❻ サンタマリア号で大阪湾周遊

The "Santa Maria" is a four-floor sightseeing ship. This ship is modeled after the Santa Maria in which Columbus discovered the North American continent. This Santa Maria in Tempōzan is about twice the size of **Columbus's Santa Maria**. You can enjoy **a 45-minute cruise** around the most famous spots in Osaka Bay. Columbus's room is on the first floor. In this room you can see items such as the instruments and materials necessary for a sea voyage.

＊　＊　＊

　サンタマリア号は 4 階建ての遊覧船です。コロンブスが北アメリカ大陸へ到達した際に乗船していた船をモデルにしています。天保山のサンタマリア号は、**コロンブスのサンタマリア号**の約 2 倍の大きさです。**45 分間のクルーズ**では、大阪湾の有名な場所の周遊をお楽しみいただけます。船の 1 階にはコロンブスの部屋があり、航海に必要な機器や資料などを見ることができます。

# ❼ 高速道路が貫通している TKP ゲートタワービル

TKP Gate Tower Building is a 16-story office building located in Osaka City. The Hanshin Expressway **runs through the 5th through 7th floors of the building**.

\* \* \*

　TKP ゲートタワービルは大阪市にある地上 16 階建てのオフィスビルです。 阪神高速道路がビルの 5 階から 7 階部分を貫通しています。

**アドバイス** ➠ 阪神高速道路 11 号池田線から大阪駅方面へと向かう、梅田出口に差し掛かるときに見られるこのビルに驚くゲストが多いです。

# ❽ 勝尾寺

## 名前の由来

Katsuoji Temple was built to pray for the Emperor Seiwa's recovery from illness. Emperor Seiwa regained his health, so this temple was named "Katsuoji." "Katsu" means victory. It is believed this temple helps people to win. **Many famous warriors, including Hideyoshi Toyotomi, visited this temple to pray for victory in battle**.

\* \* \*

　勝尾寺は清和天皇の病気平癒を祈願して建てられました。清和天皇が健康を取り戻したので、この寺は勝尾寺と名づけられました。「勝」は勝利を意味します。この寺は人々の勝利を助けると信じられています。豊臣秀吉をはじめ、**多くの有名な武将**が**戦勝祈願**に参拝しました。

## お清め橋

After passing through the Niōmon gate, there is a **purification bridge**, and after purifying yourself with the mist that comes out from both sides, you will enter the temple grounds. You will feel healed by the **negative ions** and refreshed.

\* \* \*

　仁王門を抜けると**お清め橋**があり、両脇から出る霧で身を清めてから境内に入ります。**マイナスイオン**に癒やされ、リフレッシュするでしょう。

## 本堂とお経の放送

The main deity is an eleven-headed Kannon Bodhisattva. On the 18th of every month, it is opened to the public. As you walk through the precincts of Katsuoji Temple, you will hear sutra chants. **A monk chants the sutras 17 times a day** accompanied by drums and a wooden fish, and it **is broadcast** around the precincts. Please visit the temple peacefully while listening to the sutra chanting that echoes through the grounds.

\* \* \*

　本尊は十一面観音です。毎月 18 日に御開帳されます。境内を歩くとお経が聞こえてきます。

太鼓と木魚を交えて1日17回、**住職が読経し、放送されています**。境内に響き渡るお経を聞きながら、心穏やかにお参りください。

## 勝ちだるまに祈願する

If you look at the large number of votive Daruma dolls in the temple grounds, you can see that your prayers will be answered in this temple.
1. Choose a Daruma doll that you feel a "connection" with.
2. Write the goal you want to achieve over the year on the back of the Daruma doll.
3. Write your goal in life on the bottom of the Daruma doll.
4. Put your gratitude into the incense sticks.
5. Let the smoke from the incense seep into the Daruma doll above the incense burner.
6. Pledge that you'll work hard to achieve your goal, and **paint the right eye black**.
7. When you have achieved your goal, **paint the left eye of the Daruma doll**.
8. Report the result of your prayer in the main hall, and place the "winning" Daruma doll in the votive offering box.

\* \* \*

境内に奉納された数多くのだるまから、この寺で祈願がかなうことがわかります。
1.「ご縁」を感じただるまを選んでください。
2. 1年間に達成したい目標をだるまの背中に書いてください。
3. 人生の目的をだるまの底面に書いてください。
4. 感謝の気持ちをお線香に込め、念じてください。
5. 香炉の上で、お線香の煙をだるまに染み込ませてください。
6. 目標達成のための努力することを誓い、**右目を黒く塗って目を入れてください**。
7. 目標が達成できたら、**だるまの左目を入れてください**。
8. 本堂で祈願結果の報告をし、勝ちだるまを奉納箱に収めてください。

## 境内にある弁天堂

Benzai-ten is the god of wisdom, entertainment, and music.

\* \* \*

弁才天は、知恵と芸能と音楽の神様です。

## 知恵の輪はパワースポット

1. From the entrance, walk slowly around clockwise seven times and walk to the center point.
2. Next, walk around seven times from the center point in the opposite direction.
3. Sit on the stone and pray. If you have time, please meditate.
4. Return to the entrance. You will receive a surge of strength and wisdom.

\* \* \*

1. 入り口よりゆっくりと右回りに7周。中心点まで歩いてください。
2. 中心点より逆周りに7周してください。
3. 石の上に座って合掌してください。時間があれば瞑想してください。
4. 入り口に戻ってください。湧き出る力や良い知恵をいただけます。

# ❾ 日本で2番目に高い skyscraper、あべのハルカス 300（展望台）

"Harukas" is an old Japanese word which means "**to brighten.**" Abeno Harukasu has brightened up Osaka! The Harukas Observatory is 300 meters above ground. As of 2025, it's **the second highest skyscraper** in Japan. Observation decks are located on the 58th, 59th, and 60th floors. You can enjoy 360-degree views of Osaka city. On fine days, you can enjoy the views to the ancient capital of Kyoto and to Kobe and the Rokko mountains. If you are adventurous, please experience EDGE THE HARUKAS on fine days in spring and autumn. It's a thrilling attraction! You'll feel as if you are **walking on the edge of a 300-meter cliff.** The views are superb!

\* \* \*

　「ハルカス」とは、「**明るくする**」という意味の古い日本語です。あべのハルカスは大阪を明るくしました。あべのハルカス展望台は地上300メートル。2025年現在、日本で**2番目に高い超高層ビル**です。58階、59階、60階に展望台があります。大阪市内を360度見渡すことができます。天気の良い日には、古都・京都から神戸、六甲山系まで見渡せます。冒険好きな人は、春秋の晴れの日には、ぜひ「エッジ・ザ・ハルカス」を体験してみてください。スリル満点のアトラクションです！　まるで**300メートルの断崖絶壁を歩いている**ような感覚を味わえます。絶景ですよ。

**アドバイス** ▶ 大阪城、四天王寺、住吉大社、通天閣などと組み合わせてスケジュールが組まれていることが多いです。

# Chapter 2

# 奈良

自然豊かな奈良では、東大寺、春日大社、興福寺といった人気スポットはもちろん、人々がシカと共存してきた歴史についても紹介しましょう。

（上）東大寺の大仏様（iStock.com/vanbeets）
（右）春日大社の中門・御廊（写真提供：春日大社）
（下）鹿苑（写真提供：春日大社）

## 1-1　東大寺

創建の目的、時代背景、聖武天皇、労働人口、行基、通勤するシカについて

G: Today, we're visiting Tōdaiji Temple in Nara. Nara was the capital of Japan from 710 to 784. Tōdaiji Temple was built in the middle of the 8th century by order of Emperor Shōmu. You will **be amazed** when you see the Great Buddha Hall, which is one of the largest wooden structures in the world, and the Great Buddha, which is the largest **gilt-bronze** Buddhist statue in the world.

T: Why were such large structures built?

G: Buddhism was protected by the government as a state religion. Emperor Shōmu was a devout Buddhist. Natural disasters had struck one after another, and many people were suffering from **smallpox**. Emperor Shōmu ordered Tōdaiji Temple to be built to restore the nation to health through Buddhism. Emperor Shōmu wanted all living things to be happy. A total of 2.6 million people **were involved in** the construction of the Great Buddha Hall and the Great Buddha, even though the population of Japan was only about 5 million.

T: Half of the population at that time!

G: A Buddhist monk named Gyōki was appointed leader to gather support for the construction of the Great Buddha. Gyōki improved their lives by, for example, building bridges and creating ponds. He gathered volunteer workers, funds, and materials from all over Japan. He worked with them very hard for the happiness of the people. Gyōki **passed away** before the Great Buddha was completed. A statue of Gyōki stands in front of Kintetsu Nara Station, facing in the direction of the Great Buddha Hall. He's loved by many people even today.

### Walking to the Great South Gate of the Tōdaiji Temple grounds

T: There are so many friendly deer!

G: Let's feed them after visiting the temple. Please be careful not to step on the **poop** (laughing). I often visit this temple as a tour guide. At nine, deer appear in a kind of **procession**, and leave in a group at five. They look like commuters!

T: Yes! They work here by welcoming so many visitors (laughing).

G：通訳ガイド　T：観光客

G：今日は奈良の東大寺に行きます。奈良は、710年から784年まで日本の都でした。東大寺は、8世紀半ばに聖武天皇の勅願で建立されました。世界最大級の木造建築である大仏殿と、世界最大の金銅仏である大仏様を見たら、驚くと思いますよ。

T：なぜそのような大きなものが造られたのですか？

G：仏教は国家宗教として、政府に保護されていました。聖武天皇は熱心な仏教徒でした。自然災害が次から次へと発生し、多くの人が天然痘で苦しんでいました。聖武天皇は仏教を通じて国家を健全にするために、東大寺建立の勅願を出しました。聖武天皇は生きとし生けるものが幸せになることを望みました。日本の人口はおよそ500万人でしたが、延べ260万人の人々が大仏殿と大仏の創建に携わりました。

T：当時の人口の半分ですね！

G：行基という名の仏僧が、大仏建立に支援を集めるためのリーダーに任命されました。行基は、例えば橋を建てたり、池を造ったりして人々の生活を向上させました。彼はボランティアと資金、資材を日本中から集めました。彼は人々の幸せのために、彼らとともに一生懸命働きました。行基は大仏が完成する前に他界しました。行基の像が近鉄奈良駅前に、大仏殿の方を向いて立っています。彼は今日でも多くの人に愛されています。

### 東大寺の南大門に向かって歩きながら

T：フレンドリーなシカがたくさんいますね！

G：お寺に参拝してから、餌をあげましょう。ふんを踏まないように気をつけてくださいね（笑）。私はツアーガイドとしてよく東大寺を訪れます。シカは9時にある種の行列をなして現れて、5時にグループで去っていきます。通勤者みたいですよ。

T：そうですね！　シカたちはここで多くの訪問者を歓迎して働いてくれているのですね（笑）。

## 単語の小箱

□ be amazed 驚く　□ gilt-bronze 金銅の　□ smallpox 天然痘
□ be involved in ... …に携わる　□ pass away 他界する　□ poop ふん
□ procession 行列

# 1-2 東大寺

南大門、仁王について

### In front of the Great South Gate

**G**: The Great South Gate is the main gate of Tōdaiji Temple, and it is said to be the biggest temple gate in Japan. It was once destroyed by a typhoon in 962, and the present one was built in 1203. Chōgen, who studied Buddhism and learned construction techniques in Sung Dynasty China, contributed a lot to the reconstruction. The pillars were made from whole Japanese **cypress** trees. This size of cypress no longer grows in Japan. It's said that as many as 780 average-sized Japanese houses could be built with the amount of **lumber** used in the construction of this gate. Japan is sometimes hit by earthquakes. A kind of interlocking system is used to protect the structure from damage.

**T**: It's well-designed!

**G**: Next, please look at the pair of Deva Kings standing on either side of the Great South Gate. They're guardian deities. They were also rebuilt in 1203. The artworks of the samurai period are dynamic and powerful and are often compared to those of the Renaissance. They're designed so that your eyes meet theirs when you look up at them. The Deva Kings are wooden statues made using **joint block construction**. They are made up of 3,000 pieces of wood and were created in only 69 days by a group of **Buddhist sculptors** headed by Unkei and Kaikei, the most famous Japanese sculptors.

**T**: They're superb!

**G**: Look at the Deva King on the left. His mouth is open. He seems to be **mouthing** the sound "Ah." Look at the Deva King on the right. His mouth is closed. He seems to be mouthing the sound "Un." "Ah" is the first letter in the Sanskrit phonetic system, and "Un" is the last. We have a phrase, "ah-un breathing." It means a relationship between two people is so close that they can communicate with each other without any words. In other words, the Deva Kings are guarding the temple with their "ah-un breathing." It's also said that the Deva Kings protect Buddhism and **conquer** our **worldly desires** with their weapons, called "Vajra."

G：通訳ガイド　T：観光客

## 南大門の前で

**G**：南大門は東大寺の正門で、日本で一番大きな山門と言われています。一度は962年に台風で壊れてしまい、現在の門は1203年に再建されました。宋（中国）で仏教を勉強し、建築技術も学んだ重源が、再建に大きな貢献を果たしました。柱はヒノキの一本木でできています。同じ大きさのヒノキはもう日本では生育しません。この門の建設に使われたのと同じ量の木材を使えば、日本の平均的な規模の家が780戸も建つと言われています。日本は地震に襲われることがあります。構造物を損傷から守るため、一種のインターロックシステムが使われています。

**T**：とても工夫されているのですね！

**G**：次に、南大門の両側に立つ仁王像をご覧ください。彼らは守護神です。こちらも1203年に再建されました。侍の時代の芸術作品はダイナミックで力強く、ルネサンス時代の作品とよく比較されます。見上げたときにあなたの目と彼らの目が合うように作られています。仁王には寄木造が用いられています。3,000の材木からできていて、日本で一番有名な彫刻家である運慶、快慶が率いた仏師集団によってわずか69日間で作られました。

**T**：素晴らしいですね！

**G**：左側の仁王様をご覧ください。口が開いています。「あ」の音を発音しているようです。右側の仁王様をご覧ください。彼の口は閉じています。「うん」の音を発音しているようです。「あ」はサンスクリット語の音韻体系で最初の文字、「うん」は最後です。「あうんの呼吸」という言葉があります。2人の間の息がぴったりで、お互いに言葉がなくても意思伝達する関係を意味します。言い換えれば、仁王様は「あうんの呼吸」でお寺を守っているのです。仁王様は仏教を守り、「金剛杵」という武器で人々の煩悩を打ち砕くとも言われています。

### 単語の小箱

□ **cypress** ヒノキ　□ **lumber** 木材　□ **joint block construction** 寄木造
□ **Buddhist sculptor** 仏師　□ **mouth** …を発音する、口の形だけで言う
□ **conquer** …を打ち破る　□ **worldly desires** 煩悩（worldly sins や worldly passions とも言う）

# 1-3　東大寺

鏡池、世界最大級の木造建築の大仏殿、大仏殿の屋根、観相窓について

### At the Mirror Pond

**G**: This is the Mirror Pond. It is said that the Mirror Pond reflects your mind like a mirror. Look at the beautiful reflection of the Great Buddha Hall in this pond.

**T**: Wow! It's beautiful, just like my mind! (laughing)

### In front of the Great Buddha Hall, after completing admission procedures

**G**: Here we are in front of the Great Buddha Hall. This Great Buddha Hall is the third one. It's said that the original Great Buddha Hall was completed in 751; however, it was destroyed in two wars. The present one was made in the 18th century with the support of the Tokugawa government and the cooperation of many people led by Kōkei Shōnin. The **frontage** was reduced to only two-thirds of the original size due to a lack of materials and financial difficulties. This is one of the largest wooden structures in the world. Please look at the decorations on both sides of the roof. They're in the shape of fish tails and called "Shibi." They're charms to protect the building from fire.

**T**: Fireproof charms! Nice!

**G**: Please look at the roof of the Great Buddha Hall. There are as many as 130,000 tiles on the roof. The total weight of the roof is 3,000 tons. This is almost the same weight as 2,500 average cars. It's about one-third of the total weight of the Eiffel Tower in Paris!

**T**: Amazing!

**G**: The width of the path is the distance between the two fireproof charms on the roof. Next, please look at the window under the **Chinese-style gable**. This window is opened only on January 1 and August 13, 14, and 15, which are the Buddhist festival days called "Obon." On these special days, worshippers can see the Great Buddha's face looking out from the window. The Great Buddha **illuminates** the worshippers with the light of mercy.

G：通訳ガイド　T：観光客

### 鏡池で

**G：** これは鏡池です。鏡池はあなたの心を鏡のように映し出すと言われています。この池に大仏殿がきれいに映し出されているのを見てください。

**T：** わ〜、私の心のようにきれいだわ！（笑）

### 拝観手続きを済ませた後、大仏殿の前で

**G：** 大仏殿の前にいます。この大仏殿は 3 代目です。最初の大仏殿は、751 年に完成したと言われています。しかし、二度の戦火で失われました。現在の大仏殿は、18 世紀に徳川幕府の支援を受け、公慶上人が率いる大勢の人々の協力により造られたものです。資材不足と財政難のため、正面幅はもともとの大きさの 3 分の 2 に縮小されました。これは世界最大級の木造建築物です。屋根の両側にある飾りをご覧ください。魚の尻尾の形をしていて、鴟尾と呼ばれています。火事から建物を守るお守りなのです。

**T：** 火事よけのお守りなのですね！　いいですね！

**G：** 大仏殿の屋根を見てください。屋根には 13 万枚もの瓦が乗っています。屋根の総重量は 3,000 トンです。これは、平均的な自動車 2,500 台と同じくらいの重さです。パリにあるエッフェル塔の総重量の約 3 分の 1 です。

**T：** ビックリです！

**G：** 参道の広さは屋根にある 2 つの火事よけのお守りの幅と同じです。次に、唐破風（切妻）の下の窓をご覧ください。この窓は 1 月 1 日と、「お盆」と呼ばれる仏教の特別なお祭りの 8 月 13 日、14 日、15 日に開きます。この日には参拝者たちは、窓から外を見ている大仏様の顔を見ることができます。大仏様は慈悲の光で参拝者を照らしてくださいます。

### 単語の小箱

□ frontage 間口・正面幅　□ Chinese-style gable 唐破風　□ illuminate …を照らす

141

# 1-4 東大寺

 050

シルクロード、八角燈籠、大仏開眼式、大仏様の手の形について

G: Look at the **paving stones**. The bluish stones in the middle come from India, the pink ones next to them are from China, the grayish ones are from Korea, and those on the outside are from Japan. They show the order of how Buddhism was introduced into Japan. It's been compared to the Silk Road.

T: The designer was very creative!

G: Look at this gilt-bronze **octagonal lantern**. It's the largest and oldest in Japan. This octagonal lantern dates from the construction of the Great Buddha. Unlike the Great Buddha Hall, it survived two major wars and calamities.

T: So it's seen the whole history of Tōdaiji Temple!

G: This octagonal lantern saw the ceremony to consecrate the Great Buddha in 752. It's said that a large number of people, including 10,000 monks and officials, attended the ceremony. The Indian monk Bodhisena performed the eye-opening ceremony. Many important people from Asian countries may have participated in this ceremony. By building the Great Buddha, Emperor Shōmu wanted to give a universal message for the future that all living creatures coexist.

T: It must have been a beautiful ceremony.

G: I imagine so. This octagonal lantern has beautiful reliefs of **Musical Bodhisattvas** and **Chinese lions** on it. It was repaired in the past. Do you know why it was a bit damaged?

T: The Musical Bodhisattvas are so gentle and beautiful! The deer were so attracted to them and jumped up and patted them too much.

G: (Laughing) Oh, dear! You're kidding! Unfortunately, **acid rain** has **rusted** the copper in the bronze.

**After praying in front of the Great Buddha**

G: The Great Buddha is Buddha Vairocana, the merciful Buddha of Light shining throughout the universe. The Great Buddha illuminates every creature equally. His right hand is saying, "Don't be afraid." His left hand is saying, "I will grant your prayers and wishes."

G：通訳ガイド　T：観光客

**G：** 敷石をご覧ください。中央の青みがかった石はインドから、両隣のピンクの石は中国から、灰色っぽいものは韓国から、そして外側にあるもの日本の石です。仏教がどのように日本に伝わったかの順序を示しています。シルクロードに例えられているわけです。

**T：** デザイナーはとてもクリエイティブだったのですね。

**G：** この金銅八角燈籠をご覧ください。日本で一番大きく、一番古いです。この八角燈籠は、大仏様の創建時から存在しています。大仏殿とは異なり、二度の大きな戦争や災難も生き残ったのです。

**T：** 東大寺の歴史を見てきたのですね！

**G：** この八角燈籠は752年の開眼式も見たのです。1万人の僧侶や役人を含む多くの人がこの式典に参加しました。インド人僧侶の菩提僊那が開眼供養を務めました。アジア諸国からも多くの重要人物が参加したかもしれませんね。聖武天皇は大仏様を作ることによって、万物が共存共栄する未来への普遍のメッセージを伝えたかったのです。

**T：** 美しい儀式だったに違いありませんね。

**G：** そう思います。この八角燈籠には、音声菩薩と唐獅子の美しいレリーフが施されています。過去に修繕されたことがあります。なぜ、少し傷んだかわかりますか？

**T：** 音声菩薩がとても穏やかで美しいですね！　シカが魅了されて飛びついて、なですぎてしまったとか？

**G：** （笑って）おやまあ！　冗談でしょ！　残念ながら、ブロンズの銅が酸性雨でさびてしまったのです。

### 大仏様にお祈りをしてから

**G：** 大仏様は盧舎那仏という仏様で、宇宙全体に輝く光の慈悲の仏です。大仏様はすべての生きとし生けるものを公平に照らします。大仏様の右手は「畏れることはありません」と伝えています。左手は「あなたの祈りと望みをかなえます」と伝えています。

**単語の小箱**

□ paving stone 敷石　□ octagonal lantern 八角燈籠　□ Musical Bodhisattva 音声菩薩
□ Chinese lion 唐獅子　□ acid rain 酸性雨　□ rust さびる

143

# 1-5 東大寺

〔051〕

### 大仏様の大きさ、螺髪、白毫、菩薩、蓮の花について

**T**: Awesome! The Great Buddha is so huge!

**G**: It's 15 meters tall. As for its weight, there are several theories, but according to one theory, it weighs 380 tons. The total weight of the **Statue of Liberty** is 225 tons. The Great Buddha is 1.7 times as heavy as the Statue of Liberty. The length of his middle finger is 1.3 meters, and about ten people would be able to dance on the palm of his hand.

**T**: How many curls does the Great Buddha have on his head?

**G**: The Great Buddha has 483 curls. One curl weighs about 1.2 kilograms. Curly hair, called "Rahotsu," **is a characteristic of** the Buddha.

**T**: Can I have my hair permed like the Great Buddha to reach enlightenment? (laughing)

**G**: That's a good idea! (laughing)

**T**: The Great Buddha has a huge **mole** on his forehead, like my father (laughing).

**G**: My friend, who has a mole on his forehead, is so intelligent that his nickname is "Daibutsu-san," which means the Great Buddha (laughing). No, this isn't a mole, but a kind of hair, called "Byakugō." The Great Buddha **emits merciful light** from here to save people. Facing the Buddha on the right is Nyoirin Kannon Bodhisattva. Nyoirin Kannon Bodhisattva is believed to remove your sufferings and grant your wishes. Kokūzō Bodhisattva on the left of the Great Buddha is believed to give you wisdom and knowledge.

**T**: I see. I want more wisdom! (laughing)

**G**: Compare the Great Buddha and these Bodhisattvas on both sides.

**T**: The Bodhisattvas are wearing jewelry, but the Great Buddha isn't.

**G**: Once you reach enlightenment, you don't need jewelry to make yourself shine.

**T**: I want some jewelry. I can't shine by myself, so I need jewelry (laughing).

**G**: Me, too. Please look at the **pedestal of lotus petals**. The lotus flower is a symbol of Buddhism. The lotus grows in muddy water, but the color of its flower doesn't change. This means that the lotus flower is sacred.

G：通訳ガイド　T：観光客

T： 見事ですね！　大仏様はとても大きいです！

G： 高さは 15 メートルです。重さは諸説ありますが、一説によると 380 トンあります。自由の女神像の総重量が 225 トンです。大仏様は、自由の女神像の 1.7 倍重いです。中指の長さは 1.3 メートルで、10 人くらいの人が手のひらの上でダンスできそうですね。

T： 頭にはいくつのカールがありますか？

G： 大仏様は 483 個のカールを持っています。1 つのカールは約 1.2 キロです。カールされた螺髪（らはつ）と呼ばれる髪は仏様の象徴です。

T： 悟りに達するために、大仏様のようにパーマをかけてもらえるでしょうか？

G： それはいいアイデアですね（笑）。

T： 大仏様は私の父のように、額に大きなほくろをお持ちですね（笑）。

G： 額にほくろのある私の友人は聡明で、「大仏さん」というニックネームで呼ばれています（笑）。あれはほくろではなく、白毫（びゃくごう）と呼ばれる髪の一種です。大仏様は、人々を救うために慈悲深い光をここから出しています。大仏様に向かって右側が、如意輪観音菩薩です。如意輪観音菩薩は苦しみを取り除き、あなたの願いをかなえてくれると信じられています。大仏様の左にある虚空蔵菩薩は、知恵と知識を授けてくれると信じられています。

T： なるほど。私はもっと知恵がほしいです！（笑）

G： 大仏様と両側の菩薩様を比べてみてください。

T： 菩薩様は宝飾品を身に着けていますが、大仏様は身に着けていません。

G： 悟りを開いたら、自分を輝かせるための宝石は必要ないのです。

T： 私は宝石が欲しいです。自分で輝けないので宝石が必要です（笑）。

G： 私もです。蓮の花びらの台座をご覧ください。蓮は仏教の象徴です。蓮は泥水の中で生育しますが、花の色は変わりません。これは蓮の花が神聖であることを意味します。

## 単　語　の　小　箱

□ Statue of Liberty　自由の女神像　　□ be a characteristic of ...　…を特徴とする
□ mole　ほくろ　　□ emit　…を放つ　　□ merciful light　慈悲深い光
□ pedestal of lotus petals　蓮の花びらの台座（蓮華座）

145

# 1-6 東大寺

 052

広目天、東大寺レプリカ、柱の穴くぐり、多聞天、大仏様お身拭いについて

G: Please look at Kōmoku-ten, who protects the west. He has a brush in his right hand and a **scroll** in his left hand. He can see everything in the world. It's said that he tells the heavens about your behavior.

T: Hmm. I should behave well!

G: Next, please look at this miniature replica model of the original Tōdaiji Temple. There were two seven-story pagodas. It is said that they were 70 to 100 meters high and very beautiful; however, they were burnt down in a **major civil war** and by lightning.

T: I see. Wow! What's that crowd of people?

G: They're waiting in line to **get through** a hole in a pillar. If you go through the hole, you will be healthy, happy, and intelligent! Now I'm overweight, so I can't (laughing). The size of this hole is almost the same as that of the Great Buddha's **nostril**.

T: If I was thinner, I could try, too (laughing).

G: Please look at Tamon-ten, who protects the north. The **Buddhist scriptures** say that Tamon-ten listens to the Buddhist Law very carefully.

T: Just as Kōmoku-ten reports our behavior, Tamon-ten may tell the heavens what we say.

G: I think so, too. Please look at this object in the shape of a butterfly on a bronze lotus flower vase. Insects have six legs, but this butterfly has eight legs, probably because it's a heavenly creature.

T: Mysterious! By the way, how is this Great Buddha cleaned?

G: Please look at this picture. On August 7, about 200 Buddhist **monks** and some other people purify their bodies at the bathhouse of the February Hall early in the morning. Then they gather at the Great Buddha Hall in white clothing and straw sandals. The Great Buddha's soul is taken out at 7 a.m. After that, they **chant sutras** and clean the Great Buddha.

T: Wow! They clean the Great Buddha by riding in gondolas like special baskets of woven rope. It **reminds** me **of** an **illustration** from *Gulliver's Travels*! The Great Buddha is huge!

G：通訳ガイド　T：観光客

**G：** 西を守る広目天を見てください。右手に筆、左手に巻物（経巻）を持っています。この世にあるすべての物を見ることができます。あなたの行いを天の世界に報告すると言われているのですよ。

**T：** ふむふむ。お行儀良くしなければ！

**G：** 次に、創建当時の東大寺の縮小レプリカをご覧ください。2つの七重塔が存在しました。70メートルから100メートルもの高さで、とても美しかったと言われています。しかし、それらは大きな内戦と落雷で消失してしまいました。

**T：** なるほど。わあ！　あの人混みは何ですか？

**G：** 柱の穴をくぐるために列を作って待っているんですよ。穴をくぐったら、健康で幸せで知的になれるのですよ！　今の私は太りすぎているので無理です（笑）。この穴の大きさは、大仏様の鼻の穴の大きさとほぼ同じです。

**T：** 私ももっと細ければ挑戦するのですが（笑）。

**G：** 北を守る多聞天をご覧ください。多聞天は注意深く仏法を聞くと、仏典で説明されています。

**T：** 広目天が私たちの行いを報告するように、多聞天も私たちの発言を天に報告するのかもしれませんね。

**G：** 私もそう思います。ブロンズ製の蓮の花瓶の上にいる蝶の形をした物を見てください。昆虫は脚が6本ですが、この蝶には脚が8本あります。多分、天上の生き物だからです。

**T：** 神秘的ですね。ところで、どのようにして大仏様はお身拭いされるのですか？

**G：** この写真をご覧ください。8月7日に、およそ200人の僧侶とその他の人々が、早朝に二月堂の湯屋で身を清めます。それから、白装束にわら草履姿で大仏殿に集合します。午前7時に大仏様の魂が抜かれます。その後、全員でお経を唱え、大仏様をお身拭いします。

**T：** わー！　ロープで編まれた特別なかごのようなゴンドラに乗って、大仏様のお身拭いをしていますね。『ガリバーの旅行記』の挿絵を思い出させます。大仏様は巨大ですね！

## 単語の小箱

□ scroll 巻物　□ major civil war 大きな内戦　□ get through ... …を通り抜ける
□ nostril 鼻の穴、鼻孔　□ Buddhist scriptures 仏典　□ monk 僧侶
□ chant sutras お経を唱える　□ remind A of B AにBを思い出させる　□ illustration 挿絵

# 1-7　東大寺

### 賓頭盧、万博七重塔、華厳宗について

G: This is Binzuru Pindola. It's said that he had supernatural powers and showed them off too much, so he was ordered to do training and save people outside the hall. When you have a pain in your body, please rub the **corresponding part** of Pindola, and your pain will go away.

T: Wow! I sometimes have sore feet. I'll rub Pindola's feet!

**In front of the Sōrin**

G: This is the **pinnacle** of a replica of a seven-story pagoda of Tōdaiji Temple. A replica of a seven-story pagoda of Tōdaiji Temple **was** built by the Furukawa Group and **exhibited** during Expo'70. The pavilion was constructed in the shape of a seven-story pagoda. The theme of this pavilion was "Ancient Dreams and Modern Dreams." The contrast between the modern pavilions and the seven-story pagoda was eye-catching. The replica was built to **honor** the efforts of people who overcame many difficulties and **realized** their dream of constructing the seven-story pagodas in the old days. The replica also **demonstrated** the rapid growth of the Japanese economy. Many people, including celebrities from all over the world, went up to the observatory of the pagoda and enjoyed the fine view. It is said that the pagoda also introduced Buddhist culture to guests from abroad at Expo'70. After Expo'70, this pinnacle, called Sōrin, was donated to Tōdaiji Temple and has been here ever since.

T: It feels like a present from space!

**Going up along the Cat Slope while enjoying the autumn leaves**

T: I feel deeply that all living creatures live together by helping each other.

G: I think that's a very important teaching in the Kegon sect of Buddhism. Emperor Shōmu probably wanted to realize it by creating the Great Buddha. Tōdaiji Temple is the headquarters of the Kegon sect.

G：通訳ガイド　T：観光客

G：こちらは賓頭盧ピンドラです。賓頭盧ピンドラは神通力を持つのですが、使いすぎたために、お堂の外で修行し、人々を助けるように命令されたと言われています。体の部分に痛みがあるときは、それと同じ部位をなでてください。そうすれば、あなたの痛みは消え去ります。

T：すごい！　私はときどき足が痛いです。賓頭盧さんの足をなでますね！

## 相輪の前で

G：これは、東大寺の七重塔のレプリカ用の小尖塔です。東大寺の七重塔のレプリカは古河グループによって造られ、大阪万博で展示されました。パビリオンが七重塔の形をしていたのです。テーマは「古代の夢と現代の夢」でした。現代的なパビリオンと七重塔のコントラストは目を引きました。このレプリカは、かつて多くの困難を克服し、七重塔を建設するという夢を実現した人々の努力をたたえるために造られました。また、レプリカは急速な日本経済の発展も表現していました。世界中から訪れた有名人も含め、多くの人たちが展望台に登り、美しい景色を楽しみました。この仏塔は、仏教文化を海外から大阪万博を訪れた来場者に伝えたと言われています。大阪万博終了後、この「相輪」と呼ばれる小尖塔が東大寺に寄付され，それ以来ずっとここにあります。

T：これは宇宙からのプレゼントのようですね！

## 紅葉を楽しみ、猫段を上がりながら

T：すべての生き物が、お互いに支えあい生きているんだなあと心の底から感じます。

G：それは華厳宗の教えで、とても大切なことだと私は思います。聖武天皇は大仏様を建立することでそれを実現したかったのでしょう。東大寺は華厳宗の大本山です。

## 単語の小箱

□ corresponding part 相当する場所　□ pinnacle 小尖塔、相輪
□ be exhibited 展示される　□ honor …を称える　□ realize …を実現させる
□ demonstrate …を証明する

# 1-8 東大寺

 054

鐘楼、108の除夜の鐘、太郎、二月堂前の良弁杉①について

### At the Bell Tower

G: This Bell Tower was rebuilt in the 13th century. The bell, which weighs 26.3 tons, dates from the time of the **founding** of Tōdaiji Temple. This is one of the "Three Famous Bells" of Japan. It's known for its long ring. In most temples, people begin to ring 108 chimes on New Year's Eve, but at Tōdaiji Temple, people begin to ring the bell from midnight on January 1.

T: Is 108 a significant number?

G: In Buddhism, people are thought to have 108 worldly sins, so the bells are rung to **wash away** these 108 sins. The full Buddhist rosary has 108 beads. People **affectionately** nickname it "Nara Tarō." Tarō was the most common and popular name for boys. We often call big things "Something Tarō."

T: So Tarō is like John in English-speaking countries?

G: Yes, and the most common girl's name was Hanako. Shall we go to the "Nigatsu-dō," February Hall?

### At the Rōben Cedar in front of the February Hall

G: What kind of tree is this? Do you think it's a Christmas tree? (laughing)

T: It's similar to a Christmas tree.

G: This is the "Rōben Cedar Tree." First, I'll tell you about Rōben. Rōben made enormous contributions to the construction of the Great Buddha and became the first chief abbot of Tōdaiji Temple.

T: Did Rōben plant this cedar?

G: No. Let me tell you an **anecdote** about Rōben. One day, a mother was working in a **mulberry field**, and her two-year-old son was playing near her. All of a sudden, the boy **was snatched by** a big eagle. The mother **wandered around** looking for him, but in vain.

T: Poor mother! What a **nasty** eagle!

G：通訳ガイド　T：観光客

## 鐘楼の前で

**G：** この鐘楼は 13 世紀に再建されました。26.3 トンの重さがある鐘は、東大寺の創建時からの物です。これは日本の「三大名鐘」の一つです。長い響きで知られています。ほとんどのお寺で人々は 108 つの鐘を大みそかに突き始めますが、東大寺では 1 月 1 日の午前 0 時に鐘を突き始めます。

**T：** 108 は意味のある数字なのですか？

**G：** 仏教では、人は 108 の煩悩を持っていると言われていますので、108 の煩悩を取り除くために鐘が突かれるのです。数珠も本来は 108 の玉がついているのですよ。人々は親しみを込めてこの鐘を「奈良太郎」と呼んでいます。「太郎」は最も一般的で人気のある男の子の名前でした。大きなものはよく「何々太郎」と呼ばれます。

**T：** では、太郎は英語圏の国でのジョンのようなものですか？

**G：** その通りです。そして、最も一般的な女性の名前は花子でした。二月堂に行きましょうか？

## 二月堂の前の良弁杉の前で

**G：** この木の種類は何でしょう？　クリスマスツリーだと思いますか？（笑）

**T：** クリスマスツリーに似ています。

**G：** これは「良弁杉」です。最初に、良弁についてお話しします。良弁は大仏様の建設に多大なる貢献をした人で、東大寺の最初の僧の長（初代別当）になりました。

**T：** 良弁がこの杉を植えたのですか？

**G：** 違います。良弁にまつわる逸話をお話しさせてください。ある日、お母さんが桑畑で働いていて、彼女の 2 歳になる息子は近くで遊んでいました。突然、男の子が大きなワシに連れ去られました。お母さんは子供を探して辺りをさまよいましたが、徒労に終わりました。

**T：** かわいそうなお母さん。なんて卑劣なワシなんでしょう。

## 単語の小箱

☐ founding 創立　☐ wash away ... …を洗い流す　☐ affectionately 親しみを込めて
☐ anecdote 逸話　☐ mulberry field 桑畑　☐ be snatched by ... …に連れ去られる
☐ wander around さまよう　☐ nasty 卑劣な

151

# 1-9 東大寺

良弁杉②、二月堂のお水取りと十一面観世音菩薩について

**G**: One high-ranking monk found the boy hanging in a cedar tree. He rescued the boy and brought him up. The boy also grew up to be a high-ranking monk. The mother happened to hear the story of "the boy and the eagle" and went to see him. Rōben had the **good luck talisman** that his mother had given him. It proved that Rōben was her son. Rōben then **became devoted to his mother**.

**T**: Rōben was devoted to his mother as well as the construction of the Great Buddha?

**G**: Right! "The Rōben Cedar" is performed in traditional Japanese dramas, such as Bunraku puppet plays, Kabuki dramas, and musicals.

### On the balcony of the "Nigatsu-dō," February Hall

**G**: We can look out over Nara City and the beautiful trees to Mt. Ikoma in the distance. We also have a good view of the Great Buddha Hall.

**T**: I feel I can see the mountains of the Buddha from here.

**G**: Yes! That's a very **insightful** expression. By the way, I'll explain why this hall was named "February Hall." This name comes from the Buddhist ceremony called "Shunie," or "Omizutori." This ceremony is conducted from March 1 to 14. March is February in the **lunar calendar**, so it's called February Hall. In this ritual we **repent of our sins** and pray for prosperity and happiness in front of the Eleven-headed Bodhisattva. Please look at this picture. It's a ritual performed by 11 monks. Huge torches called "Taimatsu" are carried to this balcony and rain down **sparks** of fire. Worshippers gather where the sparks fall to pray for good health. On the night of February 12 or in the **predawn hours** of the 13th, sacred water is drawn from the well under the hall and offered to the Eleven-headed Bodhisattva, which is the main statue of February Hall. In Nara, it is said that spring will come soon after this Omizutori. On the last day, the 14th, sparks from ten torches flow from the balcony like waterfalls. This has been going on ever since the eye-opening ceremony of the Great Buddha in 752.

G：通訳ガイド　T：観光客

G：高僧が、杉の木に引っかかっている男の子を見つけました。彼は男の子を助け、育てました。成長して、男の子も高僧になりました。お母さんは偶然「男の子とワシ」の話を耳にして、彼に会いに行きました。良弁は、お母さんがあげた幸運のお守りを持っていました。それが、良弁が彼女の息子であることを証明しました。良弁はそれから親孝行をしました。

T：良弁は大仏様の建立に貢献したのと同じくらい、お母さんにも親孝行したのですね。

G：その通りです！「良弁杉」は人形劇である文楽や歌舞伎、ミュージカルなどの日本の伝統的な演劇で演じられています。

## 二月堂の舞台から

G：奈良市街と美しい木々、そして遠くの生駒山まで見渡すことができます。大仏殿もよく見えますよ。

T：ブッダの山が見えるようなそんな気がします。

G：はい！洞察力のある表現ですね。ところで、なぜこのお堂が「二月堂」と呼ばれているかを説明しますね。この名前は「修二会」とか「お水取り」と呼ばれる仏教の儀式に由来しています。この儀式は3月1日から14日まで行われます。3月は太陰暦では2月ですので、二月堂と名付けられているのです。この儀式では、過ちを悔やみ、十一面観世音菩薩に繁栄と幸福を祈るのです。この写真をご覧ください。11人の僧侶によって行われている儀式です。「松明」と呼ばれる大きなトーチがこのお堂のバルコニーまで運ばれ、火の粉を大量に飛び散らせます。参拝者は火の粉が落ちる場所に集まり、無病息災を祈ります。12日の夜または13日の未明には、お堂の下にある井戸から神聖な水を汲み、二月堂の本尊である十一面観音にお供えします。奈良では、このお水取りがすむと春が近いと言われています。最終日の14日には、10本の松明からの滝のような火の粉がバルコニーから流れます。これは、大仏様の開眼がなされた752年からずっと行われています。

### 単語の小箱

□ **good luck talisman** 幸運のお守り　□ **become devoted to** *one's* **mother** 親孝行をする
□ **insightful** 洞察力のある　□ **lunar calendar** 太陰暦　□ **repent of** *one's* **sins** 過ちを悔やむ
□ **spark** 火の粉　□ **predawn hours** 未明の時間

# 1-10　東大寺

三月堂、僧侶の剃髪、柿の葉ずし、若草山のふもとのシカについて

G: This is the "Sangatsu-dō," March Hall. The name comes from the fact that an important ritual is held here in March, according to the lunar calendar. The March Hall is the oldest building in the Tōdaiji Temple grounds. This hall has many **masterpieces** from the 8th century. Fukūkensaku Bodhisattva, the main image, is a **typical Buddhist statue** of the Nara period.

T: I see. By the way, why do monks shave their heads?

G: When people wear jewelry, they try to look better than they are, so monks shave their heads so that they are not bothered by worldly passions.

T: Oh, I see. That makes sense.

### In a small Japanese restaurant

G: This is "Kaki-no-ha" sushi. Sushi with **mackerel** on it is wrapped in a persimmon leaf. The mackerel **is seasoned with** vinegar and salt. It's one of Nara's local **dishes**.

T: It's very delicious! It's easy to eat with the hands. I like the combination of the leaf and fish.

G: I'm happy to hear that. The persimmon leaf also has an **anti-bacterial effect**.

### Walking at the foot of Wakakusa-yama

T: It's refreshing to walk around the base of Wakakusa-yama. The deer are so cute. I'd like to give them some crackers and have a picture taken with them.

G: Go ahead, but please don't touch the baby deer because the mother deer may **abandon** them if they pick up a **human scent** from them. Basically, it's a rule not to touch wild animals for their own protection.

T: Thanks for the advice. We should know how to protect wild animals.

G: Also, it's important for you not to have any paper in your hand, because deer like paper. I was almost jumped on by them once. Oh, some deer are coming. Let's give them some crackers and take pictures with them.

G：通訳ガイド　T：観光客

G：これは三月堂です。その名前は、重要な儀式が太陰暦の3月に行われる事実に由来しています。三月堂は、東大寺の境内では一番古い建物です。このお堂には、8世紀からの傑作が多くあります。本尊の不空羂索観音（けんさく）は、奈良時代の典型的な仏像です。

T：なるほど。ところで僧侶はなぜ髪をそるのですか？

G：人は宝石を身に付けると、実際の自分よりも良く見せようとします。僧侶は煩悩に煩わされないよう、剃髪するのです。

T：ああ、そうか。もっともな話ですね。

## 小さな和食レストランで

G：こちらが柿の葉ずしです。サバの乗ったおすしが、柿の葉で包まれています。サバはお酢と塩で味付けされています。奈良の郷土料理の一つです。

T：とてもおいしい！　手で食べやすいです。葉とお魚の組み合わせっていいですね。

G：それは良かったです！　柿の葉には抗菌作用もあります。

## 若草山のふもとを歩きながら

T：若草山のふもとを歩くと気分がすっきりしますね。シカはとてもかわいいです。せんべいをあげて、一緒に写真を撮ってもらいたいです。

G：どうぞ、だけど赤ちゃんのシカには触らないでください。人間のにおいを感じると、お母さんシカが放棄するかもしれないですから。基本的に、野生動物保護のためには触らないことがルールです。

T：アドバイスありがとう。野生動物を守る方法を知るべきですね。

G：それから、シカは紙が好きなので、紙を手に持たないことも大切です。私は飛びつかれそうになったことがあります。あ、シカが何頭か近づいてきましたよ。せんべいをあげて、一緒に写真を撮りましょう。

単語の小箱

- □ masterpiece 傑作　□ typical Buddhist statue 典型的な仏像　□ mackerel サバ
- □ be seasoned with ... …で味付けされている　□ dish 料理
- □ anti-bacterial effect 抗菌作用　□ abandon …を放棄する　□ human scent 人間のにおい

## 瞬間英作文

1. 自然災害が次から次へと発生し、多くの人が天然痘で苦しんでいました。

2. 東大寺は8世紀半ばに聖武天皇の勅令で、仏教を通して国家を健全にするために創建されました。

3. 聖武天皇は生きとし生けるものが幸せになることを望みました。

4. 大仏様の完成は、日本の文化力と技術力を示しました。

5. 南大門は東大寺の正門で、日本で一番大きな山門だと言われています。

6. 仁王様は、阿吽の呼吸で寺を守っています。

7. 仁王様は筋肉の写実的な表現から、ミケランジェロのダビデ像と比べられます。

8. 大仏様はすべての生き物を公平に照らしています。

9. 大仏様の右手のジェスチャーは「畏れることはありません」、左手のジェスチャーは「あなたの望みをかなえますよ」を意味します。

10. 柱穴の大きさは大仏様の鼻孔の大きさとほとんど同じです。

11. 柱穴をくぐったら健康で幸せで知的になれます。

12. 広目天が私たちの行動を天に報告するように、多聞天も私たちの発言を天に報告します。

13. 僧侶は煩悩に煩わされないように剃髪します。

---

1. natural disaster 自然災害　　2. by order of ... …の命令で
3. all living things 生きとし生けるもの　　4. technological power 技術力
5. The Great South Gate 南大門　　6. ah-un breathing 阿吽の呼吸
7. realistic representation 写実的な表現　　8. illuminate … を照らす
9. grant *one's* wish …の願いをかなえる　　10. nostril 鼻の穴、鼻孔
11. intelligent 知的な　　12. heaven 天国　　13. shave *one's* head 剃髪する

解答例

1. **Natural disasters** had struck one after another, and many people were suffering from smallpox.

2. Tōdaiji Temple was built in the middle of the 8th century **by order of** Emperor Shōmu to restore the nation to health through Buddhism.

3. Emperor Shōmu wanted **all living things** to be happy.

4. The completion of the Great Buddha showed Japan's great cultural and **technological power**.

5. **The Great South Gate** is the main gate of Tōdaiji Temple and it is said to be the biggest temple gate in Japan.

6. The Deva Kings are guarding the temple with their **ah-un breathing**.

7. The Deva Kings are often compared to Michelangelo's David in their **realistic representation** of muscles.

8. The Great Buddha **illuminates** every creature equally.

9. The Great Buddha's right hand gesture signifies "Don't be afraid" and his left hand gesture signifies "I will **grant your wishes**."

10. The size of the hole is almost the same as that of the Great Buddha's **nostril**.

11. If you go through the hole, you will be healthy, happy, and **intelligent**.

12. Just as Kōmoku-ten reports our behavior, Tamon-ten may tell the **heavens** what we say.

13. Monks **shave their heads** so that they are not bothered by worldly sins.

157

# 玉虫の宝庫

## 1 すべての幸せを願う聖武天皇と人々の努力の歴史を東大寺に見る

**❶** 東大寺建立の時代背景と、聖武天皇が勅令を出された理由、延べ 260 万におよぶ労働者や、建立のリーダー・行基の仕事について説明します。

**❷** 南大門では、東大寺の正門であることや、日本で一番大きな山門と言われていること、木造の寄木造の仁王様が 69 日間で作られたことを説明します。

**❸** 中門へ行くまでの右壁の 5 本の線は、皇室と関係のあるお寺であることの証明だと説明しましょう。

**❹** 中門から大仏殿では、世界でも最大規模の大仏殿の歴史と、八角燈籠の説明。

**❺** 大仏殿では大仏様はもちろん、如意輪観音菩薩像や虚空蔵菩薩、広目天、多聞天の説明も忘れずに。東大寺創建当時のレプリカ（特に七重塔）、柱の穴の通り抜け、賓頭盧は楽し気に説明しましょう。

**❻** 七重塔のレプリカの相輪は、大阪万博に出展され、仏教を伝える役割も果たしたことを説明。

**❼** 鐘楼については、日本の三大名鐘であることや、煩悩が 108 あることを、除夜の鐘や数珠を例に挙げて説明。

**❽** 二月堂では、二月堂の前の良弁杉とお水取りの説明をします。

## 2 通訳ガイドからのアドバイス

### アドバイス1　ジョークも入れて和やかに

参拝してからシカに餌をやることや、ふんを踏まないように気をつけること（Don't step on the poop!）を伝えましょう。集団をなし、時間通りに現れたり、去ったりするシカを通勤者（commuter）に例えて話すとお客様は喜ばれます。

### アドバイス2　大仏殿の前での説明は順序良く上から下へ

① 大仏殿の屋根の両側にある、火事から建物を守る鴟尾

② 屋根を覆う 13 万枚もの瓦、屋根全体の重さは約 3,000 トン

③ 元日とお盆のときにだけ開く、唐破風の下の窓

④ シルクロードに例えられる参道の敷き石

### アドバイス3　東大寺の歴史を見てきた八角燈籠

戦火や災害を乗り越え、大仏様の開眼式から東大寺の歴史を見続けてきた、日本一大きく古い八角燈籠（octagonal lantern）は混雑していなければぜひ説明を！

### アドバイス4　大きさは何かと比較した方がわかりやすい
大仏殿の屋根の重さはエッフェル塔の3分の1、大仏様の重さは380トンで自由の女神の1.7倍、大仏様の中指は1.3メートルで10人の人が手の平で踊れそう、など。

### アドバイス5　名前の話は言葉のキャッチボールができる
日本の三大名鐘の鐘楼のニックネームは、日本で一般的だった名前の「太郎」だと説明すると、英語圏ではJohnと返ってきたことがあります。会話のキャッチボールがいいですね。また、お客様の名前を漢字で書いて教えてあげると喜ばれます。例えばMary＝真理（Truth）、Ricky＝力（Power）など。

### アドバイス6　大仏様は8世紀からのオリジナルかと聞かれたら？
大仏様の頭部、体、脚を比べてみてください。どのくらい輝いているかの違いは、作られた時代を示しています。現在の頭部は17世紀に作られ、胴体、両腕と両手は16世紀に修復されました。そして脚と台座は、建造当時の8世紀のものが多くあります。

Please compare the Great Buddha's head, body, and legs. The difference in how shiny they are tells us the period when they were made. The present-day head was made in the 17th century. The torso and both arms and hands were repaired in the 16th century. The legs and pedestal are mostly original, from the 8th century.

## 3 通訳ガイド体験日記

◎**儀式や行事は覚えよう。**
お盆の行事（万燈籠）、大仏様のお身拭い、お水取りなどの行事の説明は、知識として持っておくと便利です。実際、私はゲストから"When does the Great Buddha take a bath?"（いつ大仏様はお身拭いするのですか）と聞かれて、とっさに"Every day!"と答えてしまったことがあります。

## 4 通訳ガイドお役立ち英語表現

◎**「あーあ、あらまあ、なんとまあ」は何と言う？**
Oh, dear! と言います。シカ（deer）の話をするとき、この表現を使うと楽しんでもらえます。

# 2-1 春日大社

### 春日大社の起源、藤原家、車舎、酒樽、玉砂利について

G: Before we arrive at Kasuga Taisha Shrine, I'll tell you a little about it. According to **ancient mythology**, Kasuga Taisha's origins date back to the 8th century. In the hope of bringing prosperity to the nation, Takemikazuchi-no-mikoto, the strongest deity, was invited to the sacred mountain, Mt. Mikasa. Takemikazuchi-no-mikoto came to Mt. Mikasa on the back of a white deer, and the deer has been considered a **divine messenger** ever since. The political leader Fujiwara-no-Nagate founded Kasuga Taisha in the year 768 by order of the emperor. Takemikazuchi-no-mikoto and three deities were enshrined here to pray for the prosperity and happiness of the nation. Kasuga Taisha is a shrine with strong connections to the Fujiwara family.

T: So, Fujiwara was a samurai warrior?

G: No, there were no samurai warriors in those days. The Fujiwara family were the closest to the imperial family at that time and the actual political rulers of Japan. They were **aristocrats**.

### In front of the "Kuruma Yadori" at Kasuga Taisha Shrine

G: This is the place where the emperors and **imperial messengers** parked their court carriages when they visited and prayed at Kasuga Taisha.

T: What are the stacked-up casks for?

G: They are **sake casks**. As the deities like rice sake very much, sake is offered at shrines.

T: By the way, why **is** this path **laid with** gravel? It's a bit hard to walk on.

G: Gravel can purify everything, so you can purify yourself by walking on this **gravel path**.

### At Fuseshika-no-Temizusho, after going through Ni-no-Torii

G: Please look at this bronze statue of a deer. This deer has a scroll in his mouth. Water is coming out from the scroll to purify us.

G：通訳ガイド　T：観光客

G：春日大社に到着する前に、少し説明させてください。古代神話によれば、春日大社の起源は8世紀にさかのぼります。国家の繁栄を願い、最強の神様、タケミカヅチノミコトを神聖な山である御蓋山（みかさ）にお迎えしました。タケミカヅチノミコトが白いシカの背に乗って御蓋山にお越しになられてからずっと、シカは神様のお使いと見なされています。政治的リーダーだった藤原永手は、天皇の勅命で768年に春日大社を造営しました。国家の繁栄と幸福を願うために、タケミカヅチノミコトと3柱の神様がここに祀られています。春日大社は藤原氏ゆかりの神社なのです。

T：藤原氏は侍だったのですか？

G：いいえ、当時、武士は存在しませんでした。当時、藤原家は皇室に一番近い一族で、日本政治において事実上の支配者でした。彼らは貴族だったのです。

### 春日大社、車舎の前で

G：ここは、天皇や勅使が春日大社を訪れ、参拝する際に、お乗りになられた御所車を留め置く場所でした。

T：積まれている樽は何のためにあるのですか？

G：酒樽です。神様はお米からできたお酒がとても好きなので、お酒は神社に奉納されているのです。

T：ところで、なぜ参道には砂利が敷かれているのですか？　少し歩きにくいです。

G：砂利はすべてのものを清めるので、砂利が敷き詰められたこの参道を歩くことで、あなた自身も清められます。

### 二之鳥居を通り抜けた後、伏鹿の手水所で

G：このシカのブロンズ像をご覧ください。この鹿は口に巻物をくわえています。巻物から、清めるための水が出ています。

## 単語の小箱

□ ancient mythology　古代神話　　□ divine messenger　神様の使い　　□ aristocrat　貴族
□ imperial messenger　勅使　　□ sake cask　酒樽　　□ be laid with ...　…で敷き詰められる
□ gravel path　砂利の参道

# 2-2 春日大社

 058

### 燈籠について

**Walking along the approach, after purification at the Temizusho and worshipping at Haraido Shrine**

T: So many cute deer! How many **stone lanterns** are there here?

G: There are 2,000 stone lanterns on the approach to the shrine, and 1,000 **hanging bronze lanterns** hanging inside the shrine. Kasuga Taisha has the largest number of lanterns in Japan. They have been **donated** from the 8th century in the Heian period through to the present day. People began to donate the lanterns to please the deities. Also, people donate lanterns when they **make a wish** or when their wishes **are granted**. Moss is growing on many of the stone lanterns, which means they have a history. Each lantern **is engraved with** the donor's name and date. Please look at the stone lanterns closely.

T: Wow! The deer motifs are very cute. There are many different kinds of deer engraved on them.

G: There are many different motifs, such as cranes, **tortoises**, owls, phoenixes, moons, and family crests. Please look at the characters "春日大明神 (Kasuga Daimyōjin)" on the post of this stone lantern. "春日大明神 (Kasuga Daimyōjin)" was engraved on 15 of the stone lanterns. It is said if you find three stone lanterns engraved with "春日大明神 (Kasuga Daimyōjin)" you'll become a **billionaire** overnight.

T: Wow! I want to be a billionaire, but Kanji are difficult to read.

G: It's written on this piece of paper. Here you are. "春日大明神 (Kasuga Daimyōjin)" is the deity of Kasuga Taisha.

T: Thank you! I'll try to find them. By the way, may I ask how much one lantern costs?

G: A stone lantern costs about 2.5 million yen. A hanging lantern is about 2 million yen.

T: Wow! That's too expensive for me.

G: Not only rich people, but ordinary people donate stone lanterns too. There is one which was donated by a group of 1,000 people. It's called the "1,000 people lantern."

G：通訳ガイド　T：観光客

**手水所でお清めをして、祓戸神社で参拝してから、参道を歩きながら**

T：たくさんのかわいいシカ！　石燈籠はいくつありますか？

G：神社に続く参道には 2,000 基の石燈籠があり、神社には 1,000 基の銅製の釣燈籠があります。春日大社には日本で一番多く燈籠があります。平安時代の 8 世紀から現在に至るまで、燈籠は寄進され続けています。神様に御灯を献じて喜んでいただくために燈籠を寄進し始めました。また、奉納者は願い事をするとき、または願い事がかなったときに燈籠を寄進します。こけが多くの石燈籠に生えていますが、歴史があることを意味しています。それぞれの燈籠には、寄進者の名前と日付が彫られています。石燈籠をじっと見てください。

T：わー！　シカのモチーフはとてもかわいいです。いろいろな種類のシカが彫られていますね。

G：鶴や亀、フクロウ、鳳凰、月、家紋など、いろいろなモチーフが彫られています。この燈籠の竿に彫られている「春日大明神」の文字を見てください。「春日大明神」は、15 基の石燈籠に彫られています。「春日大明神」と彫られた石燈籠を 3 基見つけたら、一晩で億万長者になると言われています。

T：わー！　億万長者になりたいですが、漢字を読むのは難しいです。

G：この紙に書いてありますよ。「春日大明神」は春日大社の神様です。

T：ありがとう！　探してみるわ。ところで、燈籠は 1 基いくらか聞いてもいいですか？

G：石燈籠は 250 万円くらいです。釣燈籠は 200 万円くらいです。

T：わー！　私には高すぎます。

G：お金持ちだけでなく、一般の人たちも石燈籠を寄進します。1,000 人のグループから寄進された燈籠もあります。千人燈籠と呼ばれています。

**単語の小箱**

- □ stone lantern　石燈籠　　□ hanging bronze lantern　銅製の釣燈籠
- □ donate　…を寄付する　　□ make a wish　願い事をする　　□ be granted　かなう
- □ be engraved with ...　… が刻まれている　　□ tortoise　（陸生の）亀　　□ billionaire　億万長者

## 2-3　春日大社

### 永遠の燈籠、万燈籠、南門の前のパワースポットについて

T: By the way, when they get old, who pays for the repairs?

G: The **maintenance fees** are included in the price. They'll survive forever, because they're repaired by excellent **stone craftsmen**. One of them, for example, does repairs without using machines. He uses a hammer and chisel to keep the lanterns in their original beautiful shape. He has worked on the Angkor Wat temples in Cambodia and the Moai Statues on Easter Island. He **was** also **engaged in** a **conservation survey** on the Sphinx in Egypt. Thanks to the superb **craftsmanship**, the restored lanterns will survive for a long time.

T: Great! So the stone craftsmen have been engaged in major repair works in other countries, too.

G: Lanterns were lit every night until the Meiji Restoration of 1868. A large amount of **rapeseed oil** was used. Kasuga Taisha was the brightest place in Nara, but today, the lanterns are only lit on February 3, and August 14 and 15. This is called the "Bantōrō" Lantern Festival. This festival creates a mysterious fantasy world. You can experience it later on.

T: How? Today is May 10.

G: Wait and see!

### In front of the "Nanmon" South Gate

G: Please look at this gate. Do you think there's anything strange about it?

T: It doesn't have a shrine name plate.

G: Right! When the shrine's name plate was knocked down by lightning, it made a big hole in the ground. The broken name plate **was buried**, and the hole was covered over by a big stone. A part of the stone is **sticking out** of the ground; therefore, this is regarded as a place which **divine spirits** are drawn to. It's said that you can get spiritual power here. It's called a "power spot."

G：通訳ガイド　T：観光客

**T：** 古くなったら、誰が修繕費を払うのですか？

**G：** 維持費は値段に含まれています。優秀な石工によって修繕されるので、永遠に生き残ります。例えば、石工の一人は機械を使わずに修繕してくれます。彼は元の美しい形を保つために、金づちやのみを使います。彼はカンボジアのアンコールワットの寺院や、イースター島のモアイ像の修理も行いました。またエジプトのスフィンクスの保全調査にも従事しました。優れた職人技のおかげで、修繕された燈籠は長く残ります。

**T：** すごいです！　それじゃあ、石工は外国の大きな修繕工事にも取り組んだのですね。

**G：** 1868年の明治維新まで、燈籠は毎晩灯されていました。大量の菜種油が使用されていました。春日大社は奈良で一番明るい場所でしたが、今は、2月3日前後、8月14日、8月15日にだけ燈籠が灯されます。万燈籠と呼ばれています。このお祭りは神秘的で幻想的な世界をつくります。後で経験できますよ。

**T：** どうして？　今日は5月10日です。

**G：** 様子を見ましょう！

## 南門の前で

**G：** この門を見てください。何か変だと思いませんか？

**T：** 神額がないです。

**G：** その通り！　神額が雷によって落とされたとき、地面に大きな穴が開きました。壊れた神額を埋め、大きな石を穴にかぶせました。石の一部が地表に現れています。そのため、ここは神霊が引き寄せられる場所と見なされています。ここで霊的な力がもらえると言われているのです。「パワースポット」と呼ばれています。

---

単語の小箱

☐ maintenance fee 維持費　☐ stone craftsman 石工　☐ be engaged in ... …に従事する
☐ conservation survey 保存調査　☐ craftsmanship 職人技　☐ rapeseed oil 菜種油
☐ be buried 埋められる　☐ stick out 突き出る　☐ divine spirit 神霊

# 2-4 春日大社

藤の木、家紋、舞殿、林檎の庭について

### After entering through the "Nanmon" South Gate

**T**: How beautiful! What's the name of this flower?

**G**: This is a **wisteria**. The wisteria is the symbol of Kasuga Taisha. Also, the wisteria is the family crest of the Fujiwaras, who have connections with Kasuga Taisha. It's said that there are two reasons why the wisteria was chosen as the family crest of the Fujiwara family. "Wisteria" is "Fuji" in Japanese, so the family crest of the Fujiwara family is the wisteria. The second reason is that the wisteria is a symbol of an **abundant harvest**, so it's suitable for the Fujiwara family. This wisteria is said to be more than 700 years old.

**T**: How can you tell this wisteria is 700 years old?

**G**: This wisteria **is depicted** in a scroll offered to Kasuga Taisha in 1309.

**T**: I see. I like the color combinations of this shrine. I really like the **vermilion** color!

**G**: Vermilion represents happiness and **dispels** evil spirits.

### In front of the Buden

**G**: The two bays to the east usually **function as** a place of worship. The three western bays are called the "Buden." The Buden is a place where the traditional music and dances of the Imperial Court are performed on rainy days.

### In front of the "Ringo-no-niwa" Garden, after going through the special admission entrance

**G**: This garden is named "The Apple Yard." This garden is a sacred place where Shinto rituals and traditional music and dances are performed. Please look at this apple tree. People **divined** their yearly harvest through the number of apples. According to **Feng Shui** principles, the apple is a symbol of peace.

**T**: Apples have a good meaning in my country, Britain, too. "An apple a day keeps the doctor away."

G：通訳ガイド　T：観光客

## 南門を通り抜けてから

**T**：なんてきれいなんでしょう！　この花は何という名前ですか？

**G**：これはフジです。フジは春日大社のシンボルです。また、春日大社にゆかりのある藤原氏の家紋です。藤原家の家紋にフジが選ばれたのには、2つの理由があると言われています。Wisteria は日本語で「フジ」なので、藤原家の家紋はフジなのです。2つ目の理由は、フジは豊穣のシンボルなので、藤原家にピッタリだからです。このフジは樹齢 700 年以上だと言われています。

**T**：なぜ、このフジが樹齢 700 年だと言えるのですか？

**G**：このフジは、1309 年に春日大社に奉納された巻物に描かれているのです。

**T**：なるほど。私はこの神社の色の組み合わせが好きです。朱色が大好きです。

**G**：朱色は幸福を表し、悪霊を払います。

## 舞殿の前で

**G**：東二間の場所は、普段は参拝所の役割を果たします。西側三間は「舞殿」と呼ばれています。舞殿は、雨の日には宮廷の伝統的な音楽や舞が披露される場所です。

## 特別参拝所を通り抜けて林檎の庭の前で

**G**：この庭は「林檎の庭」と名付けられています。この庭は神聖な場所で、神道の儀式が行われ、伝統的な音楽と舞が披露されます。このリンゴの木を見てください。人々はリンゴの数によって、その年の収穫量を占いました。風水によれば、リンゴは平和の象徴です。

**T**：リンゴは私の国、イギリスでもいい意味を持っています。「1日1個のリンゴは医者を遠ざける」ですね。

---

### 単語の小箱

□ wisteria フジ　□ abundant harvest 豊作　□ be depicted 描かれる　□ vermilion 朱色
□ dispel …を追い払う　□ function as … …としての役割を果たす　□ divine …を占う
□ Feng Shui 風水

# 2-5 春日大社

樹齢千年の杉の木と屋根を突き抜けた木、シカ、東回廊について

G: Please look at the **cedar tree** over there. It is said to be about 1,000 years old, and the **Chinese juniper tree** next to the cedar tree is **growing through** the roof.

T: Wow! Why wasn't it cut back?

G: It's believed that deities live in trees. In Shintoism, people believe that spirits live in many objects such as mountains, rocks, trees, rivers, and so on.

T: Wow! But the top of the 1,000-year-old cedar tree seems to have been cut off.

G: No, it was struck by lightning, but it has been taken care of. By the way, do you know how a lawn is mown?

T: With a **lawn mower**, or by hand?

G: Deer can function as lawn mowers! Thanks to them we don't have to use **insecticides**, either.

T: Oh dear! (laughing) Deer are clever enough to know how to take good care of nature!

G: Look at the trees on the right-hand side. They are "Asebi," or **Japanese andromeda trees**. In Japanese we write it like this: "馬酔木 (asebi)," which literally means "Horse Gets Drunk Tree." Deer don't eat andromeda trees. Their leaves are said to taste bitter.

**Walking through the east cloister**

G: We are walking through the east **cloister**. Do you realize that the east cloister is built on a **slope**? Kasuga Taisha Shrine is at the foot of Mt. Mikasa. Mt. Mikasa is a sacred site, so it **is forbidden** to cultivate the land.

T: Yes, I can see that it's built on sloping land.

G: Nature is taken good care of.

T: The mountain wisterias and hanging lanterns are so beautiful! Why are there two different colors of lantern, gold and green?

G: As time goes by, the golden ones turn green.

G：通訳ガイド　T：観光客

G：向こうに見えるスギの木をご覧ください。樹齢およそ千年と言われています。スギの木の隣のシンパクは屋根を突き抜けています。

T：わー！　なぜ切られなかったのですか？

G：木に神様が住んでいると信じられているからです。神道では、山や岩、木、川など多くのものに生命が宿っていると信じられているのです。

T：わー！　でも、千年杉のてっぺんが切り落とされているようです。

G：いいえ、落雷でなくなってしまったのですが、大切にされていますよ。ところで、どのように芝生を刈るかわかりますか？

T：芝刈り機を使うか、手で刈るかですか？

G：シカが芝刈り機の役割もしてくれます。シカのおかげで殺虫剤も使わなくて済むんです。

T：あら、まあ（笑）！　賢いシカは自然を大切にする方法も心得ているのですね！

G：右側の木をご覧ください。馬酔木（アセビ）という日本産のアンドロメダツリーです。日本語では「馬酔木」と書くのですが、それは馬が酔う木を意味します。シカは馬酔木を食べません。葉っぱが苦いと言われています。

**東回廊を歩きながら**

G：今、東回廊を歩いています。東回廊が斜面に建っているのがわかりますか？　春日大社は御蓋山のふもとにあります。御蓋山は聖地であるため、耕地できないのです。

T：はい、傾斜した土地に建っているのがわかりますよ。

G：自然をとても大切にしているのです。

T：ヤマフジと釣燈籠がとてもきれいです！　なぜ、金色と緑色、2色の釣燈籠があるのですか？

G：時が経つにつれて、金色の燈籠が緑色になるのです。

## 単語の小箱

□ cedar tree　スギの木　　□ Chinese juniper tree　シンパク（真拍）
□ grow through ...　…を突き抜けて成長する　□ lawn mower　芝刈り機
□ insecticide　殺虫剤　□ Japanese andromeda tree　アセビ（馬酔木）
□ cloister　回廊　□ slope　傾斜　□ be forbidden　禁じられた

# 2-6　春日大社

御蓋山遥拝所、中門御廊、唐獅子、武将たちの釣燈籠について

### After praying at Mikasa-Yōhai-sho

T: Why has Mt. Mikasa been regarded as a sacred place?

G: There are two reasons for that. Firstly, Mt. Mikasa is in the east. Both the sun and the moon rise in the east and people get water from Mt. Mikasa. Because Mt. Mikasa is a **source of water**, people have believed that deities live there. Secondly, this is the sacred place where Takemikazuchi-no-mikoto arrived on a white deer. Hunting and **logging** have been prohibited here since ancient times.

### In front of the "Chūmon" Gate and Orō

G: Behind the Chūmon Gate, there is the main sanctuary. You are not allowed to enter the **main sanctuary**. Four deities are enshrined here: one in each of the four halls. The first hall is for Takemikazuchi-no-mikoto, the powerful deity of warriors who made Japan a peaceful country. The second hall is for Futsunushi-no-mikoto, who worked to build an orderly nation. The third hall is for Amenokoyane-no-mikoto, who is the deity of wisdom and ritual. And the fourth hall is for Himegami, the female deity of love, who is the wife of Amenokoyane-no-mikoto.

### After praying to the deities

G: From here you can see a picture of a **Chinese lion** and peony. The Chinese lion is a strong, divine animal and the peony is a symbol of wealth and nobility. This is regarded as a good combination and a symbol of strength.

T: I see. That makes sense!

G: Please look at these hanging lanterns donated by famous warlords in the 17th century.

T: Wow! That's more than 400 years ago! They're still in beautiful condition thanks to the skills of the craftsmen!

G：通訳ガイド　T：観光客

## 御蓋山遥拝所をお参りした後で

T：なぜ、御蓋山は神聖な場所と見なされているのですか？

G：それには2つの理由があります。1つ目には、御蓋山が東に位置するからです。太陽も月も東から上りますし、人々は御蓋山から水を得ます。御蓋山は水源なので、人々は御蓋山に神様が住んでいると信じているのです。2つ目には、ここはタケミカヅチノミコトが白いシカの背に乗って降り立った聖なる場所なのです。ここでは、狩猟と伐採は古代から禁じられています。

## 中門と御廊の前で

G：中門の後ろに本殿があります。本殿に立ち入ることはできません。4柱の神様が、4つの建物にそれぞれ祀られています。第一殿には日本を平和な国にした、力のある武の神様、タケミカヅチノミコトが鎮座されています。第二殿には、秩序ある国を建設するために働いたフツヌシノミコトが鎮座されています。第三殿には、知性と儀式の神様であるアメノコヤネノミコトが鎮座されています。第四殿は、愛の神様で、アメノコヤネノミコトの妻のヒメガミ様のためのものです。

## 神様にお祈りしてから

G：ここから唐獅子ボタンの絵が見られます。唐獅子は強い神獣で、ボタンは富と高貴の象徴です。これは良い組み合わせで強さの象徴と見なされています。

T：なるほど。理にかなっていますね！

G：17世紀の有名な武将たちによって奉納された釣燈籠をご覧ください。

T：わー！　400年以上前ですね！　職人さんの技術のおかげで、今でも美しいですね！

## 単語の小箱

□ source of water 水源　□ logging 伐採　□ main sanctuary 本殿
□ Chinese lion 唐獅子

# 2-7 春日大社

風宮神社、七種寄木(なないろのやどりぎ)、藤浪之屋の万燈籠について

### Kazenomiya Shrine and seven kinds of parasitic tree

G: We're in front of Kazenomiya Shrine. "Kaze" means wind. It's situated to the west of the main sanctuary, and protects the main sanctuary from the west wind. Kazenomiya Shrine gathers good things and **blows away** bad things.

T: I feel I can get a lot of energy from this small shrine.

G: Next, please look at these seven **parasitic trees**. The mother tree is a "Kago-no-ki," which means "**Baby Deer Tree**." The **bark** of the tree looks like the **hide** of a baby deer. Seven other trees grew from the mother tree. They are camellia, sacred bamboo, wisteria, maple, mountain cherry, elderberry, and evergreen witch hazel.

T: Wow! I've never seen such an unusual tree before.

G: Seeds were carried to the mother tree by the wind deity, and they grew out from it. You can pray for a child here and at Kazenomiya Shrine.

T: Wow! It's a sacred tree for childbirth!

### Near Hachirai Shrine

G: From here, you can see the main sanctuary. You can compare the color of the main sanctuary with that of other shrines. The most expensive vermilion color, containing mercury, is used in the main sanctuary of Kasuga Taisha. In Japan, only Kasuga Taisha uses this color.

### In Fujinami-no-ya

G: You can experience the "Bantōrō" Lantern Festival here in Fujinami-no-ya.

T: Fantastic! By the way, do the lanterns have candles inside?

G: No, they have LED **bulbs**. As they are lit up every day, it's safer.

G：通訳ガイド　T：観光客

## 風宮神社と七種寄木<small>（ななないろのやどりぎ）</small>

G：私たちは風宮神社の前にいます。風は「ウインド」を意味します。風宮神社は本殿の西側に位置していて、本殿を西風から守っています。風宮神社は、良いものを集め、悪いものを吹き飛ばしてくれます。

T：この小さな神社からたくさんのエネルギーをもらえるように感じます。

G：次に七種寄木をご覧ください。母樹の名前は「鹿子の木」で「ベイビーディアツリー」を意味します。木の皮が赤ちゃんシカの皮のようですね。ほかの7種類の木が母樹から生育しました。それらはツバキ、ナンテン、フジ、カエデ、ヤマザクラ、ニワトコ、イスノキです。

T：わー！　こんな珍しい木を見るのは初めてです。

G：種が風の神様によって母樹（鹿子の木）に運ばれ、母樹から成長したのです。ここと風宮神社で子授け祈願ができます。

T：すごい！　子授けの霊木ですね！

## 八雷神社のそばで

G：ここから本殿をご覧いただけます。本殿の色と、そのほかの神社の色を比べられますよ。水銀を含んだ最も高価な朱色が春日大社の本殿に使われています。日本では、春日大社だけがこの色を使用しています。

## 藤浪之屋で

G：万燈籠祭りをここで経験できますよ。

T：素晴らしい！　燈籠の中にはろうそくがあるのですか？

G：いいえ、燈籠 LED 電球です。毎日灯されるので、その方が安全なのです。

### 単語の小箱

□ blow away ... … を吹き飛ばす　□ parasitic tree 寄木　□ Baby Deer Tree 鹿子の木
□ bark（木の）皮　□ hide（獣の）皮　□ bulb 電球

# 2-8 春日大社

花嫁と綿帽子とウェディングベール、若宮おん祭り、蛇、藤の髪飾りについて

### In front of the Heiden

G: Look! There's a bride and groom. They're having their picture taken.

T: The bride is so cute! I want to wear a **white headdress** like hers.

G: The bride is wearing a "Wataboshi." She wears it until after the wedding ceremony. It guards her **chastity**. White is a sacred color because in ancient Japan white was considered the color of the sunlight.

T: A bride wears a wedding veil to protect herself from evil. It also symbolizes a mother's love.

G: There are some similarities between a wedding veil and a "Wataboshi." We're lucky to see a bride and a groom today! By the way, there's a **time-honored** annual festival called the Wakamiya Onmatsuri in December. People suffered for a long time from **epidemics** and **famines** caused by heavy rain. According to legend, Wakamiya was born in the form of a snake between the main deities of Kasuga Taisha, and Wakamiya **is** still **revered** as the deity of water. The Wakamiya Festival was held to pray to Wakamiya to stop the heavy rain. Miraculously, the heavy rain stopped. The Wakamiya Onmatsuri has been held for more than 870 years ever since. Rituals are held not only for Japanese people, but also for world peace.

T: It's very difficult for me to understand the Japanese deities. Is a snake a deity?

G: Yes. Snakes have been revered as deities since ancient times. Snakes grow by casting off their skins, so they are symbols of prosperity, too. They have a strong life force.

T: I see. By the way, a shrine maiden over there is wearing a hairpin in the shape of a wisteria. I'd like one like that.

G: After praying at Wakamiya Shrine, I'll take you to the gift shop.

G：通訳ガイド　T：観光客

## 幣殿の前にて

G：見て！　花婿と花嫁です。写真を撮ってもらっています。

T：花嫁はとてもかわいいです。私も彼女のような白い頭飾りを付けたいわ。

G：花嫁は「綿帽子」を身に着けています。結婚式の終了後まで綿帽子を身に着けます。それは純潔を守ることを意味します。白は古代の日本では日光の色と考えられていたので、神聖な色なのです。

T：花嫁は邪悪な物から身を守るために、ウェディングベールを着用しますよ。母親の愛も象徴します。

G：ウェディングベールと「綿帽子」にはいくつか似ているところがありますね。今日は花婿と花嫁を見ることができてラッキーです。ところで、12月には若宮おん祭りという年に一度の由緒あるお祭りがあります。人々は豪雨でもたらされた疫病と飢饉に長年悩まされていました。伝説によると、春日大社の主祭神の間に若宮がヘビの姿で誕生し、そして若宮は今でも水徳の神としてあがめられています。若宮に豪雨を止めることを祈願し、若宮おん祭りが行われました。奇跡的に豪雨は収まりました。それ以来、870年以上にわたり、若宮おん祭りは続いています。儀式は日本人だけのためだけなく、世界平和のためにも行われます。

T：私には、日本の神様を理解することは難しいです。ヘビが神様なのですか？

G：はい。ヘビは古代より神と見なされています。ヘビは脱皮を繰り返すことで大きくなっていくので、繁栄の象徴でもあります。強い生命力を持っています。

T：なるほど。ところで、向こうにいる神社の娘さんはフジの形のヘアピンをつけていますね。同じような物が欲しいです。

G：若宮神社を参拝してから、ギフトショップにお連れしましょう。

## 単 語 の 小 箱

□ white headdress 綿帽子　□ chastity 純潔　□ time-honored 由緒ある
□ epidemic 疫病　□ famine 飢饉　□ be revered あがめられる

# 2-9 奈良のシカ

シカの食べ物、注意事項、シカの出産について

G: The deer in Nara City have been designated as "Natural Monuments" and they make the Nara Park scenery all the more beautiful. I'll give you some advice about the deer. The deer are **tame** and will approach you. They'll bow to ask you for some deer crackers. Some **nasty** tourists **tease** the deer by **waving** crackers in front of them. Please don't do nasty things like that. The deer cannot digest human food, so please don't give them any. Please be careful about the use of **plastic bags** or wrappings. They've been found in the stomachs of several dead deer. There are no trash cans so that deer won't eat the trash. Please take your trash with you.

T: OK! Do the deer **live on** deer crackers?

G: They live on grass, acorns, and fallen leaves. Deer crackers are made from **wheat flour** and **rice bran**, and are **sugar-free** for their health. A part of their sales is used for protecting the deer.

**After giving some deer crackers to the deer**

T: The deer are so tame! The baby deer with its mother is so cute!

G: Very cute! But don't get close to the mother deer who's **raising her baby**. They get a bit aggressive to protect their babies. Eighty percent of **pregnant** female deer are protected and give birth to their babies from the beginning of May to the end of June in the **enclosure** called the "Rokuen," run by the "Nara Deer Preservation Foundation." When July comes, the mother deer will leave the Rokuen with their babies and return to Nara Park. Their pregnancy period is from seven to eight months. Female deer fall in love with male deer from September to November.

T: They fall in love with each other! How romantic! How many deer are there in Nara?

G: The number of deer is about 1,300, including about 200 baby deer. There are about 300 male and 800 female deer.

T: Lucky male deer!

G：通訳ガイド　T：観光客

G：奈良のシカは「天然記念物」に指定されていて、奈良公園の景色をさらに美しくしています。シカについていくつかアドバイスをしますね。シカは人に慣れていて、あなたに近付いてきます。シカは鹿せんべいをおねだりするために、お辞儀をしますよ。意地悪な旅行客が、鹿せんべいをシカの前にちらつかせてからかったりします。意地悪しないでください。シカは人間の食べ物は消化できないので、与えないでください。ビニール袋や包装紙の使用には気をつけてくださいね。それらが死んだ何頭かのシカの胃から見つかったのです。シカがごみを食べないように、ごみ箱はありません。ごみはお持ち帰りくださいね。

T：わかりました！　鹿せんべいがシカの主食ですか？

G：シカは主に芝やどんぐり、落ち葉を食べています。鹿せんべいは、シカの健康のために砂糖を使わず、小麦粉と米ぬかでできています。売り上げの一部は、シカを保護するために使われます。

### 数頭の鹿に鹿せんべいをあげてから

T：シカって本当に従順ですね！　お母さんと一緒にいる子ジカはかわいいですね！

G：とてもかわいいですよ！　ですが、子育て中のお母さんシカには近寄らないようにしてください。赤ちゃんを守るために、少し攻撃的になっています。妊娠している雌ジカの80％は保護され、5月初旬から6月末に、「奈良の鹿愛護会」の運営する「鹿苑」と呼ばれる囲いで出産します。7月になると、母ジカは赤ちゃんたちとともに鹿苑を出て、奈良公園に戻ります。妊娠期間は7か月から8か月です。雌ジカは9月から11月に雄ジカと恋に落ちます。

T：お互いに恋に落ちるのですね！　なんてロマンチックなんでしょう。奈良には何頭のシカがいますか？

G：約200頭の子ジカを含むおよそ1,300頭がいます。約300頭の雄ジカと約800頭の雌ジカがいます。

T：雄ジカは何て幸運なのでしょう！

## 単語の小箱

□ tame 人に慣れた、おとなしい　□ nasty 意地の悪い　□ tease …をからかう、じらす
□ wave …をちらつかせる　□ plastic bag ビニール袋　□ live on ... …を主食とする
□ wheat flour 小麦粉　□ rice bran 米ぬか　□ sugar-free 砂糖なしの
□ raise *one's* baby 子供を育てる　□ pregnant 妊娠した　□ enclosure 囲い

# 2-10 奈良のシカ

 066

発情期と雄ジカ、年齢の見分け方、自然サイクルの中で貢献するシカについて

G: The male deer become violent during the **mating season** from September to November, so they are taken to the Rokuen to have their **antlers** cut.

T: I see. That makes sense.

G: A strong male deer **marks out his own territory** and **encloses** many female deer. When another male deer tries to invade his territory, he **threatens** or attacks him.

T: Wow! By the way, how can you tell their age?

G: It's difficult to tell the age of a female deer, because she doesn't have antlers. As for a male deer, if he has a one-point antler, he's one year old. If he has a two-point antler, he's over two years old, and if he has a three-point antler, he's over three years old.

T: I see. By the way, there's no smell of deer **poop**.

G: It's said that one deer does 500 to 700 grams of poop a day. Scarab beetles eat their poop and break it down to **fertilize** the lawns. The lawns grow and the deer eat the grass again.

T: Wow! The natural cycle works well!

G: The deer in Nara act as **lawn mowers**! They also create a beautiful landscape for us. You can see a long way over there, right? That's because the deer eat the tree branches and leaves up to two meters in height. This line is called the "deer line."

T: The deer are landscape gardeners! It's natural art created by deer!

G: Deer have been taken good care of as messengers of the deities since ancient times. It's said that until the 17th century, killing deer, even by accident, was punished by death. There's a funny **anecdote** about Nara people. They **were in the habit of** getting up early so that they could check if there was a dead deer in front of their houses. If they found one, they moved the deer to the front of a neighbor's house.

T: They were **passing the buck**! (laughing)

G: Good expression, but Nara people are the last people to do such a thing. They have been **coexisting with** deer for more than 1,200 years and they'll carry on living with them happily.

G：通訳ガイド　T：観光客

G：雄ジカは9月から11月の発情期に暴力的になるので、鹿苑に連れて行かれて角を切られます。

T：なるほど。理にかなっていますね。

G：強い雄ジカは自分自身の縄張りを作り、多くの雌ジカを囲います。ほかの雄ジカが縄張りに侵入しようとすると、威嚇するか攻撃します。

T：わー！　ところで、シカの年齢はどのようにしてわかるのですか？

G：雌ジカは角がないので、年齢を知るのは難しいです。雄ジカの場合は、1本角があれば1歳です。2本角があれば2歳以上で、3本角があれば3歳以上です。

T：なるほど。シカのふんの臭いがしませんね。

G：1頭のシカは、一日に500グラムから700グラムのふんをすると言われています。コガネムシがシカのふんを食べて、それを分解して芝生の肥料にします。芝は成長し、シカがまたその芝を食べます。

T：わー！　自然のサイクルがうまく作用しているのですね。

G：奈良のシカたちは芝刈り機の役割もしてくれます！　私たちのために美しい景観作りもしてくれますよ。ずっと向こうまで見えるでしょう。それはシカたちが、2メートルまでの高さの枝葉を食べるからです。この線は「ディアーライン」と言われています。

T：シカは景観庭師ですね！　シカが作った自然のアートですね。

G：シカは古代から、神様のお使いとしてとても大切にされてきました。17世紀までは、誤ってでもシカを殺してしまうと、死刑になったと言われています。奈良の人についての面白い逸話があります。死んだシカが家の前にいるかどうかを確かめるために早起きをすることが、習慣になっていました。もし見つかったら、そのシカを隣人の家の前に移動させたとか。

T：責任転嫁ですね！（笑）

G：うまい表現ですが、奈良の人々はそんなことはしませんよ。人々はシカと1,200年以上も共存して、これからも、仲良く暮らしていくでしょう。

## 単語の小箱

- □ **mating season** 発情期　□ **antler** 角　□ **mark out** *one's* **own territory** 縄張りを作る
- □ **enclose** …を囲い込む　□ **threaten** …を威嚇する　□ **poop** ふん
- □ **fertilize** …に肥料を与える　□ **lawn mower** 芝刈り機　□ **anecdote** 逸話
- □ **be in the habit of ...** …を習慣とする　□ **pass the buck** 責任転嫁する（buck は雄ジカの意味）
- □ **coexist with ...** …と共存する

# 瞬間英作文

1. タケミカヅチノミコトが白いシカに乗って御蓋山に来ました。そして、それ以来、シカは神様のお使いと見なされています。

2. 春日大社は、8世紀の天皇の命令により、力のある貴族、藤原家によって造営されました。

3. 神社に向かう参道には 2,000 基の石燈籠があり、1,000 基の銅製の釣燈籠が神社の内側にあります。

4. 優れた職人技のおかげで、修繕された燈籠は長く残ります。

5. フジは春日大社のシンボルであるだけでなく、春日大社ゆかりの藤原氏の家紋でもあります。

6. 樹齢千年のスギの木の隣の木は、屋根を突き抜けて生育しています。

7. 春日大社が聖地である御蓋山のふもとにあるため、東回廊は斜面に造られています。

8. シカは人間の食べ物を消化できないので、一切与えないでください。

9. シカはかわいいですが、野生動物を保護するためには触らないことがルールです。

10. 赤ちゃんジカに人間の匂いが付くと、母ジカが育児放棄するかもしれないので、触れないでください。

11. シカは芝刈りの役割もしてくれます。

---

1. divine messenger 神のお使い　　2. aristocratic 貴族の
3. hanging bronze lantern 釣燈籠　　4. craftsmanship 職人技
5. have connections with ... …にゆかりがある
6. grow through ... …を突き抜けて成長する　　7. cloister 回廊
8. digest …を消化する　　9. for *one's* own protection 自身の保護のために
10. abandon …を放棄する　　11. function as ... …の役割をする

解答例

1. Takemikazuchi-no-mikoto came to Mt. Mikasa on the back of a white deer, and the deer has been considered a **divine messenger** ever since.

2. Kasuga Taisha was founded by the powerful, **aristocratic** Fujiwara family by order of an emperor in the 8th century.

3. Two thousand stone lanterns stand on the approach to the shrine, and 1,000 **hanging bronze lanterns** are inside the shrine.

4. Thanks to the superb **craftsmanship**, the restored lanterns will survive for a long time.

5. The wisteria is not only the symbol of Kasuga Taisha Shrine, but the family crest of the Fujiwaras, who **have connections with** Kasuga Taisha Shrine.

6. The tree next to the 1,000-year-old cedar tree is **growing through** the roof.

7. The east **cloister** is built on a slope because Kasuga Taisha Shrine is at the foot of Mt. Mikasa, which is a sacred site.

8. The deer cannot **digest** human food, so please don't give them any.

9. Deer are cute; however, it's a rule not to touch wild animals **for their own protection**.

10. Please don't touch the baby deer because the mother deer may **abandon** them if they pick up a human scent from them.

11. Deer can **function as** lawn mowers, too.

## 玉虫の宝庫

## 1 緑色の樹木と石燈籠に囲まれた、朱色の大社に生命の息吹を感じ取る

❶ **春日大社**　造営の由来と、神様のお使いとされているシカについて説明。

❷ **参道**　神様に喜んでもらうための 2,000 基の石燈籠燈籠と 1,000 基の釣燈籠について説明します。春日大明神と書かれた燈籠や、「千人燈籠」も紹介しましょう。

❸ **南門を入る**　樹齢 700 年と言われる、豊穣のシンボルであるフジの花を紹介します。フジは藤原氏の家紋にも使われていることも説明。

❹ **幣殿・舞殿**　幣殿は春日大社本殿へ向けての「参拝所」の役割も果たします。

❺ **林檎の庭**　伝統音楽と舞を披露する場所。リンゴは縁起が良いことを説明。

❻ **樹齢 1000 年のスギの木と、その隣の屋根を突き抜けているシンパク**　ゲストは驚かれます。神道ではすべての物に魂が宿ると説明すると、感動を呼びます。

❼ **東回廊**　春日大社は聖地・御蓋山のふもとにあり、整地が禁じられているため斜面に建つていることを説明。ここでも神道の魂を感じてもらいましょう。

❽ **御蓋山遥拝所**　神聖な場所なので、狩猟も伐採も古代から禁じられています。

❾ **中門と御廊前**　4 柱の神様の説明と唐獅子ボタンの説明をします。

❿ **風宮神社では鹿子の木の説明、藤波之屋では万燈篭の説明をします。**

⓫ **奈良のシカ**　神様のお使いであり、愛され続けるシカについて丁寧に伝えましょう。

## 2 通訳ガイドからのアドバイス

### アドバイス1　灯燈籠のモチーフを見て楽しもう

There are many different motifs, such as cranes, tortoises, owls, phoenixes, moons, and family crests. なのですが、異なるシカのモチーフに見入る人も多いです。 Moss is growing on many lanterns. に関しては、日本人やイギリス人は歴史を感じ美しいと思いますが、アメリカ人は美しさを感じない人が多いです。

### アドバイス2　おみくじで大凶が出たらラッキーと励ます！

Many people say that there are too many "Great fortunes" and only a few "Great misfortunes," so people who draw "Great misfortunes" are the luckiest. Also, if you are careful in everything you do, you will achieve a great success!（大吉がありすぎて大凶はほんの少しなので、大凶を引いた人は一番幸運だと多くの人が言います。また、何事にも慎重になれば、大成功を収められるでしょう）のように励ますといいでしょう。

### アドバイス3 春日大社の絵馬はシカの顔を描けるので楽しい

"Ema" are votive picture tablets which we offer to a temple or shrine. People offer Ema to a temple or shrine when they pray for something, or when their prayers are answered. At Kasuga Taisha Shrine, you can draw the face of a deer on a "Shika-ema" in the shape of a deer's head. Also, as at other shrines and temples, you write down your name and wish on the back of the Ema. (「絵馬」は願掛けの板でお寺や神社に奉納します。人々は、何かを祈る場合や願いがかなった場合に絵馬をお寺や神社に奉納します。春日大社ではシカの顔の形をした「鹿絵馬」にシカの顔を描けます。ほかのお寺や神社と同様に、裏に名前と願い事を書くのです)

### アドバイス4 蓮の生命力に興味がある人には 萬葉植物園をご案内！

Lotus seeds do not rot; even if a seed is 1,000 years old, it still buds. (蓮の種は腐らず1,000年経っても実を結ぶ) ことは、蓮の花が仏教のシンボルである理由の一つです。萬葉植物園では、2,000年以上前の種が発芽した「古代のロマン・世界最古の花」の大賀蓮を鑑賞できます。6月下旬から8月初旬に開花します。

# 3 通訳ガイド体験日記

### ◎風宮神社の前の感動を呼ぶ「鹿子の木」。

Here are seven kinds of parasitic tree. Seven different trees grew out of the "Baby Deer Tree." The bark of the tree looks like the hide of a baby deer. (これは七種寄木です。7種類の異なる木が鹿子の木から成長しました。木の皮は赤ちゃんシカの皮に似ています) に神秘を感じる人が多いです。

# 4 通訳ガイドお役立ち英語表現

### ◎ごみは何と言うの？　trash、garbage、rubbish の違いは？

シカがあさるのを防ぐため、奈良公園にはごみ箱が設置されていません。ごみは必ず持ち帰りましょう。

trash：主に一般ごみで、紙くずなどを指す場合が多い、アメリカ英語
garbage：台所から出る生ごみを指すことが多い、アメリカ英語
rubbish：一般ごみと生ごみを含む、イギリス英語

### ◎シカに関するボキャブラリーを覚えよう。

シカは単複同形で deer です。雄ジカは stag や buck、雌ジカは doe です。

# 3-1 興福寺

 067

五重塔、52段の階段、南円堂、不空羂索観音像、西国三十三所について

**G**: Here we are at Nara Station. It takes about 15 minutes to walk to Kōfukuji Temple. Kōfukuji Temple was founded by Fuhito Fujiwara as a **tutelary temple** of the Fujiwara family in 710, when the capital was transferred to Heijō-kyō. Fuhito Fujiwara was a powerful politician as well as an aristocrat.

### Looking at the five-story pagoda at Sarusawa Pond

**G**: Let's walk around Sarusawa Pond. Please look at the five-story pagoda, which is the symbol of Nara. It's 50 meters tall and the second tallest five-story pagoda in Japan. Each story represents one important natural element. From the bottom upwards, they are earth, water, fire, wind, and air. This is the best place to take a picture with the five-story pagoda in the background. Shall we take some pictures?

**T**: I'd love to.

**G**: Let's climb the 52 steps! It's said that a Bodhisattva must **go through 52 strict practices** to become a Buddha.

### In front of the Southern Round Hall (Nan'en-dō), after purification at the Temizusha

**G**: This is the Southern Round Hall. The original one was built in the 9th century. The present building is an 18th-century reconstruction. The main image is Fukūkensaku Kannon. Kensaku means rope. Fukūkensaku Kannon has a rope and catches people's wishes with it and realizes them. It's opened to the public on October 17.

**T**: By the way, who are the people wearing white kimonos, **wide-brimmed hats**, and straw sandals?

**G**: They're **pilgrims** who walk long distances. This is the 9th **station** on the 33-temple **pilgrimage** of west Japan. It's believed that experiencing **trials** will bring happiness in this world and in the **afterlife**.

**T**: Does 33 have any special meaning?

**G**: Yes, it's an important number in Buddhism. Kannon appears in 33 forms in response to each individual's needs in order to save them.

**G：通訳ガイド　T：観光客**

G： 奈良駅に到着しました。興福寺までは歩いて15分ほどです。興福寺は、平城京に遷都された710年に藤原不比等によって、藤原家の氏寺として創建されました。藤原不比等は貴族であるだけでなく有力な政治家でした。

### 猿沢の池で五重塔を見ながら

G： 猿沢の池の周りを歩きましょう。どうぞ奈良のシンボルの五重塔をご覧ください。高さは50メートルで、日本で2番目に高い五重塔です。それぞれの階は5つの重要な自然の要素を表しています。一番下から上に向かって、それぞれ地、水、火、風、空気を意味します。ここは五重塔を背景に写真撮影する最高の場所ですよ。写真を撮りましょうか？

T： お願いします。

G： 52段の階段を上りましょう！　菩薩は如来になるためには52の厳しい修行をしなければならないと言われています。

### 手水舎でお清めしてから南円堂の前で

G： これが南円堂です。もともとの建物は9世紀に創建されました。現在の建物は18世紀に再建されました。ご本尊は不空羂索観音像です。羂索はロープを意味します。不空羂索観音像はロープを持ち、人々の願いをつかみとり、かなえてくれます。10月17日に一般公開されます。

T： ところで、白い着物をやつばの広い帽子、草履を着用している人は誰ですか？

G： 長い距離を歩く巡礼者です。ここは西国三十三所の9番目に巡礼する場所です。このような試練を経験することで、現世でも来世でも幸福がもたらされると信じられています。

T： 33という数字に特別な意味があるのですか？

G： そうです。33は仏教では大切な数字です。観音様は人々を助けるために、その願いに応じて33の姿で現れます。

**単語の小箱**

- □ tutelary temple 氏寺　□ go through 52 strict practices 52の厳しい修行をする
- □ wide-brimmed hat つばの広い帽子　□ pilgrim 巡礼者　□ station 場所
- □ pilgrimage 巡礼　□ trial 試練　□ afterlife 来世

2

奈良

185

# 3-2 興福寺

### 北円堂、東金堂の薬師如来・日光菩薩・月光菩薩について

**In front of the Northern Round Hall (Hoku'en-dō), after looking at the three-story pagoda**

G: This is the Northern Round Hall. The original one was built in the 8th century, on the first **anniversary** of Fuhito Fujiwara's death. This place commands a fine view, so it's said to be the best place to console the spirit of Fuhito Fujiwara, who promoted the construction of the capital at Heijō-kyō. The present one is a reconstruction from 1210 and **retains** the elegant style of the Nara period in the 8th century.

**Looking at Medicine Buddha at the Eastern Golden Hall (Tōkondō)**

G: This is the Eastern Golden Hall. Emperor Shōmu constructed this hall in the 8th century to pray for the recovery of his sick aunt, Empress Genshō. The present one is a 15th-century reconstruction. Yakushi Nyorai, the Medicine Buddha, is in the center. He has a medicine pot in his left palm. Visitors pray to the Medicine Buddha for recovery from illness and for good health.

T: I'll pray to the Medicine Buddha because my mother is sick.

G: There is a pair of Bodhisattvas, one on either side of the Medicine Buddha. When facing the altar, to the right is the Sunlight Bodhisattva and to the left is the Moonlight Bodhisattva. They are **attendants** of the Medicine Buddha.

T: I assume the Medicine Buddha is a doctor, the Sunlight Bodhisattva is a day-shift nurse, and the Moonlight one is a night-shift nurse?

G: (Laughing) Nice! Look at the Twelve Divine Generals who protect the Medicine Buddha. They're often compared to security guards!

**Looking at the five-story pagoda and the Eastern Golden Hall**

T: I really like this five-story pagoda. I could look at it all day.

G: The original five-story pagoda was built by Empress Kōmyō, the wife of Emperor Shōmu, in the 8th century, so the area around the five-story pagoda and the Eastern Golden Hall is called the "**Sacred Area of Marital Harmony**." The present one is a 15th-century reconstruction.

G：通訳ガイド　T：観光客

## 三重塔を見た後、北円堂の前で

G：こちらが北円堂です。初代北円堂は8世紀、藤原不比等の一周忌に建てられました。この場所は見晴らしが良いので、平城京建設を促進した藤原不比等の霊を慰めるのに最高の場所だと考えられています。現在の北円堂は1210年に再建され、8世紀の奈良時代の優雅な様式を保っています。

## 東金堂で薬師如来を見ながら

G：これは東金堂です。聖武天皇が、病臥した叔母の元正天皇の回復を祈り、8世紀に創建しました。現在の建物は15世紀に再建されました。中央にいるのは薬師如来です。左手に薬壺をお持ちです。参拝者は、薬師如来に病気の回復や健康を祈願します。

T：母が病気なので薬師如来にお祈りします。

G：薬師如来の両側に、2体の菩薩がいます。向かって右側が日光菩薩、左側は月光菩薩です。2体は薬師如来の脇侍です。

T：薬師如来はお医者さんで、日光菩薩は日勤の看護師、月光菩薩は夜勤の看護師さんでしょうか？

G：（笑って）素晴らしいですね！　薬師如来を守る十二神将をご覧ください。ガードマンによく例えられます。

## 東金堂と五重塔を眺めながら

T：この五重塔が大好きです。ずっと見続けていたいです。

G：もともとの五重塔は、聖武天皇の妻の光明皇后によって8世紀に建立されました。それで五重塔と東金堂のあたりは「夫婦和合の聖域」と呼ばれています。現在のものは15世紀に再建されました。

### 単語の小箱

□ anniversary 記念日　□ retain …を保つ　□ attendant 従者、お供
□ Sacred Area of Marital Harmony 夫婦和合の聖域

# 3-3 興福寺

中金堂のお釈迦様・薬王菩薩・薬上菩薩、国宝館の阿修羅像について

### In the Central Golden Hall (Chūkin-dō)

G: This is the Central Golden Hall, which was originally founded by Fuhito Fujiwara, who promoted the relocation of the capital to Heijō-kyō in the 8th century. It burned down seven times. In 2018, this new one was completed and opened to the public. Buddha Shakyamuni, the founder of Buddhism, **is enshrined** in the center. This image of Shakyamuni is the **principal image** of Kōfukuji Temple. The right-hand one is Yakuō Bodhisattva, the Medicine King. The left-hand one is Yakujō Bodhisattva, the Supreme Healer. They're said to be the brothers who give us medicine!

T: Good brothers!

G: The Four Heavenly Kings protect the four directions. The small statue on the left is Daikokuten, the Great Black Deity, who is the god of prosperity and wealth.

T: I see. By the way, what's this pillar?

G: This is the "Hossō Pillar." Kōfukuji Temple is the head temple of the Hossō Sect. Fourteen famous monks of this sect are depicted here.

### Looking at Ashura in the National Treasure Museum

G: This is the famous statue of Ashura with three faces and six arms.

T: I've seen Ashura in Nara posters and sightseeing brochures.

G: Right! Most of the temple buildings were burned down during **fighting** in 1180; however, the 8th-century "Tenpyō culture" **dry lacquer statues** of the Eight Guardians, including Ashura, survived. Ashura isn't wearing armor. It's said he experienced **fierce** fighting and realized how meaningless it was. I'm attracted by his pure and innocent face.

T: I'm attracted by his pure and innocent face, too.

G: The dry lacquer technique **enabled sculptors to** portray **subtle** facial expressions. During the samurai era, a group of sculptors created the dynamic and now world-famous statuary known as "Kamakura sculpture." You can have a good look at it here.

T: It's really exciting to see the dynamism of Kamakura sculpture **up close**.

G：通訳ガイド　T：観光客

## 中金堂にて

**G：** ここは、8世紀に平城京への遷都を推進した藤原不比等によって建立された中金堂です。7度、火事で焼け落ちました。2018年にこの新しい中金堂が完成し、一般公開されました。仏教の創始者であるお釈迦様が真ん中にいらっしゃいます。このお釈迦様の像が興福寺のご本尊でもあられます。右側は薬王菩薩、左側が薬上菩薩様です。私たちにお薬をくださる兄弟だと言われています！

**T：** 良い兄弟ですね！

**G：** 四天王像は4つの方角を守ってくださっています。左側にいらっしゃる小さな像は大黒天で、繁栄と富の神様です。

**T：** なるほど。ところでこの柱は何ですか？

**G：** これは法相柱です。興福寺は法相宗の本山です。法相宗の有名な僧侶14人がここに描かれています。

## 国宝館にて阿修羅像を見ながら

**G：** こちらは有名な三面六臂の阿修羅像です。

**T：** 奈良のポスターや観光パンフレットで見たことがあります。

**G：** そうなんですね！　1180年にほとんどのお寺の建物は戦火で焼失しましたが、8世紀に作られた「天平文化」の阿修羅を含む乾漆八部衆立像は生き残りました。阿修羅はよろいを身に着けていません。阿修羅は激しい戦を経験したので、それがどれだけむなしいか悟っていたと言われています。私は阿修羅の純真無垢な顔に魅了されます。

**T：** 私も阿修羅の純真無垢な顔に魅了されます。

**G：** 乾漆造のおかげで、彫刻家たちは繊細な顔の表情を表現できるようになりました。侍の時代に、彫刻家たちは力強く、今では世界的に有名な彫刻「鎌倉彫」を作りました。ここでじっくり見られますよ。

**T：** 鎌倉彫の力強さを近くで見られるなんてワクワクしますね！

## 単語の小箱

- □ be enshrined 祀られている　□ principal image 本尊　□ fighting 戦
- □ dry lacquer statue 乾漆造の像　□ fierce 激しい
- □ enable A to B AがBすることを可能にする　□ sculptor 彫刻家
- □ subtle 繊細な、微妙な　□ up close 近くで

## 瞬間英作文

1. 菩薩は如来になるために、52 の厳しい修行を経験しなければならないと言われています。

2. 三重塔と北円堂は 13 世紀初頭に再建された、興福寺境内で一番古い建物です。

3. 興福寺の阿修羅像や五重塔は、奈良の観光パンフレットによく登場します。

4. 興福寺は三面六臂の阿修羅像で有名です。

5. 私の 75 歳の祖母は、いろいろなお寺で小さな朱印帳いっぱいに印を押してもらい、幸せをかみしめています。


解答例

1. It's said that a Bodhisattva must go through 52 **strict practices** to become a Buddha.

2. The three-story pagoda and the Northern Round Hall were reconstructed at the beginning of the 13th century and are the oldest buildings in the Kōfukuji Temple **compound**.

3. Kōfukuji Temple's Ashura statue and five-story pagoda often **appear** in Nara sightseeing brochures.

4. Kōfukuji Temple is famous for its statue of Ashura **with three faces and six arms**.

5. It makes my 75-year-old grandmother happy to receive a red stamp from each temple to **fill up** her little stamp book.

---

1. strict practice 厳しい修行　　2. compound 境内　　3. appear 登場する、現れる
4. with three faces and six arms 三面六臂の　　5. fill up ... …を埋める

# 玉虫の宝庫

## 1 凛とした空気が特徴的な興福寺で、文化財にごあいさつ

次の順に回るのがお勧めです。
①猿沢の池（五重塔を背景に写真）→② 五十二段→③南円堂→④三重塔→⑤北円堂→⑥東金堂（五重塔と並べてみる）→⑦ 中金堂→⑧ 国宝館

## 2 通訳ガイドからのアドバイス

### アドバイス1　ジョークも交えて軽やかに！

東金堂で薬師如来を医師、日光菩薩と月光菩薩を昼夜シフトの看護師さん、十二神将をガードマンに例えるとゲストはほぼ笑んでくれます。

### アドバイス2　景観条例と高層ビルのない奈良

The tallest building in Nara is the five-story pagoda of Kōfukuji Temple. と説明すると景観条例について聞かれます。そこで、There are no tall buildings in Nara because the height of buildings is regulated by the "landscape ordinance."（奈良に高い建物がないのは、建物の高さが景観条例で規制されているからです）と説明します。

## 3 通訳ガイド体験日記

◎阿修羅を含む乾漆像が生き残った理由が答えらえなかった。

This is because dry lacquer statues were light enough to carry out. Each one weighs about 15 kilograms.（乾漆造の像は軽いので救い出しやすかったからです。一体15キロほどです）と説明しましょう。

## 4 通訳ガイドお役立ち英語表現

◎「薬師如来様の両側に菩薩様が鎮座しています」という表現は？
○　There is a Bodhisattva on both sides of the Medicine Buddha.
×　There is a pair of Bodhisattvas on both sides of the Medicine Buddha.

下の英文では、薬師菩薩の両側に2人ずつ合計4人の菩薩様がいらっしゃることになってしまいます。注意しましょう。

## その他の名所めぐり

# ❶ ならまち

## 歴史

Naramachi is an area centered on the former grounds of Gangōji Temple, a World Heritage Site. The history of Naramachi goes back to the 8th century. Originally a town of shrines and temples, Naramachi has developed from a town of commerce to a town of tourism. Naramachi is an ideal place for strolling around and seeing how small businesses such as sake shops, greengrocers, **candle** stores, and **India ink** stores were run from the late Edo to the Meiji period, 200 to 150 years ago.

\* \* \*

　ならまちは世界文化遺産の元興寺の旧境内を中心とする地域です。ならまちの歴史は 8 世紀にさかのぼります。元は社寺の町で、商業の町から観光の町へと発展していきました。ならまちを散策しながら、江戸時代後半から明治時代の 200 年から 150 年前に、酒屋、青果店、ろうそくや墨の小売店といった小さな商売がどのように栄えたかを垣間見ることができます。

## 町屋の間口が狭い理由は？

This is a merchant house, characterized by its narrow frontage and great depth. It is said that there are two reasons for this. One is that a tax was imposed according to the width of the frontage in the olden days. The other reason is that merchants wanted their houses to face on to the main streets for business reasons.

\* \* \*

　こちらは商人の家で、間口が狭く、奥行きが深いという特徴があります。これには 2 つ理由があると言われています。まず、かつては間口の広さによって税金がかけられたこと。また、商人が商売を考慮して建物を表通りに面したかったからです。

**アドバイス ▸▸** 町屋は京都、高山、山口、堺、宮島、有馬などにもあるので、応用できるようにしましょう。

## 町屋の正面に格子戸がある理由は？

There are **lattice sliding doors** at the front of the "machiya" houses. There are two reasons for them. One is that lattice sliding doors control the sunlight and airflow. The other is that they make it hard for people to look into the house from outside.

\* \* \*

　町屋の前面には**格子戸**がついています。その理由は 2 つあります。1 つは、格子戸が日差しや風量を調整するからです。もう 1 つは、外から家の中を見えにくくするためです。

## 町屋に箱階段がある理由は？

Please look at the stairs, which are used as **chests of drawers**. They're also called "**box staircases.**" They were designed to make full use of the space.

192　その他の名所めぐり ❖ 奈良

＊　＊　＊

引き出し収納として使われている階段をご覧ください。「**箱階段**」と呼ばれています。空間を十分に生かすように工夫された造りになっています。

## 軒につるしてある赤いものは何？──「身代わり申」

Please look at the red fabric ornaments hanging from the eaves of the houses. They're **charms** which represent a monkey messenger of "Kōshin-san." The monkey suffers pain on your behalf, so it is called a "Migawari Saru"—a monkey that sacrifices itself for you.

＊　＊　＊

家の軒先からつり下げられた赤い布製の飾りをご覧ください。これは「庚申さん」のお使いのサルをかたどった**お守り**です。災いを代わりに受けてくれることから、「身代わり申」と呼ばれています。サルがあなたのために自分自身を犠牲にしてくれるのです。

# ❷ 法隆寺

## 日本初の世界文化遺産に選ばれた理由は？

It is said that Hōryūji Temple was originally built by Prince Shōtoku and Empress Suiko in AD 607. The temple complex contains **the oldest existing wooden structure in the world**. It was registered as Japan's first World Heritage Site, together with Himeji Castle, in 1994.

＊　＊　＊

法隆寺は聖徳太子と推古天皇によって607年に創建されたと言われています。お寺の境内には、**現存する世界最古の木造建築物**があります。法隆寺は1994年、姫路城とともに、日本で初めて世界文化遺産として登録されました。

**アドバイス** ➡ 日本の仏教興隆に大きな役割を果たした聖徳太子については p. 90 を参照。

## 世界最古の木造建築として現存する理由とヒノキの効果

There are two reasons why Hōryūji Temple looks the same as it did more than 1,300 years ago. One is that it is away from the center of Nara, so it **escaped damage in the civil wars**. The other reason is that Hōryūji Temple is made of **cypress wood**. Miraculously, cypress wood increases in strength for 200 years after being cut down. The cypress wood used in Hōryūji Temple has almost the same strength as new cypress wood. The cypress tree is said to be **the king of trees**. Cypress wood is **insect- and germ-resistant**. Many Japanese temples and shrines are made of cypress. Cypress wood also has **aromatherapeutic effects**. It feels great to soak in a Japanese bathtub made of cypress wood. I recommend you buy items made of cypress, such as chopping boards, chopsticks, and small boxes as souvenirs.

＊　＊　＊

　法隆寺が 1,300 年以上前と同じように見えるのは、理由が 2 つあります。まず、奈良の中心地から離れているため**内戦**での**戦火を逃れられた**こと。それから、**ヒノキ**でできているということです。驚くべきことに、ヒノキは伐採後 200 年間も強度を増します。法隆寺に使用されたヒノキ材は、新しいヒノキ材と同じ強さを保っています。ヒノキは**木の王様**と呼ばれており、**防虫・防菌作用**があります。日本の寺社仏閣の多くはヒノキでできています。ヒノキはまた、**アロマセラピー効果**があります。ヒノキ製の風呂につかると気持ちが良いのはそのためです。お土産には、ヒノキで作られたまな板、お箸、小箱などをお勧めします。

**アドバイス** ▶ 旅程に世界最古の木造建築・法隆寺が入ってなくても説明してほしいところです。吉野杉とヒノキは奈良県の二大ブランドなので、木製のお土産を勧めると喜ばれます。

## ❸ 若草山の山焼きとその理由

In January, the Wakakusa-yama Hill "Grass Burning Ceremony" is held. Wakakusa-yama Hill is enveloped in a sea of red flames. The grass burning takes about 20 minutes. This is an important event because the ashes of dead leaves are used as a **fertilizer** to grow trees. It also **exterminates harmful insects**. Grass burning is also carried out in other rural areas for **the improvement of the harvest**. It's also enjoyed as a spectacular event, and more than 100,000 spectators come to see it.

＊　＊　＊

　1 月には若草山焼きが行われます。若草山は赤い炎の海で包まれます。山焼きには 20 分ほどかかります。これは重要な行事で、というのも、枯葉の灰が木を生育させる**肥料**として使われるからです。**害虫駆除**もできます。山焼きはほかの農村地域でも**収穫を向上させる**ために行われています。また、山焼きは壮大な行事として楽しまれており、10 万人以上の見学者が集まります。

Chapter
3

兵庫

兵庫では、異国情緒あふれる神戸と、世界遺産の姫路城を中心に取り上げました。ゲストにさまざまな日本の顔を知っていただきましょう。

（上）風見鶏の館（写真提供：風見鶏の館）
（右）神戸ポートタワーとメリケンパーク（©一般財団法人神戸観光局）
（下）姫路城への道（iStock.com/font83）

## 1-1 神戸の街

靴の文化、世界初の缶コーヒー、チョコレートについて

### On the way to Kitano Ijinkan Gai from Sannomiya Station

G: Kobe is the second largest port in Japan after Yokohama. Today, we're visiting Kitano Ijinkan Gai. It takes about 15 minutes to walk there.

T: My guide book says that Kobe is a fashionable town and has an exotic atmosphere.

G: Yes! Japan had a **national isolation policy** from 1639 to 1853. However, in 1858, the **Treaty of Amity and Commerce between the United States and Japan was concluded**. The Port of Kobe was opened in 1868, and was greatly influenced by western culture.

T: I've heard that the quality of the shoes is excellent and the coffee and chocolates are very delicious in Kobe.

G: The **manufacture** of shoes began when Kobe Port opened and foreigners started living in the **foreign settlement**. In those days, the Japanese wore different types of footwear. Enthusiastic shoe **craftsmen** gathered and created high quality shoes. Coffee beans were first imported into Japan in 1877 and coffee **spread out** from port towns like Kobe. "UCC Milk Coffee" was launched in 1969 as the world's first **canned coffee** beverage. As for chocolates, a Russian who escaped from the Russian Revolution came to Kobe and **popularized** chocolate. There are famous coffee, chocolate, and shoe specialty stores.

T: Please take me to the shoe, chocolate, and coffee specialty shops!

G: OK! The Kitano district, which we're visiting today, became a mixed residential area where both foreign and Japanese people could live in harmony after the opening of Kobe Port. Foreigners were allowed to rent and build houses. You can enjoy the western-style townscape.

T: How many residences of early foreign settlers are open to the public?

G: About 14 are open to the public. There was a time when the beautiful townscape seemed to be fading; however, it became a famous tourist spot after Kitano Ijinkan Gai's "Weathercock House" was used as the **backdrop** to a TV drama.

G：通訳ガイド　T：観光客

## 三宮駅から北野異人館街に行く道で

**G：** 神戸は、横浜に次ぐ日本で2番目に大きな港です。今日は北野異人館街へ行きます。歩いて15分くらいかかります。

**T：** 旅行ガイドには、神戸はおしゃれな街で異国情緒が豊かだと書かれています。

**G：** そうです！　日本は1639年から1853年まで鎖国政策を取っていました。しかしながら、1858年に日米修好通商条約が結ばれました。神戸の港は1868年に開港し、西洋文化の影響を強く受けたのです。

**T：** 靴の品質が抜群で、コーヒーとチョコレートがおいしいと聞いたことがあります。

**G：** 靴の製造は、神戸港が開港し、外国人たちが外国人居留地に住み始めたときに始まりました。当時、日本人は違ったタイプの履物をはいていました。熱心な靴職人が神戸に集まり、高品質な靴を作りました。コーヒー豆は1877年に日本に初めて輸入され、神戸のような港町から広がっていきました。1969年には、世界初の缶コーヒーとして「UCC ミルクコーヒー」が発売されました。チョコレートに関して言うと、ロシア革命から逃れてきたロシア人が神戸に来て、チョコレートを広めました。有名なコーヒー、チョコレート、靴の専門店があります。

**T：** その有名な靴、チョコレートやコーヒー専門店に連れて行ってくださいね。

**G：** わかりました。私たちが今日来ている北野地区は、神戸港の開港後、外国人と日本人の両方が住むことのできる雑居区になりました。外国人は家を借りたり、建てたりすることが許されました。西洋の街並みをお楽しみいただけますよ。

**T：** いくつの異人館が一般公開されていますか？

**G：** 約14の異人館が公開されています。美しい街並みがすたれてきたような時代もありましたが、北野異人館街の風見鶏（の館）がテレビドラマの背景に使われた後、人気の観光地になりました。

3

兵庫

## 単語の小箱

☐ **national isolation policy** 鎖国政策
☐ **Treaty of Amity and Commerce between the United States and Japan** 日米修好通商条約
☐ **be concluded** 結ばれる　☐ **manufacture** 製造　☐ **foreign settlement** 外国人居留地
☐ **craftsman** 職人　☐ **spread out** 広がる　☐ **canned coffee** 缶コーヒー
☐ **popularize** …を広める、…を人気のあるものにする　☐ **backdrop** 背景

197

# 1-2 神戸の街

風見鶏の館、日本のジャズ発祥の地について

G: Here we are at the Weathercock House. The rooftop weathercock and **red-brick exterior** of this house are symbols of the Kitano district. The weathercock is a symbol of Christianity, tells us the wind direction, and **dispels evil spirits**.

**Walking around the Weathercock House**

G: This house was built by a German trader, Gottfried Thomas, in 1905. The Weathercock House is itself a work of art. Now we are in the room which **functioned** both **as** a **reception room** and a showroom. Performances such as jazz concerts are held here.
T: Wow! I'm a big jazz fan. I like "Fly Me To The Moon"!
G: Me too! Jazz came to Japan in the early 1900s, and Japan's first jazz band was formed in Kobe. Many jazz clubs started up in the Kitano district. The "Kobe Jazz Street," one of the biggest traditional jazz festivals in Japan, is held along the road from Sannomiya to Kitano.
T: Sounds exciting! I want to experience a Japanese jazz concert!
G: Next, I'll show you the dining room. This dining room is modeled on a European castle. The chandelier is in the shape of a crown. It**'s** also **equipped with** a wine cellar.
T: I never expected to experience Germany in Japan.

**On the first floor, after enjoying the cherry blossoms from the guest room on the second floor**

G: This is Thomas's study. It's said Thomas bought the furniture with the carved dragons on it in Yokohama and took good care of it. He might have exported this type of furniture to Germany.
T: Did Thomas live in this house for the rest of his life?
G: No. World War I **broke out** in 1914, and Germany was an enemy country, so he wasn't allowed to live in Japan. When World War II broke out, the Americans and the British were forced to leave Japan. This area has experienced **ups and downs**! Now it's peaceful and beautiful.
T: It's really fantastic to experience a variety of countries here in Kitano.

G：通訳ガイド　T：観光客

G：風見鶏の館に到着しました。この家の屋根の上の風見鶏と赤レンガの外観は、北野地区のシンボルです。風見鶏はキリスト教のシンボルで、風向きを教えてくれ、悪霊を追い払ってくれます。

## 風見鶏の館を歩きながら

G：この館は、ドイツの貿易商ゴットフリート・トーマスによって1905年に建てられました。風見鶏の館は、それ自体が芸術作品です。今は応接室と展示室の役割をした部屋にいます。ここでジャズコンサートなどの演奏も行われます。

T：すごい！　私もジャズが大好きです。私はFly Me To The Moonが好きです。

G：私もですよ！　ジャズは日本に1900年代の初めに伝わり、日本初のジャズバンドは神戸で誕生しました。多くのジャズクラブが北野地区で始まりました。日本最大の伝統あるジャズフェスティバルの一つ、「神戸ジャズストリート」は三宮から北野の道路に沿ってで行われます。

T：ワクワクしますね！　日本のジャズコンサートを経験したいです。

G：次に食堂をお見せしますね。この食堂は、ヨーロッパのお城をモデルにしています。シャンデリアは王冠の形です。ワインセラーも備え付けられています。

T：日本でドイツを体験できるなんて期待していなかったです。

## 2階の客室から桜を楽しんだ後、1階で

G：ここがトーマスの書斎です。龍の彫られた家具を横浜で購入し、大切にしていたと言われています。彼はこうした家具をドイツに輸出していたかもしれませんね。

T：トーマスはずっとここで過ごしたのですか？

G：いいえ。1914年に第一次世界大戦が勃発し、ドイツは敵でした、だから彼は日本に住めなくなりました。第二次世界大戦が勃発すると、アメリカ人やイギリス人たちは日本を去らなければなりませんでした。この地域は浮き沈みを経験しているのです！　今は平和で美しい地域です。

T：北野でさまざまな国を経験できるなんて素晴らしいです。

### 単語の小箱

- [ ] red-brick exterior　赤レンガの外観　　[ ] dispel evil spirits　悪霊を払う
- [ ] function as ...　…の役割を果たす　　[ ] reception room　応接室
- [ ] be equipped with ...　…を装備する　　[ ] break out　勃発する
- [ ] ups and downs　浮き沈み、好不調

# 1-3 神戸の街

### 神戸牛、世界初の缶コーヒー、EXPO'70、神戸港について

**G**: What kind of beef would you like, red beef or Japanese black beef? The Japanese black beef is **marbled**, tender and has a mild taste. It **melts** in the mouth. The red meat has a low **fat content**.

**T**: The Japanese black beef, please. This is my first time to try it.

### While drinking coffee after dinner

**T**: The Japanese black beef is the best beef I've ever eaten.

**G**: When I ask foreign guests what food they liked best during their stay, they always answer, "Kobe beef and sushi."

**T**: I see. This coffee is delicious, too. I'd like to know about the history of canned coffee.

**G**: Tadao Ueshima, the founder of Ueshima Coffee, loved coffee. One day, Ueshima was drinking glass-bottled milk coffee on the platform while waiting for a train. The train came, so he rushed back to the shop to return the glass bottle without finishing it. He thought this was wasteful. He **hit upon the idea of** putting coffee in cans. He conducted experiments in Kobe, and after a process of trial and error invented canned milk coffee. The world's first canned coffee was launched in 1969. The timing was good. Expo'70 Osaka was held in 1970. Many visitors to Expo'70 Osaka fell in love with the new canned milk coffee.

**T**: Oh, that was really lucky! Canned coffee is really handy to carry around.

**G**: That's true. It was a time when Japan was in the middle of the "Era of High Economic Growth."

**T**: So, Kobe people imported western culture through the Port of Kobe and improved on it!

**G**: Yes! The Port of Kobe has played an important role! Kobe survived the **tragedy** of the Great Hanshin-Awaji Earthquake in 1995. The Port of Kobe was destroyed; however, it has now **revived** and is attracting people with its iconic red Kobe Port Tower and Meriken Park. Under the "Phoenix Plan" for reconstructing the city, its infrastructure has been rebuilt stronger than before.

**T**: Thank you for your explanation! I feel like visiting Kobe Port tomorrow!

G：通訳ガイド　T：観光客

G： どういった牛肉がいいですか？　赤身の肉、または黒毛和牛ですか？　黒毛和牛は霜降りで柔らかく、まろやかです。口の中で溶けますよ。赤身肉は脂肪分が少ないです。

T： 黒毛和牛をお願いします。初めて食べます。

### 夕食後、コーヒーを飲みながら

T： 黒毛和牛は、私が今まで食べた中で一番おいしい牛肉です！

G： 海外のお客様に滞在中に気に入った食べ物を尋ねると、いつも「神戸牛とすし」と答えます。

T： なるほど。このコーヒーもおいしいですね。缶コーヒーの歴史を知りたいです。

G： 上島珈琲の創業者、上島忠雄氏はコーヒーを愛していました。ある日、上島氏はホームで電車を待ちながら、ガラスの瓶に入ったミルクコーヒーを飲んでいました。電車が来たので、全部飲み終えないまま、ガラス瓶を返却するためにお店に急いで戻りました。彼はこれは無駄なことだと思いました。そこで、コーヒーを缶に入れることを思いつきました。彼は神戸で実験を行い、試行錯誤の結果、缶入りミルクコーヒーを発明しました。世界初の缶コーヒーが 1969 年に発売されました。タイミングは良かったです。大阪万博が 1970 年に開催されたのです。多くの万博来場者は新しい缶ミルクコーヒーが大好きになりました。

T： まあ、それは本当にラッキーでしたね！　缶入りコーヒーは持ち歩くのに本当に便利ですね。

G： そうですね。日本経済は「高度経済成長期」の真っただ中でした。

T： では、神戸の人たちは神戸港を通して西洋文化を受け入れ、それを改良していったのですね！

G： そうです！　神戸港は、大切な役割を担ってきています！　神戸は 1995 年の阪神・淡路大震災の悲劇を生き延びました。神戸港も破壊されましたがよみがえり、今は象徴的な赤い神戸ポートタワーや、メリケンパークとともに人々を魅了しています。復興のための「フェニックスプラン」の下で、インフラはより強いものになったのです。

T： 説明どうもありがとう！　明日、神戸港に行きたくなりました。

### 単語の小箱

□ marbled 霜降りの　□ melt 溶ける　□ fat content 脂肪含有量
□ hit upon the idea of ... …というアイデアを思いつく　□ tragedy 悲劇
□ revive よみがえる

3

兵庫

201

## 瞬間英作文

1. 日本は 1639 年から 1853 年まで鎖国政策を取っていました。

2. 神戸港は 1868 年に開港し、西洋文化の影響を強く受けました。

3. 神戸港の開港後、北野地区は外国人と日本人が一緒に暮らせる雑居地になりました。

4. 日本初のプロのジャズバンドが 1923 年に神戸で結成されました。

5. 世界初の缶入りミルクコーヒーは、1970 年の大阪万博の来場者たちの間で人気が出ました。


### 解答例

1. Japan had a **national isolation policy** from 1639 to 1853.

2. The Port of Kobe was opened in 1868, and **was** greatly **influenced by** western culture.

3. The Kitano district became a mixed residential area where both foreign and Japanese people could **live in harmony** after the opening of Kobe Port.

4. Japan's first professional jazz band **was formed** in Kobe in 1923.

5. **The world's first** canned milk coffee became popular among the visitors to Expo'70 Osaka.

---

☐ national isolation policy 鎖国政策　　☐ be influenced by ... … に影響を受ける
☐ live in harmony 仲良く暮らす　　☐ be formed 結成される
☐ the world's first ... 世界初の…

# 玉虫の宝庫

## 1 異国情緒豊かな神戸異人館街

❶ 異人館への往路で、神戸港開港と影響を受けた西洋文化について話しましょう。

❷ 風見鶏の館は、1階：応接室→居間→食堂、2階：客室→朝食室→子供部屋→ベランダ→ショップ、というのが基本経路となります。客室とベランダからの景色が素晴らしい！

## 2 通訳ガイドからのアドバイス

**アドバイス　お客様のリクエストに合わせて臨機応変に**

ガイド当日に突然、"No temples, no shrines!"（神社仏閣はもういや）とおっしゃったゲストを神戸異人館街にご案内し、喜ばれました。

## 3 通訳ガイド体験日記

### ◎缶コーヒー、自動販売機は日本の文化の一つ

There are many vending machines because Japan is a safe country. Canned coffee is a part of Japanese culture.（日本は安全な国なので多くの自動販売機がありますね。缶コーヒーは日本の文化の一つですね）とアメリカ人ゲストが気づかれたのは驚きでした。冷凍食品、化粧品から仏像まで販売されている自販機も日本文化ですね。

### ◎神戸の履き倒れ！

Kobe people go bankrupt by overspending on shoes. のように「神戸の履き倒れ、大阪の食い倒れ、京都の着倒れ」の話をすると喜ばれます。大阪 1-5 も参照（p. 20）。

## 4 通訳ガイドお役立ち英語表現

### ◎「専門店」の言い方は？

神戸では早くからチョコレート、コーヒーや靴が広まったため、専門店が多いです。「専門店」を英語で言うと specialty shop が正しく、special shop は「特別な店」という意味になるので誤りです。

specialty shop は名詞が名詞を修飾する複合名詞です。ほかの例も見てみましょう。

例：chocolate specialty shop（チョコレート専門店）、coffee specialty shop（コーヒー専門店）、waste basket（くずかご）、safety training（安全トレーニング）、quality management（品質管理）

# 2-1　姫路城

日本初の世界文化遺産、姫路城が白い理由、菱の門、明治維新と廃城令について

G: Here we are at Himeji Castle. Himeji Castle became Japan's first World Cultural Heritage site in 1993. Please look at Himeji Castle, also called the "**White Heron Castle**."

T: It really looks like a flying white heron!

G: It is said that Terumasa Ikeda, the builder of the present-day Himeji Castle, wanted to **show off his power** with this beautiful, shining, white exterior. It was completed in 1609.

T: I've seen some white castles in Europe, but Himeji Castle is the best!

G: Himeji Castle is covered with **white plaster**. They were lucky to be able to get the materials from the Seto Inland Sea, which is near Himeji Castle. The white plaster is made from slaked lime, shell lime, hemp fiber, and seaweed glue.

T: So, the white plaster is made from raw materials from the sea?

G: Yes! It's fireproof and waterproof. The fish-like tiles on either side of the roof are said to be charms against fire. Himeji Castle looks like a five-story castle, but it actually has seven stories. Today, I hope you'll enjoy seeing the architectural techniques and **ingenuity** of Himeji Castle.

## At the Diamond Gate

G: This is called the Diamond Gate. This name comes from the flower-shaped ornaments which look like diamonds. This is the most beautiful gate in the castle grounds. It's only 130 meters from the Diamond Gate to the main tower in a straight line; however, you have to walk up a 330-meter zigzag pathway, which is like a maze. There are 21 gates.

## The Meiji Restoration and the order to abandon the castles

G: This is a monument in honor of Colonel Nakamura, who persuaded the government to preserve Himeji Castle. With the Meiji Restoration of 1868, the **feudal system was abolished** and an order to abandon the castles **was issued**. Most of the castles **were torn down**, but Himeji Castle survived, thanks to Colonel Nakamura.

G：通訳ガイド　T：観光客

G：姫路城に着きましたよ。姫路城は 1993 年に、日本で初めて世界遺産になりました。「白鷺城」とも呼ばれている姫路城をご覧ください。

T：本当に飛ぶシラサギに見えますね！

G：現在の姫路城の築城者、池田輝政が、美しく輝く白い外観によって自分の権力を示したかったと言われています。1609 年に築かれました。

T：ヨーロッパで白いお城を見たことがありますが、姫路城が一番です。

G：姫路城には白漆喰が塗られています。幸運なことに、近くにある瀬戸内海から材料を調達できました。白漆喰は消石灰、貝灰、麻の繊維、海藻から作られたのりできているのです。

T：では、白漆喰は海から採取できる原料でできているのですね？

G：そうです！　耐火性も、耐水性もあります。屋根の両側にある魚のような瓦は火災除けのお守りだと言われています。姫路城は 5 階建てに見えますが、実は 7 階建てです。今日は、姫路城の建築技術と、その工夫をお楽しみいただければと思います。

## 菱の門にて

G：これは菱の門と呼ばれています。この名前はダイヤモンドのような花の形の装飾に由来しています。この門は、城内では一番美しいです。菱の門から天守閣までは、直線距離でわずか 130 メートルなのですが、迷路のようなジグザグの道を 330 メートル歩かなければなりません。21 もの門があります。

## 明治維新と廃城令

G：これは、政府に姫路城を保存するように説得した中村大佐の顕彰碑です。1868 年の明治維新で封建制度は崩壊し、廃城令が出されました。ほとんどの城が取り壊されましたが、中村大佐のお陰で姫路城は生き残りました。

## 単語の小箱

☐ **White Heron Castle** 白鷺城　☐ **show off** *one's* **power** 権力を誇示する
☐ **white plaster** 白漆喰　☐ **ingenuity** 創意、工夫　☐ **feudal system** 封建制
☐ **be abolished** 廃止される　☐ **be issued** 発令される　☐ **be torn down** 取り壊される

# 2-2　姫路城

第二次世界大戦と姫路城、いの門、将軍坂、狭間(さま)、はの門について

### World War II and Himeji Castle

G: During the Second World War, Himeji was bombed and downtown Himeji City **was burned to the ground**. A bomb hit the castle, but luckily it failed to explode. The castle miraculously survived. Himeji Castle encouraged a lot of people to live in a more positive way.

### At the "I Gate"

G: Please look at the tile in the shape of a butterfly. The butterfly was the family crest of Terumasa Ikeda, the builder of the castle in its present form.

### Looking at the "Sama" on the slope from the "Ro Gate" to the "Ha Gate"

G: Let's go up the hill called the "Shogun Slope." The Shogun Slope is where scenes in historical TV dramas and movies, including "You Only Live Twice," starring Sean Connery, have been filmed.

T: Wow! What are these openings in the wall? Are they decorations?

G: They're called "Sama." It's a **strategic defense system**. If the enemy attacked, the defenders could **shoot arrows and bullets at** them. The **rectangular** ones are called "Arrow Sama" and the circular, triangular, and square ones are called "Gun Sama." There are still 997 Sama in the walls of the main tower and **turrets**, and in the earthen walls.

### In front of the "Ha Gate"

G: Please look at the pillars of this gate. The pieces of wood **are mortised together**. No nails are used.

T: This kind of interlocking joint system is attracting attention from around the world.

G: Yes. It's also earthquake-proof. The damaged part of the pillar is removed and a new length of wood is mortised into it. It's not necessary to change the whole pillar, and this technique also maintains its strength. It's a good example of traditional Japanese craftsmanship.

G：通訳ガイド　T：観光客

## 第二次世界大戦と姫路城

G：第二次世界大戦中、姫路市は空襲を受け、市街地は焼け野原になりました。爆弾は姫路城にも落ちましたが、幸いにもそれは爆発しませんでした。姫路城は奇跡的に生き延びたのです。姫路城は、多くの人々がより前向きに生きるよう、勇気付けました。

## 「いの門」の前で

G：蝶の形の瓦をご覧ください。蝶は姫路城を現在の形にした築城者の池田輝政の家紋です。

## 「ろの門」から「はの門」へと続く坂に沿って狭間（さま）を見ながら

G：さあ、「将軍坂」と呼ばれる坂を上りましょう。将軍坂はテレビ時代劇や、ショーン・コネリーの主演映画『007は二度死ぬ』などが撮影された場所です。

T：すごい！　この壁の開口部は何ですか？　飾りですか？

G：「狭間」と呼ばれています。戦略的な防御システムです。敵軍が攻撃してきたら、兵士は敵に矢を放ったり、弾丸を撃ったりできます。長方形のものは「弓狭間」、円形や三角形、正方形のものは「鉄砲狭間」と呼ばれています。現在でも、天守閣や櫓（やぐら）、土塀の壁面に997個の狭間が残っています。

## 「はの門」の前で

G：門の柱をご覧ください。木片がほぞ継ぎにされています。釘は使われていません。

T：こういったつなぎ方は、世界中から注目を集めていますね。

G：はい。地震にも強いです。柱の傷んだ部分を取り除き、新しい部分をほぞ継ぎによって接続しています。柱全体を交換する必要がなく、これもまた柱の強度を保つ技術です。日本の職人技の良い例なのです。

### 単語の小箱

☐ be burned to the ground　焼け野原になる　☐ strategic　戦略的な
☐ defense system　防衛システム
☐ shoot arrows and bullets at ...　… に矢を放ち、銃弾を撃つ　☐ rectangular　長方形の
☐ turret　櫓　☐ be mortised together　ほぞ継ぎにする

# 2-3 姫路城

十字瓦、キリスト教の伝来と禁止、鎖国、にの門について

### Looking at the tile marked with a cross, after going through the "Ha Gate"

G: Please look up at the second roof from the top. You can see a tile with a **cross** on the **eave**. It's said that the cross may be related to Kuroda, who was a Christian lord and lived in this castle in the 16th century. It's also said that the cross wards off evil spirits.

### The history of Christianity in Japan

T: I'm interested in the history of Christianity in Japan.

G: Christianity was introduced into Japan in 1549 and banned in 1612. The Edo government was afraid that Christianity would destroy feudalism. There were several **rebellions** after the ban on Christianity. This led Japan to adopt a **policy of seclusion from the rest of the world** in 1639. Japan traded only with the Netherlands, China, and Korea. China and Korea had no connection with Christianity. The Dutch didn't have any intention of **spreading Christianity**. The ban on Christianity **was lifted** in 1873, 19 years after Japan opened its doors to the world in 1854.

### At the "Ni Gate"

G: The Ni Gate is one of the strongest and most easily defended gates. It has two stories. They can attack the enemy from the upper floor. The first floor looks like an underpass and bends at a right angle. Since it is narrow and the ceiling is low, a group of enemy soldiers would have trouble **passing through**. This is an iron-covered door, so the attackers can't break down the gate or burn it down.

T: This gate is very narrow and low. It's dark, too. The attackers would feel they were caught like mice in a trap.

G: Yes. As you approach the main tower, the gates become narrower and lower. You'll experience confusing routes and slopes, too.

T: In other words, it'll be harder to **break in**!

G：通訳ガイド　T：観光客

### 「はの門」を通り抜け、十字架の印のついた瓦を見ながら

**G：** 上から2番目の屋根をどうぞご覧ください。軒の上に十字架のついた瓦が見えますよ。十字架は、16世紀に姫路城に住んでいたキリシタン大名の黒田氏と関係があるかもしれないと言われています。また、十字架は魔除けだとも言われています。

### 日本におけるキリスト教の歴史

**T：** 日本におけるキリスト教の歴史に興味があります。

**G：** キリスト教は1549年に日本に伝わり、1612年に禁止されました。江戸幕府はキリスト教が封建制度を破壊することを恐れたのです。キリスト教を禁止してからいくつかの反乱がありました。このことは、日本が1639年に鎖国政策を取ることにつながりました。日本はオランダと中国、朝鮮とだけ貿易をしました。中国や韓国はキリスト教と関係ありませんでしたし、オランダにキリスト教を布教する意図はなかったのです。キリスト教禁止令は、日本が1854年に開国し、その19年後の1873年に解かれました。

### 「にの門」にて

**G：** にの門は、最強で最も防御力のある門の一つです。2階建てです。兵士らは上の階から敵を攻撃できます。1階は地下道みたいですし、直角に曲がっています。天井が低く狭いので、敵の兵士の一団は通り抜けるのに苦労します。門扉には鉄板が張られているので、襲撃者は打ち破ったり、焼き落とすことができません。

**T：** この門はとても低く狭いですね。それに暗いです。敵は罠にかかったネズミのように感じるでしょう。

**G：** はい。天守閣に近づくにしたがって、門はさらに狭く、低くなります。混乱させるようなルートや坂道もありますよ。

**T：** つまり、突破するのがだんだん難しくなるのですね！

## 単語の小箱

- □ cross 十字架　□ eave 軒　□ rebellion 反乱
- □ policy of seclusion from the rest of the world 鎖国政策
- □ spread Christianity キリスト教を広める　□ be lifted 解除される
- □ pass through ... …を通り抜ける　□ break in ... …へ侵入する

3

兵庫

209

# 2-4 姫路城

油塀、姥が石、水一門について

 076

### Pointing at the Oil Wall on the right-hand side after going through the "Ho Gate"

G: Please look at this "Oil Wall," which goes back 400 years. It's so strongly made that it's **bulletproof** and waterproof. It's the only one of its kind which has survived in these castle grounds. It's said that it's made of clay, sand, **pea gravel**, and rapeseed oil.

### The "Old Widow's Stone" in the stone wall

G: Please look at the stone covered with a wire net. This stone is called the "Old Widow's Stone." When the main castle tower was under construction, they had difficulty collecting stones. According to legend, a poor old woman who made a living by selling roasted rice cakes donated her **millstone**.

T: Her millstone was a very important tool for making a living?

G: Yes. Ways of thinking have changed, but the 16th century was a time when it was a virtue to devote one's life to others. Hideyoshi, the lord of the castle, praised her highly, and then many people donated stones, so the construction **made rapid progress**. The story of the Old Widow's Stone is taught to children at some schools in Himeji.

### After going through the Mizu-no-ichi Mon (Water Gate 1)

G: There are six gates named "Water Gates." They were so named because they were important checkpoints when water was carried along the route from the **well** in the "Waist Quarter" to the main tower. Water is indispensable for human life, and it protects us from fire. Since we entered the Diamond Gate, we have been going up. Now we're walking on a gentle downward slope. How would enemy soldiers feel?

T: They'd think they'd **gone the wrong way**. The attackers would slow down.

G: That's a good point. It would make it easier for the defenders to attack the enemy. We can see how familiar the architects at that time were with **visual effects** and **psychology**.

G：通訳ガイド　T：観光客

## ほの門をくぐり右側の油壁を指さして

G：この 400 年の歴史を持つ「油壁」をご覧ください。防弾かつ防水と、とても丈夫に造られています。この城に残るこの種類の唯一の壁です。粘土、砂、玉砂利と菜種油を混ぜ合わせて造られたと言われています。

## 石垣にある「姥が石」

G：金網で囲まれている石を見てください。この石は「姥が石」と呼ばれています。天守閣を建設しているとき、石を集めるのが非常に困難だったのです。伝説によると、焼き餅を売って生計を立てていた貧しい老婆が、石臼を寄付したと言われています。

T：臼は生計を立てるための重要な道具ですよね？

G：はい。考え方は変化していますが、16 世紀は人のために命をささげるのが美徳と考えられた時代ですから。城主の秀吉は、老婆のことを褒め称え、それから多くの人が石を寄付し、建設は急速に進展を遂げました。姫路には「姥が石」の話を子供たちに教えている学校もあります。

## 水一門を通り抜けてから

G：「水の門」と名付けられた門が 6 つあります。そう名付けられたのは、6 つの水門が、腰曲輪の井戸からルートに沿って天守に水を運ぶ重要なチェックポイントだったからです。水は私たちの生活にとって不可欠であり、火事から私たちを守ってくれます。菱の門から入ってきて、ここまで上ってきました。私たちは今緩やかな下り坂を歩いています。敵兵はどのように感じるでしょうか？

T：道を間違えたと思うかもしれませんね。敵はスピードを緩めるかもしれません。

G：いい点を突いていますね。守備の兵士たちは、敵を攻撃しやすくなるでしょう。当時の建築家がいかに心理学や視覚効果に通じていたかがよくわかりますね。

3

兵庫

## 単語の小箱

- [ ] bulletproof 防弾の　　[ ] pea gravel 玉砂利　　[ ] millstone 石臼
- [ ] make rapid progress 急速に前進する　　[ ] well 井戸
- [ ] go the wrong way 間違った道を行く　　[ ] visual effect 視覚効果　　[ ] psychology 心理学

211

# 2-5 姫路城

 077

天守閣地階（流し台・トイレ・武具庫・柱）、１階（六葉釘隠し・石落とし）

### Sink and toilet in the basement of the main castle tower

G: First, let me show you the basement. There are two unique devices in the basement. One is this wooden kitchen sink. The other is the toilet. They're behind the wooden doors just around the corner; however, there is no **indication** they've been used.

T: So, where did people in the castle **do a poo**? (laughing)

G: They did a poo in a small container and threw it away somewhere far away.

### East and West Main Pillars and Weapon Room in the basement

G: Here you can see the bases of the East and West Main Pillars which support the 6,000-ton main tower of Himeji Castle. Look at the Weapon Room. In peacetime, the main tower was mainly used for storing weapons. Some tourists from abroad are disappointed to see inside the main tower because, unlike European castles, it's not beautifully decorated. The main tower was not a living area; it was the last **stronghold**. I hope you enjoy looking at the defense systems.

### Six-leaf nail cover on the first floor

G: Please look at this six-leaf nail cover. The nail head is covered with a six-leaf design. It's made of **lacquered** wood. The spaces between the leaves are heart-shaped.

T: How cute! It not only hides the nail but also functions as a decoration.

G: You **hit the nail on the head**!

### Stone drop on the first floor

G: Please look at this "stone drop." It is designed so that the defenders can open the cover, monitor the enemy, throw stones at them or shoot at them. Stone drops are located in three corners of the first floor.

G：通訳ガイド　T：観光客

## 天守閣の地階の流し台とトイレ

G：まずは地階からご案内しましょう。地階には2つのユニークなものがあります。一つはこの木製の流し台です。もう一つはトイレです。角の木製のドアの後ろにありますが、使用された形跡はないようです

T：じゃあ、お城の人たちはどこでうんちをしたのですか？（笑）

G：小さい容器に排泄して、離れた場所に捨てていたのです。

## 天守閣地階の東西の大柱と武具庫

G：6,000トンの姫路城天守を支えている東大柱と西大柱の基部をここで見ることができます。武具庫をご覧ください。平和な時は、天守は主に武器を保管する場所として使われます。ヨーロッパのお城と違って美しく装飾されていないので、海外からのお客様の中には、天守閣の内部を見てがっかりする人もいます。天守閣は住居ではなく、最後のとりでです。天守閣内部の防御システムをお楽しみいただければと思います。

## 1階の「六葉釘隠し」

G：この六葉釘隠しをご覧ください。釘の頭が6枚の葉のデザインで覆われています。漆塗りの木でできています。葉の間のスペースはハート型です。

T：かわいいですね！　釘を隠すだけでなく、装飾の機能も果たしますね。

G：的を射ていますね！

## 1階の「石落とし」

G：こちらの「石落とし」をご覧ください。防御側がふたを開けて、敵を監視し、石を投げたり撃つことができる仕組みになっています。石落としは1階の三隅にあります。

3

兵庫

### 単語の小箱

□ indication 兆候、形跡　□ do a poo 排便する　□ stronghold とりで、要塞
□ lacquered 塗装された、漆塗りの　□ hit the nail on the head 的を射たことを言う

213

# 2-6 姫路城

筋交、2階の出窓格子の石落とし、破風の間、武具庫、武具掛け、西の大柱

### Brace on the first floor

G: Please look at this earthquake-proof structural **reinforcement**. It **extends** through the first floor and second floor. It prevents the building from **collapsing** due to **lateral forces**.

### Stone drops on the second floor

G: This large **lattice window** is provided with stone drops.
T: So, if a stone is dropped from here, it'll make a hole in the roof of the first floor?
G: No, there is a hole specially made in the roof, so the stones will hit the enemy soldiers.

### Gable Room, Weapon Room, and weapon racks on the second floor

T: What's this room for? May I take a rest for a few minutes in this room?
G: OK. Let's sit down. This **Gable** Room commands a good view, so warriors can monitor the enemy soldiers from here. One of the lattice windows can be opened. You can see the Weapon Room and weapon racks on this floor.

### Warrior hiding places on the third floor

G: This is a hiding room for warriors, where they can hide and **ambush** the attackers. There are four of these secret places in each corner of this floor.
T: It's a good design! They can attack the enemy by surprise!

### West Main Pillar and the East Main Pillar on the third floor

G: The West Main Pillar consists of two pieces of lumber. You can see the joint. The old West Main Pillar was replaced by the present one during the major repair works from 1956 to 1964. It **is on display** near the ticket office. The East Main Pillar is original, except for the section in the basement. It has supported the castle for 400 years.

G：通訳ガイド　T：観光客

## 1 階の筋交

G：この耐震性のある構造的補強材をご覧ください。それは 1 階から 2 階に伸びています。建物が水平方向の力によって押し潰されるのを防ぎます。

## 2 階の石落とし

G：この大きな出窓格子窓に石落としが据え付けられています。

T：ここから石が落とされたら、1 階の屋根に穴が開きますよね？

G：いいえ、屋根に特別に作られた穴があるので、石は敵兵士に当たるのです。

## 2 階の破風の間、武具庫と武具掛け

T：この部屋は何の部屋ですか？　この部屋で少し休憩してもよろしいですか？

G：じゃあ、座りましょうか。この破風の間は見晴らしがいいので、兵士たちは敵兵をここから監視できます。格子窓の一つが開きます。このフロアでは武具庫も武具掛けも見られますよ。

## 3 階の武者隠し

G：これは兵士が隠れて攻撃者を待ち伏せする、隠れ部屋です。この秘密の場所はこの階の四隅にあります。

T：いい装置ですね！　敵に不意打ちを食らわせられますね！

## 3 階の西大柱と東大柱

G：西大柱は 2 本の木材からできています。その結合部を見ることができますよ。旧西大柱は 1956 年から 1964 年にかけて行われた大修理で、現在のものに取り替えられました。旧西大柱は入場券売り場のそばに展示されています。東大柱は、地下にある部分（最下部）以外はオリジナルのもので、400 年にわたり城を支えています。

## 単 語 の 小 箱

□ reinforcement 補強　□ extend 広がる　□ collapse 崩壊する
□ lateral force 水平方向の力　□ lattice window 格子窓　□ gable 破風
□ ambush …を待ち伏せる　□ be on display 展示中である

# 2-7 姫路城

石打棚、高窓、長壁神社、幻の窓について

 079

### Stone-throwing platforms and high windows (smoke vents), and the inner chamber on the fourth floor

G: Look at this stone-throwing platform. The windows are high up on this floor, so soldiers climb up the **staircase** on to the platform to observe, throw things at, or shoot at the enemy. If the soldiers shoot, this room will be filled with smoke. However, there are also higher windows which function as smoke vents. These windows are designed to **allow** the smoke **to** escape.

T: I see. What's this under the stone-throwing platform?

G: It's a chamber for storing food and weapons in case of siege.

### On the fifth floor

G: The windows are small and the eaves are low. The fifth floor is in the ceiling of the fourth floor, so the main tower seems to have five stories. Do you know why the fifth floor was built in the ceiling of the fourth floor?

T: To confuse the enemy! It's dark.

### Osakabe Shrine on the sixth floor

G: This is a residential-style floor. This floor has two functions. In peacetime, the feudal lord and his **retainers** could enjoy a fine view from here. There was no fighting, so no one committed suicide here. Here's Osakabe Shrine. It's a shrine to the guardian god of Himeji Castle. It **wards off** fire and disasters.

### Hidden windows on the sixth floor

G: The sixth floor was originally planned with windows in each of the four corners, but the design was changed to strengthen the earthquake resistance.

T: I'm really impressed by the abilities of the architects and the craftsmanship of the carpenters.

G：通訳ガイド　T：観光客

## 4階の石打棚と高窓（煙出し）と内室

**G**：この石打棚をご覧ください。この階では窓が高い場所にあるので、兵士は階段を上って石打棚に上がり、敵を監視し、物を投げ、鉄砲を撃ちます。兵士が撃つと、この部屋は煙でいっぱいになるでしょう。しかし、煙出しの働きをする高窓もあります。この高窓は煙が外に出るようにできています。

**T**：なるほどね。石打ち棚の下にあるのは何ですか？

**G**：これは籠城時に備えて、食べ物や武器を保管する内室です。

## 5階にて

**G**：窓は小さく、軒は低いです。5階は4階の天井の中にあるので、天守は5階建てのように見えます。なぜ5階が4階の天井の中に建てられたのかわかりますか？

**T**：敵を混乱させるためですね！　暗いですね。

## 6階の長壁神社

**G**：住居形式のフロアです。この階には2つの機能があります。平和な時は、大名とその家来たちがここからの眺望を楽しんだかもしれません。戦がなかったので、ここでは誰も自害しませんでした。こちらに長壁神社があります。姫路城の守護神のための神社です。火事や災害を防ぎます。

## 6階の幻の窓

**G**：6階は四隅に窓を設置する予定だったのですが、耐震力を強めるためにデザインが変更されました。

**T**：建築家の技術と、大工の腕前には本当に感動します。

## 単語の小箱

□ staircase 階段　□ allow A to *do* A が…することを防ぐ　□ retainer 家来
□ ward off ... …を防ぐ

## 2-8 姫路城

姫路城の傾き、旧番所、備前門入口の石棺、備前から太鼓櫓までの坂道など

### Master carpenter Sakurai and the tilt of the main tower

G: There's a story about the master carpenter, Sakurai. He **devoted himself to** building Himeji Castle for about nine years. After its completion, he found the main castle tower was **leaning to** the southeast. He thought his **measurements** had been wrong. He **got depressed** and killed himself by jumping from this top floor with a chisel in his mouth. Later it was proved that the cause of the **tilt** was **land subsidence**.

T: I think he was too much of a perfectionist.

### In Bizen-maru square below the main tower

G: Here used to be Terumasa Ikeda's mansion. He was the builder of the present-day Himeji Castle.

### Pointing at the Kyūbansho (former guardhouse)

G: This is the former guardhouse. Some guards probably checked people here. Please look at the peach-shaped tile on the top of the roof behind it over there. The peach is a symbol of **fertility** and a charm to protect you from evil. There's an old tale about a boy who was born from a peach. "Peach Boy" grew up and defeated some demons.

### Pointing at the Sekkan (stone coffin) at Bizen Gate

G: Look at the stone coffin used here in the wall. Coffins were used because of a shortage of stone. This shows that there used to be ancient burial mounds around this area.

### Pointing at the Obi no Yagura (Belt Turret)

G: Look at the building on your left. It's built in the tea ceremony style. It was possibly used as a resting place for visitors.

### On the slope from Bizen Gate to the Taiko Yagura (Drum Turret)

G: This is another movie location, where members of the ninja training school were practicing in the Bond movie.

G：通訳ガイド　T：観光客

## 大工棟梁・桜井と姫路城の傾き

G：大工の棟梁である桜井についてのお話があります。彼は約9年間、姫路城の築城に身をささげました。完成後、彼は天守閣が南東に傾いているのに気づきました。自分の測量が間違っていたのだと思いました。彼は落ち込み、最上階からのみをくわえて飛び降り自殺したのです。後に、この傾きの原因は地盤沈下だったと判明しました。

T：私は、彼が完璧主義過ぎると思いますよ。

## 天守閣の下に位置する「備前丸広場」で

G：ここは池田輝政の屋敷があった場所です。池田は現在の姫路城の築城者です。

## 旧番所を指さして

G：こちらが番所です。たぶん、何人かの番人が人々を検査していたのです。その後ろに見える、屋根の上にある桃の形をした瓦をご覧ください。桃は多産の象徴で、魔除けのお守りとも言われています。桃から生まれた男の子についての昔話があります。「桃太郎」は成長して、鬼を退治しました。

## 備前門の石棺を指さして

G：この壁の中で使われている石棺をご覧ください。石棺は石不足のために使われています。このことは、この辺りに古代の古墳があったことを意味します。

## 帯ノ櫓を指さして

G：左側にある建物をご覧ください。茶室の造りになっています。訪問者の休憩場所として使われていたのかもしれません。

## 備前門から太鼓櫓への坂で

G：ここもまた映画のロケ地で、『007』に登場する忍者の訓練施設のメンバーが練習していました。

### 単語の小箱

- □ devote *oneself* to ... …に身をささげる
- □ lean to ... …に傾く
- □ measurement 測量、寸法
- □ get depressed 落ち込む
- □ tilt 傾き
- □ land subsidence 地盤沈下
- □ fertility 多産

219

# 2-9　姫路城

鏡石、扇の勾配、るの門、西の丸、千姫について

### In front of the "Kagami-ishi" (Mirror Stones), after going through the "Ri Gate," "Kami Yamazato-maru," and the "Nu Gate"

G: Please look at these stones, which look like human faces. It's said that big, round stones called "Mirror Stones" drive away evil spirits. On the left-hand side, you can see a stone in the shape of a heart. If you keep a photo of it in your smartphone, it'll bring you happiness.

T: Wow! I'll take a picture and keep it.

### At the "Fan curve" stone wall

G: Look at this stone wall, which has a curve called a "**fan curve**."

T: It's a beautiful curve, but it's almost impossible for enemy soldiers to **scale the wall**?

G: Right! This design also prevents the stone walls from collapsing from the internal pressure.

### At the "Ru Gate"

G: Please look at this stone gate, called a "**Burying** Gate."

T: It looks like a tunnel. I have a feeling spies went in and out of this gate.

G: It's a shortcut to the main tower, but it would be easy to block up the gate and **keep** the enemy **out**.

### Princess Sen and the Nishi-no-maru

G: We're in the West Quarter, Nishi-no-maru, where Princess Sen lived. The story of Princess Sen is very famous. She was a granddaughter of Ieyasu Tokugawa, who founded the Tokugawa shogunate. Her first husband was Hideyori Toyotomi, but he committed suicide after the fall of **Osaka Castle**.

T: I heard about her in Osaka Castle yesterday. I want to know more about poor Princess Sen.

G: Princess Sen got remarried, to Tadatoki Honda, and lived happily here, but Tadatoki died of tuberculosis. After his death, she became a nun and spent the rest of her life in Edo, which is present-day Tokyo.

G：通訳ガイド　T：観光客

### 「りの門」と「上山里丸」、「ぬの門」を通り抜けた後、鏡石の前で

G：人の顔に見えるこれらの石をご覧ください。大きな丸い石は「鏡石」といって、悪霊を追い払うと言われています。左側にハートの形をしている石があります。スマートフォンに写真を入れておくと、幸福を運んでくれると言いますよ。

T：わー！　写真を撮って、スマートフォンに入れておきます。

### 扇の勾配にて

G：「扇の勾配」と呼ばれるカーブを持つこの石垣をご覧ください。

T：美しい曲線ですね、ですが敵兵がよじ登ることはほとんど不可能ですよね？

G：その通りです！　この様式は、石壁が内側の圧力で壊されないようにもなっています。

### 「るの門」にて

G：「埋め門」と呼ばれる石の門をご覧ください。

T：トンネルみたいですね。この門からスパイが出入りしていたような気がします。

G：天守閣への近道なのですが、門をふさいで、敵を中に入れないようにするのはたやすいでしょうね。

### 千姫と西の丸

G：私たちは、千姫が生活していた西の丸にいます。千姫のお話はとても有名です。千姫は、徳川幕府を創設した徳川家康の孫娘でした。千姫の最初の夫は豊臣秀頼でしたが、大坂城が陥落した後に自害しました。

T：昨日、大坂城で彼女について聞きました。かわいそうな千姫についてもっと知りたいです。

G：千姫は本多忠刻と結婚し幸せに暮らしていましたが、忠刻は結核で他界しました。彼の死後、千姫は尼になり、現在の東京である江戸で余生を送りました。

兵庫

### 単語の小箱

□ fan curve 扇の勾配　□ scale the wall 壁をよじ登る　□ bury …を埋める
□ keep ... out …を締め出す
□ Osaka Castle 大坂城（明治期までは「大坂城」、明治以降は「大阪城」という表記が一般的）

# 2 - 10　姫路城

百間廊下、化粧櫓、武者だまり、三国堀について

### In the Hyakken Rōka (Long Corridor Building)

G: The Long Corridor Building is the women's quarters. Princess Sen used to walk here with her servants in the 17th century. All the maids were proud of serving a **prestigious** family. This building is also fitted with gun or arrow loopholes called "Sama" and some stone drops.

### At the door of the room in Kesshō Yagura Turret

G: Princess Sen visited this room once a day and prayed here to the shrine on a hill nearby. This is a typical Japanese-style room.

### Musha-Damari (Warrior Mobilization Area), on the way back to the Diamond Gate

G: Please look at this space surrounded by an **earthen wall**. This is where the warriors could gather in time of war and wait for their leader's instructions. It's about 65 square meters. It's said that it's large enough to hold 120 **armed soldiers** or 20 horses.

T: Very **efficient**! It enabled them to fight **effectively** against the enemy.

G: Everything was planned strategically, but there was no fighting at Himeji Castle.

### At Sangoku Moat

G: Sangoku Moat is strategically positioned. If the enemy soldiers rushed through the Diamond Gate, they would be confused as to which way they should go. They might be attacked from the Warrior Mobilization area. The defenders might shoot through the Sama openings in the walls.

T: I see. They'd have no time to work out which way they should go. So, this pond without a fence acted as a trap!

G: Right! Well, we're scheduled to go to Kōkoen Garden, which was built on a site where there used to be samurai residences. We have a lunch reservation for 12:30. If you like, you can have a **conger eel** set menu. It's a local **specialty** of Himeji.

G：通訳ガイド　T：観光客

## 百間廊下で

G：百間廊下は女性の住居です。17世紀、千姫はこの廊下を女中たちと一緒に歩いていました。すべての女中は名門家に仕えることを誇りに思っていました。この建物は、「狭間」と呼ばれる銃や弓の穴や、石落としを備えています。

## 化粧櫓の中の一室の戸口にて

G：千姫は1日に一度この部屋を訪れ、近くの丘にある神社にここで拝んでいました。これは典型的な日本式の部屋です。

## 菱の門に戻る途中の武者だまり

G：土壁で囲まれたこのスペースをご覧ください。ここは戦争時に武士が集まり、リーダーの指示を待つはずだった場所です。およそ65平方メートルあります。よろい武者が120人、または馬が20頭入るスペースがあると言われています。

T：とても効率的ですね。敵と効果的に戦うことを可能にしたのですね！

G：すべては戦略的に練られています。しかし、姫路城で戦いはなかったのです。

## 三国堀にて

G：三国堀は戦略的に配置されています。敵が菱の門を急いで通り抜けたら、彼らはどちらに行けばよいか迷うでしょう。武者だまりから攻撃されるかもしれません。防御する側が壁の「狭間」から撃ってくるかもしれません。

T：なるほど。敵はどちらに行けばよいのか熟考する時間はないですね。だから、柵のないこの池は落とし穴として機能した！

G：その通り！　ええと、これから、侍の住居があった場所に建てられた好古園という庭園に行きます。12時半にランチの予約をしています。お望みなら、アナゴのセットメニューを食べられますよ。姫路の特産品なんです。

3

兵庫

## 単語の小箱

□ prestigious 名門の　□ earthen wall 土塀　□ armed soldier よろい武者
□ efficient 効率的な　□ effectively 有効に　□ conger eel アナゴ　□ specialty 特産品

## 瞬間英作文

1. 姫路城は飛んでいるシラサギと似ているので「白鷺城」と呼ばれています。

2. 天守閣へは迷路のようなジグザクの道を 330 メートル歩かなければなりません。

3. 狭間は、敵に弓や銃を撃つための重要な防衛システムとして作られました。

4. 天守閣に近づくにしたがって、門は狭く低くなります。

5. 天守閣は居住空間ではなく最も重要なとりでなので、防御システムをお楽しみいただければと思います。

6. 6,000 トンの姫路城天守閣を支えている、東大柱と西大柱の下部を地階で見られます。

7. 石落としは 1 階の三隅に設置されています。

8. この破風の間は見晴らしがいいので、兵士たちは敵の兵士をここから監視できます。

9. スパイダーマンですら天守閣には忍び込めないでしょう。

10. 兵士たちが隠れて待ち伏せする武者隠しが 3 階には 4 か所あります。

11. 4 階では、兵士たちは石打棚に上がって、敵を監視し、物を投げ、鉄砲を撃ちます。

12. 長壁神社は姫路城の守護神のための神社で、火事や災害を防ぎます。

13. 好古園は侍の住居のあった場所に建築されました。

---

1. white heron シラサギ　　2. maze-like 迷路のような　　3. shoot arrows 矢を撃つ
4. main tower 天守閣　　5. stronghold とりで　　6. basement 地階
7. stone drop 石落とし　　8. Gable Room 破風の間　　9. sneak into … …に忍び込む
10. warrior hiding place 武者隠し　　11. stone-throwing platform 石落とし
12. guardian god 守護神　　13. residence 住居

解答例

1. Himeji Castle is called the "White Heron Castle" because it looks like a flying **white heron**.

2. You have to walk up a **maze-like**, 330-meter zigzag pathway to the main tower.

3. Sama were created as an important defense system for **shooting arrows** and bullets at enemies.

4. As you approach the **main tower**, the gates become narrower and lower.

5. The main tower was not a living area but was the last **stronghold**, so I hope you enjoy looking at the defense systems.

6. In the **basement**, you can see the bases of the East and West Main Pillars, which support the 6,000-ton main tower of Himeji Castle.

7. **Stone drops** are located in three corners of the first floor.

8. This **Gable Room** commands a good view, so warriors can monitor the enemy soldiers from here.

9. Not even Spiderman would be able to **sneak into** the main tower.

10. There are four **warrior hiding places**, where warriors could hide and ambush the enemy on the third floor.

11. Soldiers climb up on to the **stone-throwing platform** to observe, throw things at, or shoot at the enemy on the fourth floor.

12. Osakabe Shrine is a shrine to the **guardian god** of Himeji Castle, who wards off fire and disaster.

13. Kōkoen Garden was built where there used to be samurai **residences**.

## 玉虫の宝庫

# 1 人々に生きる勇気を与えた姫路城

❶ 姫路城の歴史と外壁が白い理由について説明しましょう。

❷ **菱の門** 天守閣まで直線距離で 130 メートルだが、迷路のようになっているので 330 メートルも歩くことを説明。

❸ **いの門** 姫路城を現在の形に改修、築城した池田家の家紋の蝶の説明。

❹ **将軍坂** 「ろの門」から「はの門」へ続き、時代劇や『007 は二度死ぬ』などの撮影現場であることを紹介。絶好の写真スポットでもあります。

❺ **はの門→十字瓦** はの門でほぞ継ぎの説明をし、十字瓦の前では日本とキリスト教の関係について説明。

❻ **にの門** 最も防御力のある門で、2 階建てであることと門扉に鉄板が張られていることを説明します。

❼ **油塀→水一門** 400 年の歴史を持つ強固な油塀と、姥が石の説明をします。

❽ **水一門** 下り坂になるので敵がスピードを緩めることや、建築デザイナーが心理学に通じていたことの説明をします。

❾ **天守閣** 各階の特徴を説明。

❿ 天守閣を降りた場所で池田輝政の住居があった備前丸広場→見張りがいた旧番所→石棺が石垣に使われている備前丸入口→左側に茶室がある帯櫓→映画のロケ地である太鼓櫓への坂→「りの門」と上山里丸を抜けて「ぬの門」から降りて、右側に悪霊を追い払うと言われる鏡石→敵がよじ登ることのできない扇の勾配→敵の侵入を許さない「るの門」

⓫ **西の丸** 千姫の話→百間廊下では狭間や石落とし、女中の説明→化粧櫓では千姫がここから神社を拝んだエピソードを話しましょう

⓬ **武者だまり** 効率的に造られたレイアウトで、よろい武者 120 人、または馬が 20 頭入るスペースがあると言われています。不戦の姫路城では使われませんでした。

⓭ **三国堀** 戦略的に配置されていて、天守とそれを囲む堀、三国堀を一度に撮影！

# 2 通訳ガイドからのアドバイス

### ▶ アドバイス1　人々に勇気と希望を与えた Lucky castle！

廃城令（An order to abandon the castles）が発布された（was issued）ものの、中村重遠大佐の説得もあり、取り壊されずに済んだことを紹介しましょう。また、第二次大戦中に姫路市街地が焼け野原になった (Himeji City was burned to the ground) こと、姫路城にも焼夷弾が落とされたが不発弾だった (A bomb hit the castle, but it failed to explode) ことを紹介し、姫路城が人々に前向きに生きる勇気を与えてくれたことを強調しましょう。

### アドバイス2　映画ロケ地は興味を持たれる！

将軍坂は絶好の写真スポット。備前門から太鼓櫓への坂、好古園が映画のロケ地だった話や忍者の話は興味を持たれます（忍者の話は p. 58 参照）。

### アドバイス3　景色や防御システムだけでなく人物の話も！

水一門の前の「姥が石」にまつわる、自分の生活の糧を作る石臼 (millstone) を寄付して姫路城に尽くした話や、千姫の女中に生涯独身で姫に尽くした人もいた話、築城に献身した棟梁の桜井が自殺した話は興味を引きます。

### アドバイス4　運命に翻弄された千姫の愛する人との悲劇の別れ

徳川家康の孫の千姫と豊臣秀頼の政略結婚については p. 40 と p. 56 を参照。愛する秀頼の死後、千姫は本多忠刻と再婚し、十万石もの持参金（dowry）で西の丸再整備や化粧櫓などの建設をしました。しかし、愛する忠刻は病死し、幸せは短くはかないものでした。

## 3 通訳ガイド体験日記

◎池田輝政の 1609 年築城の白い姫路城の説明後に歴史好きなゲストが付け加えた話（白い城と黒い城の比較）。

Hideyoshi Toyotomi built the black, three-story Himeji Castle keep in 1581. After the decisive Battle of Sekigahara in 1600, Japan became a peaceful country, so white castles became popular.

豊臣秀吉は 1581 年に三層の黒い姫路城天守閣を築城。1600 年の関ケ原の戦い以降、日本は平和な国になり、白い城が流行ですね〜と話されました（ゲストは播磨の豪族・赤松氏が初期の姫路城を 14 世紀に築いたこともご存じでした）。

## 4 通訳ガイドお役立ち英語表現

◎ toilet のアメリカ英語とイギリス英語の意味の違い。

アメリカ英語では toilet は「便器」を、イギリス英語では「お手洗い、便器」を意味します。姫路城天守閣地階の未使用の便器は、アメリカ英語でもイギリス英語でも toilet です。イギリス人とアメリカ人感覚の違いが顕著な笑い話をご紹介します。

【英】 Where can I find a toilet?（お手洗いはどこですか？）

【米】 There's a toilet in the restroom.（便器はお手洗いにあるよ）

# その他の名所めぐり

## ❶ 灘の酒

### 日本一の灘の酒と飲み方　熱燗でも冷酒でも OK

Hyōgo, which includes Nada-Gogō, is the **No. 1 sake-producing area in Japan**. Japanese sake is an alcoholic beverage made from fermented rice and water. You can enjoy sake hot or cold.

\*　\*　\*

　灘五郷を含む兵庫の酒の生産量は日本一です。日本酒は発酵米と水からできるアルコール飲料です。熱くても冷たくてもいただけます。

### 灘の酒がおいしい理由　山田錦米と六甲の水

① There are two reasons why the sake made in Nada-Gogō is so delicious. Firstly, the local "Nishiki Yamada" rice is well suited to making sake, **thanks to its low protein content, dense white core, and uniform size, which is bigger than the rice that we eat.** Also, it absorbs water and dissolves easily. Secondly, the "Miyamizu" water, which flows down from Mt. Rokkō, is **hard water** and is **rich in minerals**, so it produces a full-bodied sake. Before the development of modern technology, **the cold winds from Mt. Rokkō** contributed a lot to the production of delicious sake. These cold winds could lower the fermentation temperature and slow the rice fermentation process in winter. It is important to brew it at low temperatures, because it not only improves the quality of the sake but also prevents the growth of bacteria.

② To sum up: Hyōgo is the top producer of sake in Japan; sake is made from rice and water; and Nada is proud of the good quality of its rice and water.

\*　\*　\*

　①灘五郷で造られた酒がおいしい理由は２つあります。第一に、地元の錦山田米が酒造りにふさわしいからです。錦山田米はプロテイン含有量が低く、**心白（米の中心の白い部分）が濃く、食用米より大きく形が均一です。**また、水を吸収しやすく、溶けやすくもあります。次に、六甲山から流れる「宮水」は**硬水**で**ミネラルが豊富**なので、コクのある酒を造ります。現代の技術が開発される前は、**六甲山の頂上から吹く冷たい風**が、おいしい酒造りに大きな影響を与えていました。この冷たい風は、冬に発酵温度を下げて、ゆっくりと発酵を進めます。低い温度で醸造することは酒質を高めるだけでなく、雑菌の繁殖も防ぎます。

　②簡潔に説明しましょう。兵庫の酒の生産量は日本一です。酒は米と水でできています。灘は良質の米と水を誇っています。

アドバイス ➡ 詳しい説明が必要な場合は①を、簡単な説明は②で OK です。

### 白鶴酒造資料館　リアルな酒蔵職人の人形

The Hakutsuru Sake Brewing Company's brewery has been open to the public since 1982 in its original form as the Sake Brewery Museum. The wooden structure of this

228　　その他の名所めぐり ✣ 兵庫

historic sake brewery was built about 100 years ago. You will be impressed by the **life-size dolls** making sake. They really look like **sake brewers**. You can also see the sake production tools that they actually used to use. A huge vat made of cypress wood was used for fermentation. It's also wonderful that you can learn the sake-making process by watching the panoramic screen in the projection mapping theater—a world first in the sake-making business. In the sake-tasting area, you can enjoy the freshest and most incredibly delicious sake. On the second floor, you can see in detail **the various traditional methods and processes of making sake**. The windows were to let in the cold winds from Mt. Rokkō.

＊　＊　＊

　白鶴酒蔵は、1982 年よりかつての酒造を酒蔵資料館として一般公開しています。この歴史ある木造建築の酒造は約 100 年前に建設されました。酒造りをする**等身大の人形に感心される**と思います。**本物の酒造職人**のように見えますね。実際に使われていた酒造りの道具もご覧いただけます。ヒノキ造りの大きなおけは、発酵に使われていました。また、業界では世界初のプロジェクションマッピングシアターで、パノラマスクリーンを見て酒造りの過程を学べるのは素晴らしいです。試飲（利き酒）コーナーでは、とても新鮮で驚くほどおいしい酒を飲むことができます。2 階では、**酒造りの伝統的な方法と過程**を詳しくご覧いただけます。ここの窓は、六甲山からの冷たい風が入るように作られていました。

**アドバイス** ➡ 試飲を楽しむ人が多いです。コロナ前は法被・鉢巻き姿で撮影もできました。

# ❷ 明石海峡大橋

## 世界で 2 番目に長いつり橋　経済発展にも大きく貢献

The Akashi Kaikyō Bridge, which connects Kobe City and Awaji City on Awaji Island, is **the second longest suspension bridge in the world**. This bridge is 3,911 meters long. The length of the center span is 1,991 meters. The main towers are 300 meters above sea level. This bridge has greatly contributed not only to the tourism industry but also to **the development of the economy**.

＊　＊　＊

　明石海峡大橋は、神戸市と淡路島の淡路市を結ぶ**世界で 2 番目に長いつり橋**です。この橋の全長は 3,911 メートルで、中央支間長は 1,991 メートルです。主塔の高さは海抜 300 メートルです。明石大橋は観光業だけでなく、**経済の発展**にも大きく貢献しています。

## 舞子海上プロムナード　迫力満点のガラス張りの丸木橋

The Maiko Marine Promenade is situated on the Kobe side of the Akashi Kaikyō Bridge. It's about 47 meters above sea level and 150 meters from the shore. It has a total length of about 317 meters. It's thrilling to walk along **the glass floor of the "log-bridge"** high above the sea! In the 8th-floor observation lounge there is a camera system, which will give you the feeling of being on top of one of the bridge's 300-meter-tall main towers.

\* \* \*

　舞子海上プロムナードは明石海峡大橋の神戸側にあります。海抜47メートル、陸地からの高さは150メートルです。全長は317メートルあります。海のはるか上で**ガラス張りの床の丸木橋**を歩くのは迫力満点！　8階の展望ラウンジには展望カメラシステムがあり、明石海峡大橋の300メートルの主塔の一つに登った気分が味わえます。

# ❸ メリケンパーク

## 歴史と名前の由来は？

Meriken Park is a waterfront park in Kobe's port area. In 1868, a wharf for the new port was built near the American Consulate, so it was named "Meriken Wharf." **"American"** sounded like **"Meriken"** to Japanese people. Meriken Park opened in 1987 to commemorate the 120th anniversary of the opening of Kobe Port. It is famous for the red Kobe Port Tower and the Kobe Maritime Museum. In 2017, Meriken Park was renovated to commemorate the 150th anniversary of the opening of Kobe Port.

\* \* \*

　メリケンパークは神戸の湾岸エリアにある臨海公園です。1868年に新しい港の埠頭がアメリカ総領事館のそばに建てられたので、「メリケン波止場」と名づけられました。日本人には「American」が「Meriken」と聞こえたのです。メリケンパークは1987年、神戸港開港120周年を記念してオープンしました。赤い神戸ポートタワーや神戸海洋博物館で有名です。2017年には、神戸港開港150年周年を記念してリニューアルされました。

**アドバイス** ▶ 小麦粉はアメリカから輸入されたので「メリケン粉」と呼ばれるようになった話も楽しんで聞いてもらえます。日本人には「アメリカン」が「メリケン」に聞こえたのです。

## 神戸ポートタワー　世界初のパイプ構造の建物

When the seventh mayor of Kobe visited Rotterdam on an inspection trip, he got an idea from the Euromast, which overlooks the harbor. Kobe Port Tower was completed in 1963. The red Kobe Port Tower was **the world's first "pipe structure" building**. It's called the **"Steel Tower Beauty"** because it is shaped like a beautiful woman in the form of a steel tower. You can enjoy a spectacular view of the bay area and its surroundings from this 108-meter-tall Port Tower.

\* \* \*

　神戸の7代目の市長がロッテルダムを視察旅行で訪問したとき、港を一望できるユーロマスト塔にヒントを得ました。神戸ポートタワーは1963年に完成しました。赤い神戸ポートタワーは**世界初のパイプ構造の建物**です。美しい女性のような鉄塔の形から、「鉄塔の美女」と呼ばれています。この108メートルのポートタワーから、ベイエリアとその周辺の素晴らしい景色をお楽しみいただけます。

## 神戸海洋博物館　神戸港開港の 120 周年記念に開館

The Kobe Maritime Museum was opened in 1987 to celebrate the 120th anniversary of the opening of the Port of Kobe. The white "space frame" roof of the museum gives you the impression of a sailboat racing across a vast ocean, right? In this museum you can experience **the history and future of the sea, ships, and ports** by looking at navigational instruments, ships' gear, ships' records, dioramas, videos, and graphics.

＊　＊　＊

　神戸海洋博物館は 1987 年に神戸港開港 120 周年を記念して開館しました。博物館の白い「スペースフレーム（立体的な骨組み）」の屋根は、大海原を駆け巡る帆船をイメージしますよね。この博物館では航海計器、船具、船の記録、ジオラマ模型、ビデオ、グラフィックなどを通して、**海や船、港の歴史と未来**を体験することができます。

## 神戸港震災メモリアルパーク　次世代の人々に伝えるために

Meriken Park was devastated by the Great Hanshin-Awaji Earthquake in 1995. Kobe Memorial Park, a part of Meriken Park, has been left unrepaired so that future generations can understand how much effort was made to restore the ruined city of Kobe to its present state.

＊　＊　＊

　メリケンパークは 1995 年の阪神・淡路大震災で破壊されました。メリケンパークの一部である神戸港震災メモリアルパークは、荒廃した神戸を現在の姿に復旧させるのに費やした努力の大きさを次世代の人々に理解してもらうため、修理せずに残されています。

## モニュメント　"BE KOBE" とオルタンシアの鐘

It's a lot of fun to look around the various monuments!
• Please look at the "BE KOBE" monument. With the renovation of the park in 2017, a monument in the shape of "BE KOBE" was installed. This message was made in 2015 to commemorate the 20th anniversary of the Great Hanshin-Awaji Earthquake of 1995. The message **"BE KOBE" conveys the spirit of challenge and love of Kobe people**.
• Please look at the "Bell of Hortensia." Hortensia means **hydrangea**. The hydrangea is **the symbolic flower of Kobe City**. This was modeled after a wind instrument in commemoration of the first Kobe Fashion Festival of 1989.

＊　＊　＊

　さまざまな記念碑を見るのはとても楽しいです。
　・「BE KOBE」の記念碑をご覧ください。2017 年の公園のリニューアル時に「BE KOBE」の形のモニュメントが設置されました。このメッセージは 1995 年の神戸・淡路大震災 20 年周年を記念して、2015 年に造られました。**「BE KOBE」は神戸の人々のチャレンジ精神や愛を伝えています**。

・「オルタンシアの鐘」をご覧ください。オルタンシアとは**アジサイ**のことです。アジサイは**神戸のシンボルの花**です。これは1989年の神戸ファッションフェスティバルを記念して、吹奏楽器をモデルに造られました。

# ❹ 布引ハーブガーデン

It takes about ten minutes to get to Nunobiki Herb Gardens by ropeway. On the way, you can enjoy the panoramic view of Kobe City, as well as some beautiful spots such as **Nunobiki Falls** and **Gohonmatsu Dam,** which has been designated as an Important Cultural Property. It is one of the largest herb gardens in Japan, with around 75,000 herbs and flowers of about 200 kinds blooming throughout the year.

＊　＊　＊

　布引ハーブガーデンにはロープウェイで約10分で到着します。途中、**布引の滝**や重要文化財に指定された**五本松ダム**のような美しい場所や、神戸のパノラマをお楽しみいただけます。ここは日本最大級のハーブ庭園で、約200種、7万5,000もの草花が四季を通して咲き誇っています。

# ❺ 有馬温泉

Arima Onsen is **one of the three most famous hot spring resorts in Japan**. Hideyoshi Toyotomi, one of the most famous warlords, loved Arima. Walking around the streets of the onsen area will give you a nostalgic feeling. You can enjoy two different types of hot springs.

One is "Kin-no-Yu," which means "golden hot spring." Many foreign guests are surprised by this **golden color**. It's rich in iron and salt and has **moisturizing and warming effects,** which are good for **skin ailments**. The other is "Gin-no-Yu," which means "silver hot spring." It contains radium and carbonate and **is effective for muscle and joint relief**. If you don't have enough time to soak in a bath, **you can warm yourself up in an outdoor footbath next to the Kin-no-Yu bathhouse**. Also, it takes 12 minutes to go up Mt. Rokko from Arima by ropeway.

＊　＊　＊

　有馬温泉は**日本三名泉**の一つです。最も有名な武将の一人である豊臣秀吉も有馬温泉を愛しました。温泉街をめぐれば、ノスタルジックな気分に浸れます。2種類の温泉を楽しめますよ。
　一つは「金の湯」で「金の温泉」を意味します。海外のお客様の多くはこの**黄金色**に驚きます。鉄分と塩分が豊富で、**保湿効果や保温効果**、そして**皮膚疾患**に効果があります。もう一つは「銀の湯」で「銀の温泉」を意味します。ラジウムと炭酸塩を含み、**筋肉や関節の疲労回復**に効果があります。ゆっくり浸かる時間がない場合は、**金の湯の隣にある屋外の足湯**で体を温めるのもいいでしょう。また、有馬から六甲山へはロープウェイで12分です。

# Chapter 4
## 大阪から日帰り旅行

近年、大阪を拠点としたロングツアーが増えています。一足延ばして、厳島神社、平和記念公園、伊勢神宮、白川郷なども、ぜひご案内しましょう。

（上）伊勢神宮の内宮正宮（twilllll/Shutterstock.com）
（右）夏の合掌造り集落（写真提供：岐阜県白川村役場）
（下）平和記念公園と原爆ドーム（JWCohen/Shutterstock.com）

# 1-1 宮島

神の島、宮島の人口面積と歴史、姉妹都市モン・サン＝ミッシェルについて

### On the ferry to Miyajima

**G**: Now we are heading for Miyajima Island, which has **been worshipped** as an island of the deities. Miyajima is one of the three most beautiful scenic spots in Japan. We can only get there by ferry, which makes it even more exciting. It takes about ten minutes.

**T**: Why has Miyajima been worshipped?

**G**: It's said people felt a **divine presence** on Miyajima, centered on Mt. Misen, and worshipped it. It was regarded as a divine island, so in the olden days people **were** not **allowed to** live on Miyajima.

**T**: When did people begin to live on Miyajima?

**G**: From the 13th to the 15th century, houses were built for priests and monks, and this led to people living on the island. The population of Miyajima is now 1,600. The island is 31 kilometers in **circumference**. The **area** of Miyajima is 30 square kilometers. The number of tourists visiting Miyajima has been increasing since it was designated as a World Heritage Site in 1996. As many as 4.5 million tourists visit Miyajima annually. By the way, please look at the shape of the mountain from here. It looks like Kannon lying down in this picture, right? Kannon saves us in this world.

**T**: It's really exciting. I've always wanted to see Itsukushima Shrine floating on the water from up close. I've been to see Mont-Saint-Michel in France.

**G**: Hatsukaichi City, which includes Miyajima, is a sister city of Mont-Saint-Michel. They signed a **Tourism and Friendship Agreement** in 2009. We're approaching the Great Torii built in the sea!

G：通訳ガイド　T：観光客

## 宮島へ向かうフェリー船の中で

G：神の島とあがめられている宮島へ向かっています。宮島は日本三景の一つです。フェリーでしか行けないので、そのことが私たちをより一層ときめかせます。約10分で到着します。

T：なぜ、宮島はあがめられているのですか？

G：人々が弥山を中心とする宮島に神威を感じ、信仰したと言われています。神の島と見なされていたので、昔は人々は宮島に住めなかったのです。

T：いつ人々は宮島に住み始めたのですか？

G：13世紀から15世紀にかけて神官や僧侶たちの住まいが創建されました。それがきっかけとなり、人が住むことになりました。現在、宮島の人口は1,600人です。島の周囲は31キロメートルで、宮島の面積は30平方キロメートルです。1996年に宮島が世界文化遺産に認定されてから、宮島への観光客は増加し続けていて、年間450万人もの観光客が宮島を訪れます。ところで、ここから、山の形をご覧ください。この写真の横になられている観音様のように見えるでしょう？　観音様は、私たちをこの世で助けてくださっています。

T：とてもワクワクしますね。海中に浮く厳島神社をずっと目の前で見たいと思っていました。フランスのモン・サン＝ミッシェルは見に行ったことがあります。

G：宮島が位置する廿日市市とモン・サン＝ミッシェルは姉妹都市です。両市は2009年に観光友好都市提携を結びました。海に建てられた大鳥居が近づいてきましたよ。

※宮島は「観音様の寝姿」と呼ばれています。山の形をよく見ると、観音様が寝ている姿に見えるからです。

**4**

日帰り旅行

## 単語の小箱

□ be worshipped あがめられる　□ divine presence 神威
□ be allowed to *do* 〜することができる、許される　□ circumference 円周
□ area 面積　□ Tourism and Friendship Agreement 観光友好都市提携

235

# 1-2 厳島神社

シカのための鹿戸、海に立つ大鳥居の構造について

### After getting off the ferry and going through the Stone Torii Gate

T: The deer are so cute!

G: Look at the toilet door. It can only be opened by pulling. It's called a "Deer Gate," and it **prevents** deer **from** entering the toilet. Deer like tissue paper. They're very cute, but don't **feed** them. Miyajima is working on an important project to return the deer to the mountains. They can live more happily in **natural surroundings**.

T: I see. Wow! The Great Torii Gate floating in the sea has a mysterious beauty!

G: The Great Torii stands on the **foreshore**, but when the tide is high, it seems to be floating in the sea. When the tide is low, we can walk up to the Great Torii. The tide changes about every six hours. You're not allowed to **gather clams** under the Great Torii.

T: Was Itsukushima Shrine built on the foreshore to make it look beautiful?

G: The island itself was considered a deity, so it was built on the foreshore. In the olden days, people were not allowed to cultivate the land.

T: I see. My book says it's **freestanding**. How is it constructed?

G: The two main pillars are supported by four legs. The Great Torii is about 16 meters high. It weighs 60 tons. From 30 to 100 pine wood piles are driven into the sand under each pillar, and these piles are covered by **flagstones**. The Torii rests on this firm foundation under the sand. These piles keep the Torii firmly in place. The **crossbeams** are filled with **fist-sized stones**, which weigh about 4 tons. The Torii is so heavy that it cannot be washed away.

T: I see. We can learn a lot from the **wisdom of our ancestors**! What's the Torii made of?

G: The two main pillars are made from **camphor trees**, which are about 600 years old. Camphor trees don't **rot** so easily and they **repel** insects. They're coated with vermilion lacquer, which also protects them from **corrosion**. The present Great Torii is the ninth one, and it was rebuilt in 1875.

G：通訳ガイド　T：観光客

## フェリーを降りて石の鳥居をくぐってから

T： シカはなんてかわいいのでしょう。

G： トイレの扉をご覧ください。この扉は引くことによってのみ開きます。島では「鹿戸」と呼ばれて、シカがトイレに入ることを防いでいます。シカはティッシュペーパーが好きなのです。とてもかわいいですが、餌を与えないでくださいね。宮島ではシカを山に戻す大切なプロジェクトに取り組んでいます。自然環境の中でならもっと幸せに暮らせます。

T： なるほど。わ～！　海に浮かぶ大鳥居は神秘的で美しいですね。

G： 大鳥居は前浜に立っていますが、満ち潮時は海に浮かんでいるように見えるのです。干潮時は大鳥居まで歩けます。干潮と満潮は約6時間ごとに繰り返されます。大鳥居内では潮干狩りをすることは許されていません。

T： 厳島神社は、美しく見えるようにと前浜に建てられたのですか？

G： 島自体が神様と見なされていたので、前浜に建てられたのです。昔は開墾を許可されていなかったのです。

T： なるほど。私の本には鳥居は自力で立っていると書かれています。どのような造りになっていますか？

G： 2本の主柱は四脚造りです。鳥居の高さは16メートル、重さは60トンで、30から100の松の杭が各柱の下の砂の中に打たれています。これらの杭は敷石で覆われています。鳥居は、砂の下の堅固な基礎の上に立っています。横梁の中にはこぶし大の約4トンの重さの石が入っています。とても重いので流されることはありません。

T： なるほど。先人の知恵を学べますね。鳥居は何でできているのですか？

G： 2本の主柱は樹齢約600年の楠でできています。楠は腐りにくく、虫を寄せ付けません。また朱塗りなので腐食を防ぎます。現在の大鳥居は9代目で、1875年に再建されました。

## 単語の小箱

□ **prevent A from** *doing* A が～するのを妨ぐ　□ **feed** …に餌を与える
□ **natural surroundings** 自然環境　□ **foreshore** 前浜　□ **gather clams** 潮干狩りをする
□ **freestanding** 自立している　□ **flagstone** 敷石　□ **crossbeam** 横梁
□ **fist-sized stone** こぶし大の石　□ **wisdom of** *one's* **ancestors** 先人の知恵
□ **camphor tree** 楠（クスノキ）　□ **rot** 腐る　□ **repel** …を寄せ付けない　□ **corrosion** 腐る

237

# 1-3 厳島神社

**厳島神社歴史、平清盛、寝殿造り、床板の間の空間について**

T: I'd like to know about Itsukushima Shrine.
G: It's said that the original Itsukushima Shrine was founded in 593. Itsukushima Shrine **is dedicated to** three female sea deities. It was in the 12th century that Kiyomori Taira, a political leader as well as a warlord, created the shrine in its present size and style. Kiyomori Taira promoted trade between Sui Dynasty China and Japan. Miyajima faces the Seto Inland Sea, which was a very important trade route to Sui Dynasty China.
T: I see. Kiyomori Taira designed Itsukushima Shrine in its present form and enlarged it, right?
G: Right. Itsukushima Shrine is in the **aristocratic architectural style of the Heian period**, which is one reason why it was chosen as a World Heritage Site. In this style, there is a pond in front of the aristocrat's house, where aristocrats enjoyed boating. The shrine is modeled on an aristocrat's house, and the sea plays the role of the pond, while the **open-air stage**, called the "Hirabutai," plays the role of the garden. Graceful curving lines can be seen everywhere.

### In front of Marōdo Shrine, after purification at the Temizusha

G: Marōdo Shrine is the primary **auxiliary shrine**. Many of Itsukushima Shrine's ceremonies start from this shrine.

### Walking along the East Corridor, after praying at Marōdo Shrine

G: The **corridors** are about 270 meters long. There are eight floor boards between each pillar.
T: By the way, why do the floor boards have spaces between them?
G: It's to allow the seawater to pass up through the spaces **at high tide**, and this reduces the water pressure against the boards. This prevents damage to the structure.
T: Amazing! In other words, it helps to protect the shrine, right?
G: Yes. Next, please look at this pond. When the tide falls, it creates this pond in the shape of a mirror, so it's called the "Mirror Pond."

G：通訳ガイド　T：観光客

T： 厳島神社について知りたいです。

G： 最初の厳島神社は 593 年に創建されたと言われています。厳島神社には 3 体の海の女神様が祀られています。12 世紀初頭に、武士で政治のリーダーでもある平清盛が、現在の規模とスタイルの厳島神社を造りました。平清盛は中国の宋と日本の貿易を促進しました。宮島は中国との重要な交易路だった瀬戸内海に面しているのです。

T： なるほど。平清盛が現在の形を考案し、厳島神社を大きくしたのですね。

G： そうです。 厳島神社は平安時代の寝殿造りで、それは厳島神社が世界遺産に選ばれた理由の一つなのです。この建築様式では貴族の家の前に池があり、貴族たちは舟遊びを楽しみました。神社は貴族の家をモデルとして、海が池の役割を果たし、平舞台と呼ばれる屋外ステージは庭の役割を果たしています。優雅な曲線が至る所に見られます。

**手水舎でお清めをしてから客 神社の前で**

G： 客神社は一番の摂社です。厳島神社の多くの儀式はここから始まります。

**客神社でお祈りをした後、東回廊を歩きながら**

G： 廊下は 270 メートルの長さです。柱と柱の間には 8 枚の床板があります。

T： ところでなぜ、床板の間に隙間があるのですか？

G： 海水が高潮時に床板の間を通り抜けるようにするためで、このことは板に対する水圧を弱めます。これで建物が損傷するのを防げるのです。

T： すごいです！　つまり、神社を守る助けとなるのですね？

G： そうです。次にこの池をご覧ください。引き潮のときに鏡の形の池が造られるので、鏡池と呼ばれています。

4

日帰り旅行

## 単語の小箱

□ be dedicated to ... …が祀られている
□ aristocratic architectural style of the Heian period 平安時代の寝殿造り
□ open-air stage 平舞台、野外舞台
□ auxiliary shrine 摂社（本社に付属し、その祭神と縁故の深い神様を祀った神社のこと）
□ corridor 廊下　□ at high tide 高潮時に

# 1-4 厳島神社

本社、高舞台、火焼(ひたさき)、大国神社について

 086

### In front of the Gohonsha (Main Shrine)

G: The Main Shrine consists of a main hall, an offering hall, a worship hall, and a purification hall in a straight line.

### In front of the Takabutai (elevated stage), after praying at the worship hall

G: As the power of the Taira clan — the founders of the present shrine — increased, **courtiers** also started to worship here. Itsukushima Shrine became more and more famous and gorgeous. This is the place where court dances called "Bugaku" are performed. Please look at this picture of "Bugaku."

### At the Hirabutai, the open-air stage

G: Now we are standing on the open-air stage. Please look at the two shrines on the right and left. The deities of these shrines protect the shrine from the right and left sides. Next to them, there are orchestra halls, where music is played when Bugaku dances are performed on the Takabutai.

### In front of the Hitasaki

G: This place, named the "Hitasaki," is where **votive lamps** were lit in olden times. During the festival called "Kangensai," gorgeously decorated ships arrive here. Please stand here. This is the best place for pictures with the Great Torii Gate in the background. The deep blue sea extends all around you.

T: Thanks! The vermilion Torii gate **fuses into** the light blue sea and sky.

### At Daikoku Shrine

G: This is Daikoku Shrine. The deity of marriage is enshrined here. Offerings to the Main Shrine were temporarily placed here and then taken to the Main Shrine.

G：通訳ガイド　T：観光客

### ご本社の前で

G：ご本社は本殿、幣殿、拝殿、祓殿がまっすぐに並んで建っています。

### 拝殿でお祈りした後、高舞台の前で

G：この神社を創建した平家の力が強くなるにつれて、宮廷の人々も参拝するように
なりました。厳島神社はますます有名に、豪華になりました。こちらは「舞楽」
と呼ばれる宮廷の踊りが演じられる場所です。この舞楽の写真をご覧ください。

### 平舞台にて

G：今、私たちは平舞台に立っています。右側と左側にある2つの神社をご覧くださ
い。これらの神社の神様は、社殿を右と左から守ってくださっています。その横
には楽房があり、高舞台で舞楽が披露される際には音楽が演奏されます。

### 火焼前で

G：火焼前というこの場所は、昔は灯明がたかれていたと言われています。「管絃祭」
と呼ばれるお祭りでは、華やかに飾られた船がここに着船します。どうぞ、ここ
に立ってください。ここは大鳥居を背景に、写真撮影には最高の場所です。青い
海があなたの周りに広がりますよ。

T：ありがとう。朱色の鳥居が水色の海と空に融合していますね。

### 大国神社にて

G：こちらが大国社です。縁結びの神様とも言われています。ご本社へのお供え物は
いったんここに置かれてから、ご本社に運ばれました。

単語の小箱

□ courtier 宮廷の人　□ votive lamp 灯明　□ fuse into ... …に融合する

241

# 1-5 厳島神社

天神社、能、能舞台に陶器のかめが不要な理由について

 087

### In front of Tenjinsha Shrine, after talking about votive picture tablets

G: This is Tenjinsha Shrine, where Michizane Sugawara, a 9th century scholar, is enshrined. He is revered as the patron of learning.

### Looking at the Noh stage while walking along the West Corridor

G: Please look at the Noh stage. It's said that Noh is the oldest performing art in the world. "Nōgaku" was registered as a UNESCO Intangible Cultural Heritage in 2001.

T: Why is there a painting of a tree behind the stage?

G: It's a pine tree, which **reflects** the time when Noh plays were performed outdoors in front of shrines with pine trees in the background.

T: I know something about Kabuki. I'd like to know more about Noh.

G: Please look at this picture. It began to flourish in the 14th century. The main Noh characters, called "Shite," generally wear masks that match their roles and sometimes change their masks according to the development of their characters. Facial expressions **are represented by manipulation** of fans and other symbolic gestures. This Noh stage is different from other Noh stages.

T: I think that has a lot to do with the sea.

G: Right! Several **ceramic jars** are placed under Noh stages to produce **resonance**. However, this stage doesn't need ceramic jars because the seawater under the floor produces sounds.

T: Wow! The sound of the waves must be very beautiful!

### Leaving Itsukushima Shrine, after talking about the Arched Bridge

G: Only **imperial messengers** could cross this bridge. Well, shall we leave Itsukushima Shrine and go on to the Senjōkaku?

G：通訳ガイド　T：観光客

### 絵馬について説明後、天神社の前で

**G：**こちらは天神社で、9 世紀の学者である菅原道真が祀られています。道真は学問の守護神として尊敬されています。

### 西の回廊を歩きながら、能舞台を見て

**G：**どうぞ能舞台をご覧ください。能は世界で一番古い舞台芸術だと言われています。能楽は 2001 年にユネスコ無形文化遺産に登録されました。

**T：**なぜ舞台の後ろに木の絵があるのですか？

**G：**あれは松の木で、松の木のある神社を背景に屋外で能が演じられていたことを反映しているのです。

**T：**歌舞伎については少し知っています。もっと能について知りたいです。

**G：**この写真をご覧ください。能は 14 世紀に盛んになり始めました。「シテ」と呼ばれる能の主役は通常、役割に合ったお面をかぶり、そして性格の変化に応じてお面を変えることもあります。顔の表情は、扇やそのほかの象徴的なジェスチャーで表現されます。この能舞台は一般的な能舞台と異なっています。

**T：**海と関係があると思います。

**G：**その通りです！　能舞台の下には陶器のかめがいくつも置かれていて、反響音を出します。しかし、この舞台には陶器のかめは必要ないのです。なぜなら、床の下の海水が音を出すからです。

**T：**すごいです！　波の音は美しいに違いありませんね。

### 反橋の説明をして厳島神社を出る

**G：**勅使だけがこの橋を渡れました。さあ、厳島神社を出て千畳閣へ行きましょうか？

4

日帰り旅行

### 単語の小箱

- □ votive picture tablet 絵馬　□ reflect …を反映する
- □ be represented by ... …に表される　□ manipulation 操作　□ ceramic jar 陶器のかめ
- □ resonance 共鳴　□ imperial messenger 勅使

243

# 1-6 厳島神社

 088

美しさの理由、豊国神社（千畳閣）、かき、もみじまんじゅうなどについて

### On the way to the Senjōkaku

T: Itsukushima Shrine is really impressive because it has stayed so beautiful.

G: As you can see, the pillars **are** partially **submerged** at high tide, so they **decay** rather easily. Besides that, Itsukushima Shrine **is** constantly **exposed to sea breezes**. It has been hit by typhoons and **mudslides** many times. Eight hundred and fifty years have passed since Itsukushima Shrine was constructed in its present style. Constant maintenance, inspections, and repairs have been carried out, so we can still see the style of the Heian court aristocrats' residences here today.

### At the Senjōkaku, after talking about the five-story pagoda

G: Hōkoku Shrine is dedicated to the warlord Hideyoshi Toyotomi and his loyal retainer Kiyomasa Katō. Hōkoku Shrine's nickname is "Senjōkaku," which means "Hall of One Thousand Tatami Mats." Actually, it's the size of 857 mats. The average size of a tatami mat is 1.2 times that of a single bed, so this shrine can **accommodate** about 730 single beds. It's the largest wooden structure on Miyajima Island. There are no ceiling boards, because it wasn't completed due to Hideyoshi's death. This place is as popular as the landmark five-story pagoda.

### At a gift shop, after an oyster lunch on Omotesandō Street

T: I want to eat that set menu of raw, grilled, and **fried oysters** again!

G: Hiroshima's cultivation of oysters and its lemon production rank number one in Japan!

T: Great! By the way, could you recommend some gifts?

G: I recommend this **rice scoop**. Rice scoops are a **specialty** of Hiroshima. It is said that rice scoops lead you to victory, so they're also used as **good luck talismans**. How about this Momiji Manjū in the shape of a maple leaf? The maple, "Momiji," is the symbol of Hiroshima Prefecture. It's very delicious!

T: Wow! I'll buy both.

G：通訳ガイド　T：観光客

## 千畳閣に行く途中で

T：厳島神社は、今も美しさを保っていたのでとても感銘を受けます。

G：ご覧のように、柱の一部は満潮時に水につかるので腐りやすいです。その上、厳島神社は絶えず海風にさらされています。台風にも土砂崩れに何回も襲われました。厳島神社が現在の様式となってから 850 年が経ちました。絶えず保守点検と修復が実施されていますので、平安時代の宮廷貴族の屋敷の様式を見られるのです。

## 五重塔について話してから豊国神社（千畳閣）で

G：豊国神社には、武将である豊臣秀吉と彼の家臣の加藤清正がお祀りされています。この豊国神社は畳が 1,000 畳という意味で「千畳閣」と呼ばれています。実際の大きさは 857 畳です。標準的な畳の大きさはシングルベッドの 1.2 倍の大きさなので、この神社は 730 台のシングルベッドが入る大きさがあります。これは宮島で一番大きな木造の建造物です。天井の板がないのですが、秀吉公が死亡したために建物は完成しなかったのです。この場所は、ランドマークである五重塔と同じくらい人気があります。

## 表参道でかきランチを食べた後、お土産屋さんで

T：私は、生がき、焼きがき、かきフライのセットをもう一度食べたいです。

G：広島のかきの養殖とレモンの生産量は日本で第 1 位なのですよ。

T：すごいですね！ところで、お勧めのお土産はありますか？

G：このしゃもじをお勧めします。広島の特産品です。しゃもじは勝利へ導いてくれると言われているので、お守りとしても使えますよ。もみじの形をした、このもみじまんじゅうはいかがですか？　もみじは広島のシンボルなのです。とってもおいしいですよ。

T：わあ、両方買います。

4

日帰り旅行

## 単語の小箱

□ be submerged 沈められている　□ decay 腐る
□ be exposed to ... …にさらされる　□ sea breeze 海風　□ mudslide 土砂崩れ
□ accommodate …を収容する　□ fried oyster かきフライ　□ rice scoop しゃもじ
□ specialty 特産品　□ good luck talisman 幸運のお守り

245

## 1-7　平和記念公園

城下町から軍事都市への変遷、原爆ドーム（平和記念碑）①について

### In the tram, on the way to the Peace Memorial Park

G: I hope you enjoyed Miyajima. Next, we're visiting the Peace Memorial Park. Hiroshima Prefecture is situated in the southwestern part of Japan's main island of Honshu and in the center of the Chūgoku region. The population of Hiroshima City is about 1.2 million. Hiroshima is the 10th largest city in Japan. Hiroshima Castle was built in the 16th century and Hiroshima **flourished** as a castle town.

T: A castle town! I want to visit Hiroshima Castle next time. I'm very impressed with the kindness of the people and the beauty of Hiroshima. By the way, I've been wondering why America **chose Hiroshima for the atomic bomb**.

G: There are several reasons for this. Hiroshima became a military target probably because it had an army base and factories that made weapons. Unlike other big cities, such as Tokyo and Osaka, Hiroshima had not been hit by a **major air raid**, so it was used to demonstrate the power of the atomic bomb. Also, there were no allied **POW camps** in Hiroshima.

### In front of the Atomic Bomb Dome (Peace Memorial)

G: Here we are in front of the Peace Memorial called the "Atomic Bomb Dome." This building **remained** after the dropping of the world's first atomic bomb in 1945. It was registered on the UNESCO World Heritage List in 1996.

T: It's very shocking to see the **skeleton** of a tower.

G: This building was once the Hiroshima Prefectural Industrial Promotion Hall. This western-style building was designed by a famous Czech architect and completed in 1915. This building was 160 meters away from the **hypocenter**. The atomic bomb **exploded** about 600 meters above the ground and the blast struck the hall almost directly from above, so part of its thick walls and the steel of its dome survived. Everyone in the hall was killed instantly. It is estimated that the atomic bomb took the lives of 140,000 people in that year.

G：通訳ガイド　T：観光客

## 市電に乗って平和記念公園へ

**G：** 宮島をお楽しみになったと思います。今から、平和記念公園を訪問します。広島は本州の南西部にあり、中国地方の中心地にあります。広島市の人口は約120万人で、日本で10番目に大きな都市です。16世紀には広島城が築城され、広島は城下町として栄えました。

**T：** 城下町ですか！　次回は広島城にも行きたいです。私は広島の人たちの親切さと街の美しさに感動しました。ところで、なぜ、アメリカは原爆投下に広島を選んだのでしょうか？

**G：** これにはいくつかの理由があります。というのは、広島には軍隊の基地があり、兵器を製造する工場があったので、おそらく軍事標的になったのです。東京や大阪と違い、広島は大空襲を受けなかったので、原爆の威力を実証する場所になりました。また、広島には連合国の捕虜収容所もなかったのです。

## 原爆ドーム（平和記念碑）の前で

**G：** 私たちは「原爆ドーム」と呼ばれている平和記念碑の前にいます。人類史上初の1945年の原爆投下後にこの建物が残りました。この建物は1996年にユネスコの世界文化遺産のリストに登録されました。

**T：** 骸骨のようなタワーを見てとてもショックです。

**G：** この建物は、かつて広島産業奨励館でした。この西洋建築のビルは有名なチェコの建築家によってデザインされ、1915年に完成しました。建物は爆心地から160メートル離れていました。原爆は上空600メートルでさく裂し、爆風が建物のほぼ真上から当たったので、厚い壁の一部とドームの鉄製の部分が残りました。館内にいた人たちは即死でした。原爆は投下された年に、14万人の命を奪ったと推定されています。

4

日帰り旅行

## 単語の小箱

☐ flourish 栄える　☐ choose Hiroshima for the atomic bomb 広島を原爆の標的にする
☐ major air raid 大空襲　☐ POW camp 捕虜収容者（POW は prisoner of war の略語）
☐ remain 残る　☐ skeleton 骸骨　☐ hypocenter 爆心地　☐ explode 爆発する

247

# 1-8 　平和記念公園

原爆ドーム（平和記念碑）②、平和の灯について

T: I came here to see the Atomic Bomb Dome, which I studied about in my history textbook in school. This dome teaches us about the misery of war.

G: Public opinion was divided for many years. Some people felt that this building should be destroyed because it reminded them of the **tragedy** and **devastation** of the atomic bombing. Other people felt this building should be preserved to express opposition to the use of the atomic bomb.

T: I can understand the opinions of both sides.

G: Hiroko Kajiyama, who died of **leukemia** at the age of 16, wrote in her diary that this structure should be kept to **raise awareness of** the horror of the atomic bomb. It's said that this encouraged a volunteer group to **call for** its **preservation**. In 1966, Hiroshima City Council decided to preserve the Atomic Bomb Dome. Since then, several preservation projects have been carried out. It still looks as it did immediately after the bombing.

T: I'm starting to understand why the Japanese people are preserving this building in the hope of peace.

G: In a **desire for peace**, the Atomic Bomb Dome was listed as a World Heritage Site in 1996. It **conveys** the **horror** of the first use of a nuclear weapon. It appeals for **lasting peace** as a world peace monument.

## Looking at the Peace Flame

T: Good! When was this Peace Memorial Park completed?

G: Construction of the Peace Memorial Park and facilities began in 1950 and was completed in 1955. This is the "**Peace Flame**." This monument symbolizes people's desire for peace. Look at the **pedestal**. It looks like two palms opening up to the sky. In the center of the monument, you can see a fire which will keep on burning for peace. The flame will keep on burning until the day that nuclear weapons disappear from the earth.

G：通訳ガイド　T：観光客

T：私は学校の歴史の教科書で学んだ原爆ドームを見るために、ここに来ました。このドームは私たちに戦争の悲惨さを教えてくれます。

G：何年もの間、世論は2つに分かれていました。この建物は人々に原爆投下による惨状と破壊を思い出させるので、取り壊すべきだと言う人たちがいました。また、この建物は原爆の使用に反対するために保存するべきだと思う人たちもいました。

T：両方の意見を理解できますね。

G：16歳で白血病により他界した少女、楮山ヒロ子は日記で、この建物を原爆の恐ろしさを訴えるために保存すべきだと書き残しました。このことは、ボランティアグループが保存を求めて声を上げるのを鼓舞したと言われています。1966年、広島市議会は原爆ドームを保存することを決定しました。それ以来、いくつかの保存プロジェクトが実行されています。原爆ドームは今でも被爆直後の形をとどめています。

T：日本人が平和を祈願して、この建物を保存する気持ちがわかり始めてきました。

G：平和を祈るために原爆ドームは1996年に世界遺産に登録されたのです。人類史上初めて使用された核兵器の怖さを伝えています。原爆ドームは、世界平和の記念碑として恒久平和を訴えているのです。

### 平和の灯を見ながら

T：いいですね。この平和記念公園はいつ完成したのですか？

G：平和記念公園および施設の建設は1950年に始まり、1955年に完成しました。

G：これは平和の灯です。この記念碑は人々の平和への願いを意味します。台座をご覧ください。両手の手のひらを大空に広げているように見えます。この記念碑の中央に、平和のために燃え続ける炎を見ることができます。炎は核兵器が地球から消える日まで燃え続けます。

## 単語の小箱

□ tragedy 惨劇　□ devastation 破壊　□ leukemia 白血病
□ raise awareness of ... …の意識を高める　□ call for ... …を声を上げて求める
□ preservation 保存　□ desire for peace 平和への強い願い　□ convey …を伝える
□ horror 恐怖　□ lasting peace 恒久平和　□ Peace Flame 平和の灯　□ pedestal 台座

# 1-9　平和記念公園

原爆死没者慰霊碑、オバマ大統領のスピーチ、広島平和記念資料館について

### In front of the Memorial Cenotaph for the Atomic Bomb Victims

G: This is the "**Memorial Cenotaph** for the Atomic Bomb Victims." The **inscription** reads, "Let all the souls here rest in peace; For we shall not repeat the evil." The registration books for the atomic bomb victims are kept in a stone chest in the cenotaph.

T: How many atomic bomb victims are registered?

G: About 310,000 — all the atomic bomb victims who **passed away**. To protect their souls from rain and dew, it was designed in the shape of an ancient Japanese clay house figurine. Every year, at 8:15 a.m. on August 6, people pray for the atomic bomb victims and the annual peace memorial ceremony for the atomic bomb victims is held.

T: 8:15 a.m. on August 6 is the time when the atomic bomb was dropped?

G: Yes. It's when time stopped for the atomic bomb victims. On the evening of August 6, a **floating lantern ceremony** is held along the Motoyasu River **opposite** the Atomic Bomb Dome to **comfort** the souls of the atomic bomb victims.

T: I saw that in my history textbook.

G: Good. Former American president Obama offered flowers here in 2016. In his speech, he said, "We are part of a single human family." He also said we should pursue a world without nuclear weapons.

T: Yes, I think that he came to Hiroshima to talk about it.

G: Many Japanese were impressed with his visit and speech. The number of foreign tourists has been increasing since his visit to Hiroshima.

### In front of the Peace Memorial Museum

G: This is the Peace Memorial Museum. The main hall is supported by pillars. It's said that this symbolizes the strength of people who rise up from the **ruins**. Inside, the history of Hiroshima before and after the bombing **is exhibited** in movies, photos, and **victims' belongings**. They show how terrible the atomic bombing was.

G：通訳ガイド　T：観光客

### 原爆死没者慰霊碑の前で

G：これは原爆死没者慰霊碑です。「安らかに眠って下さい　過ちは繰返しませぬから」と碑文には書かれています。原爆で死亡した人の名簿が、慰霊碑の中の石棺に納められています。

T：何人の原爆犠牲者が登録されているのですか？

G：原爆で亡くなられた約31万人です。原爆死没者の霊を雨露から守るために、古代日本の埴輪の家形のデザインにしています。毎年、8月6日の午前8時15分に原爆死没者に祈りがささげられ、恒例の原爆死没者のための平和記念式典が行われます。

T：8月6日の午前8時15分は原爆が落とされた時間ですか？

G：はい。　原爆死没者の時間が止まった時なのです。8月6日の夕方には原爆ドーム対岸の元安川で、原爆死没者の霊を慰めるために灯篭流しが行われます。

T：歴史の教科書で見たことがあります。

G：いいですね。アメリカのオバマ元大統領も、2016年にここに献花されましたよ。大統領はスピーチの中で「われわれは人類という一つの家族の一員だ」と言いました。私たちは核兵器のない世界を達成しなければならない、とも言いました。

T：はい。オバマ大統領はそれを語るために広島に来たのだと思います。

G：多くの日本人はオバマ氏の訪問とスピーチに感銘を受けました。オバマ氏の訪問以来、広島を訪れる外国人旅行者の数は増加し続けています。

### 広島平和記念資料館

G：これが広島平和記念資料館です。本館は柱で支えられています。これは、廃墟の中から立ち上がる人間の強さを表現していると言われています。館内では、被爆前後の広島の歴史が、映像や写真、被爆者の持ち物を通じて展示されています。原爆がどれほどひどいものかを示しています。

4

日帰り旅行

### 単 語 の 小 箱

□ memorial cenotaph 慰霊碑　□ inscription 碑文　□ pass away 亡くなる
□ floating lantern ceremony 灯篭流し　□ opposite 反対側の　□ comfort …を慰める
□ ruin 廃墟　□ be exhibited 展示される　□ victims' belongings 被爆者の持ち物

# 1-10 平和記念公園

広島平和記念資料館、原爆の子の像、禎子について

### After leaving the Peace Memorial Museum

T: I felt as if I was in the middle of the city after the atomic bombing. I really felt the misery of war. Now I can truly understand the importance of peace.

G: The lives of the people who somehow survived the atomic bomb were changed, too.

T: I can imagine they **went through indescribable hardships**.

G: Yes. Look at the layout of the Atomic Bomb Dome, the Peace Flame, the Memorial Cenotaph for the Atomic Bomb Victims, and the Peace Memorial Museum.

T: They're in a straight line, right?

G: Yes. I think this is the path to permanent peace.

### In front of the Children's Peace Monument

G: Please look up at the bronze statue of a girl who's lifting a golden origami crane with both hands above her head. Her name is Sadako Sasaki.

T: It looks like she is opening her hands to a peaceful future!

G: When Sadako was two years old, the atomic bomb was dropped on Hiroshima. At that time, Sadako was in her house, which was 1.7 kilometers away from the hypocenter. Sadako grew up as an **apparently** healthy girl. Sadako was very kind and cheerful and was popular among her friends. At the age of twelve, she had strange **swellings** on parts of her body and went to see the doctor. She **was diagnosed with** leukemia, a kind of blood cancer, and admitted to hospital.

T: She **developed leukemia** about ten years after the atomic bomb?

G: Yes. The doctor didn't tell her about the leukemia. However, she happened to find out the name of her disease. Even when Sadako felt very sick, she **pretended to** be fine so as not to make the people around her sad.

T: Sadako was such a considerate girl!

G：通訳ガイド　T：観光客

## 広島平和記念資料館を後にして

T： 私は原爆が投下された街の真ん中にいるように感じました。戦争の悲惨さを強く感じました。今、平和の大切さをつくづく感じています。

G： どうにか原爆を生き残ることのできた人々の人生も、変わってしまったのです。

T： そうした人々が、言葉では言い表せないような苦労をしたことが想像できます。

G： そうですね。原爆ドームと平和の灯、原爆死没者慰霊碑、平和記念資料館の配置を見てください。

T： 一直線上に並んでいますね。

G： はい。これが恒久平和への道だと思うのです。

## 原爆の子の像の前で

G： 金色の折り鶴を両手で頭の上に掲げている、女の子のブロンズ像を見上げてください。彼女の名前は佐々木禎子です。

T： 平和な未来へと手を広げているように見えますね！

G： 禎子が2歳のとき広島に原爆が落とされました。当時、禎子は爆心地から1.7キロ離れた家にいました。禎子は元気な女の子に育ったように見えました。とても優しく明るくて、友達の間でも人気がありました。12歳のときに体の一部に妙な腫れができたので、お医者さんに診てもらいました。血液のがんの一種である白血病と診断され、病院に入院しました。

T： 被爆から約十年後に白血病を発症してしまったのですね？

G： そうです。医師は禎子に白血病だと告知はしませんでしたが、彼女はたまたま病名を知ってしまいました。禎子はどんなに体調が悪いときでも、周囲の人たちを悲しませないように元気に振る舞いました。

T： 禎子はとても思いやりのある女の子だったのですね！

単 語 の 小 箱

□ go through ... …を経験する　□ indescribable hardships 言葉で表現できない苦労
□ Children's Peace Monument 原爆の子の像　□ apparently 見かけは　□ swelling 腫れ
□ be diagnosed with ... …と診断される　□ develop leukemia 白血病を発病する
□ pretend to ... …のふりをする

4

日帰り旅行

253

# 1-11 平和記念公園

禎子と千羽鶴について

G: An ancient Japanese **legend** promises that if you make a thousand paper cranes, your wishes will **be granted**, such as long life and recovery from illness or injury. Sadako believed that she could live by making 1,000 paper cranes. There was not enough paper to fold, so Sadako used small **medicine wrappers** or paper candy wrappers. Her friends also made paper cranes, praying for her recovery with all their hearts. Sadly, despite their prayers, Sadako passed away after fighting leukemia for eight months.

T: I think Sadako lives in many people's hearts. Also, Sadako encourages people who suffer from an **incurable disease** to live positively.

G: Yes. After her death, her classmates made great efforts to have a cenotaph built for Sadako and the other child victims of the atomic bomb. They got a lot of support and managed to **raise funds**. There were donations from more than 3,200 schools in Japan, and from nine countries. The Children's Peace Memorial was completed and opened to the public on May 5, 1958. It **is dedicated to** all the children who died as a result of the atomic bombing. The inscription on the stone block under the monument reads: "This is our cry, this is our prayer: for building a peaceful world."

T: We shouldn't bear grudges; we should pray for peace, right?

G: Absolutely! In 2013, an origami crane made by Sadako was donated to the visitor center at Pearl Harbor and displayed as a **permanent exhibit**. Origami cranes are a symbol of peace.

T: I'd like to make an origami crane.

G: Here's some paper for you. I'll teach you how to make an origami crane. After making it, let's place the crane in the booth behind the Children's Peace Monument and pray for peace.

## On the way back to Hiroshima Station

T: There's something nostalgic about this tram car. Today I visited two World Heritage Sites connected by this tram. They look totally different, but both of them pray for peace!

**G**：通訳ガイド　**T**：観光客

**G**：日本の古い言い伝えでは、折り鶴を千羽折れば、長生きできる、病気やけがが治るなどの願いがかなうと言われています。禎子は千羽鶴を折れば生きられると信じていました。十分な紙がなかったので、禎子は小さな薬の包み紙やキャンディーの包み紙を使いました。彼女の友達も心を込めて、回復を祈りながら鶴を折ってくれました。悲しいことに、祈りは届かず、禎子は8か月にわたる白血病との闘病の末、亡くなりました。

**T**：禎子は多くの人の心の中で生きていると思います。不治の病で苦しむ人々にも、前向きに生きる勇気を与えてくれています

**G**：その通りです。彼女の死後、クラスメートたちは禎子や原爆の犠牲となった子供たちのために碑を造ろうと、大変な努力をしました。クラスメートたちは多大なる支持を受けて、資金集めを達成できました。全国の 3,200 の学校と、9つの国から寄付金が集まりました。原爆の子の像は完成し、1958 年 5 月 5 日に公開されました。原爆によって亡くなったすべての子供たちにささげられています。像の下に置かれた石碑には「これはぼくらの叫びです　これは私たちの祈りです　世界に平和をきずくための」という碑文が刻まれています。

**T**：私たちは恨みを残さず、平和を祈ることが大切ですね。

**G**：その通りです。2013 年には禎子の作った折り鶴が、真珠湾のビジターセンターに寄付され常設展示されています。折り鶴は平和のシンボルなのです。

**T**：折り鶴を作りたいです。

**G**：ここに紙があります。折り鶴の作り方を教えますね。作ったら、折り鶴を原爆の子の像の後ろのブースにささげて平和を祈りましょう。

### 広島駅への帰路で

**T**：この路線電車にノスタルジーを感じます。今日はこの路面電車がつなぐ2つの世界遺産を訪れることができました。全く違う場所のように見えますが、両方とも平和を祈っているのですね。

---

## 単語の小箱

□ legend 伝説、言い伝え　□ be granted かなえられる　□ medicine wrapper 薬の包み紙
□ incurable disease 不治の病　□ raise funds 資金を集める
□ be dedicated to ... …にささげる　□ permanent exhibit 常設展示

4

日帰り旅行

255

## 瞬間英作文

1. 人々は弥山を中心とする宮島に神威を感じ、信仰しました。

2. 原爆ドームは世界平和記念碑として、恒久平和を訴えているのです。

3. 折り鶴は平和の象徴です。

4. 禎子は不治の病で苦しむ患者に、前向きに生きる勇気を与えてくれます。

5. 2013 年には禎子の作った折り鶴が、真珠湾のビジターセンターに寄付され常設展示されています。

### 解答例

1. People felt a **divine presence** on Miyajima, centered on Mt. Misen, and worshipped it.

2. The Atomic Bomb Dome appeals for **lasting peace** as a world peace monument.

3. Origami cranes **are a symbol of** peace.

4. Sadako encourages people who suffer from an **incurable disease** to live positively.

5. In 2013, an origami crane made by Sadako was donated to the visitor center at Pearl Harbor and is displayed as a **permanent exhibit.**

---

1. divine presence　神威　　2. lasting peace　恒久平和
3. be a symbol of ...　…の象徴だ　　4. incurable disease　不治の病
5. permanent exhibit　常時展示

# 玉虫の宝庫

## 1 宮島から平和記念公園へのツアーの一例

JR 新大阪駅（7 時 30 分頃発）新幹線普通車指定席（約 2 時間）→ JR 広島駅（9 時 30 分頃着）→ JR 在来線普通車自由席（約 25 分）で JR 宮島口駅→徒歩→フェリーに乗船し宮島へ（約 10 分）→宮島到着（11 時から 14 時まで 3 時間程度の自由時間）→厳島神社参拝→千畳閣→表参道（ランチ）→宮島港（14 時）→広電宮島口→平和記念公園（約 2 時間）市内自由散策および早めの夕食（広島名物もんじゃ焼きなど）→広島 18 時発→大阪 20 時 30 分頃着

## 2 通訳ガイドからのアドバイス

### アドバイス　平和への願いを込めて

平和記念公園はきれいに整備されていて、空気が透き通っています。(The Peace Memorial Park is beautifully maintained, and the air is crystal clear.) 原爆ドームを残してほしいと旅立ったヒロ子さんや、回復を信じて千羽鶴を折り続けた禎子さん、被爆者の方、多くの人の平和への願いが込められています。海外のゲストに同情（sympathy）ではなく共感（empathy）してもらえるように、心のこもったガイディングをしましょう。

## 3 通訳ガイド体験日記

### ◎期待外れの状況でも、お客様に楽しんでもらえるように！

海に浮かぶ大鳥居を期待する人に、引き潮の場合は Luckily, as the tide is low, we can walk up to the Great Torii!（幸運にも引き潮なので大鳥居まで歩けますよ！）とお伝えするなど、工夫をしましょう。

## 4 通訳ガイドお役立ち英語表現

### ◎歴史的建造物をガイドしながら「昔の人ってすごいな」と思うときに。

「私たちは先人の知恵から多くを学べます」は、We can learn a lot from the wisdom of our ancestors. のように言います（1-2 参照）。

# 2-1 伊勢神宮

外宮（豊受大御神）、内宮（天照大神）、宇治橋、式年遷宮について

### On the way to the Naikū

G: Ise Jingū consists of the Inner Shrine, "Naikū," the Outer Shrine, "Gekū," and 123 small shrines. The Naikū **is dedicated to** Amaterasu-Ōmikami. Amaterasu-Ōmikami, the ancestral kami of the imperial family, has **been revered** as the **universal tutelary kami** of Japan. The Gekū is dedicated to Toyouke-no-Ōmikami, who is responsible for offering food to Amaterasu-Ōmikami and is revered as the kami of food, clothing, shelter, and industry. The Naikū has a history of 2,000 years and the Gekū has a history of 1,500 years. The **Main Sanctuaries** of the Naikū, Gekū, 14 **associated shrines**, and Ujibashi Bridge are rebuilt every 20 years. The sacred apparel, furnishings, and divine treasures are also remade. When everything is ready, the Holy Mirror, a symbol of Amaterasu-Ōmikami, is moved to the new Main Sanctuary by Shinto priests. This is called the "Shikinen Sengū." The first one was conducted in 690 and the 62nd one was in 2015.

### Looking at Ujibashi Bridge

G: Ujibashi Bridge is considered to **connect** the everyday world **and** the sacred world. It's about 102 meters long. This bridge is also rebuilt every 20 years. Both the inner and outer Torii gates are made from recycled wood from the Main Sanctuaries.

T: I'm curious to know why they are rebuilt every 20 years.

G: It's said that Emperor Tenmu decided to do so. It's said that there are two reasons. One is to please the kami and **revitalize** the whole of Japan. The other is that the architectural style called "Yuiitsu-shinmei-zukuri" should be handed down to new generations. You can see it later. Let's cross the bridge. We have to **keep to the right**.

### After bowing to the Torii gate and crossing the Ujibashi Bridge

G: The Naikū is the most sacred site in Japan. Visitors have to walk along the 1-kilometer **approach** to reach the Main Sanctuary.

G：通訳ガイド　T：観光客

## 内宮に行く途中

G：伊勢神宮は「内宮」と「外宮」、そして 123 の小さな神社から成り立っています。内宮には天照大神がお祀りされています。天照大神は皇室のご祖神で、日本の総氏神としてあがめられています。外宮には豊受大御神がお祀りされていて、天照大神の食事を司り、衣食住の神、そして産業の神としてあがめられています。内宮は 2,000 年の歴史があり、外宮には 1,500 年の歴史があります。内宮と外宮の正宮、14 の別宮と宇治橋は、20 年ごとに建て替えられます。御装束神宝も新たに作られます。準備が整うと、天照大神の御神体の神聖な鏡が神官たちによって新しい正宮に遷されます。これを「式年遷宮」と呼びます。690 年に初めて行われ、2015 年に 62 回目が行われました。

## 宇治橋を見ながら

G：宇治橋は、日常と神聖な世界を結ぶと見なされています。長さは約 102 メートルです。この橋も 20 年に一度架け替えられます。内側の鳥居も外側の鳥居も、正宮のリサイクル木材で造られています。

T：なぜ 20 年に一度建て替えられるのか、知りたいです。

G：天武天皇がそうお決めになられたと言われています。2 つの大きな理由があると言われています。1 つ目の理由は神様に喜んでいただき、日本全体を活性化させることです。2 つ目は「唯一神明造」と言われる建築様式が新しい世代に受け継がれていくべきだからです。後でご覧になれますよ。橋を渡りましょう。右側通行しなければなりません。

## 鳥居に一礼して宇治橋を渡った後で

G：内宮は日本で一番の聖域です。参拝者は正宮に到着するには 1 キロ続く参道を歩かなければなりません。

4

日帰り旅行

### 単語の小箱

□ be dedicated to ... …にささげられる　□ be revered あがめられる
□ universal tutelary kami 総氏神　■ Main Sanctuary 正宮　□ associated shrine 別宮
□ connect A and B A と B を結ぶ　■ revitalize …を活性化する
□ keep to the right 右側通行する　■ approach 参道

# 2-2 伊勢神宮

 095

五十鈴川で自然のお清め、瀧祭宮、神楽殿、正宮の階段前について

### At the Isuzu River (site for ablution), after purification at the Temizusha and bowing in front of the Torii

G: Here too, you can purify yourself with river water flowing from the woods. The rainfall in the forests creates small streams and they flow into the rivers.

T: Both the air and water are **transparent**! I can see the riverbed!

G: Let's pray to the god Takimatsuri-no-kami. This kami, who **protects** the Isuzu River, is enshrined here.

### At the Kagura-den

G: If you have a personal wish, you can pray by offering a ceremonial dance to the Amaterasu-Ōmikami. It's important to entertain the kami.

T: By the way, I'm interested in a kind of fortune-telling paper. Where can I get one?

G: You've got the highest level of fortune because you came to pray at Ise Jingū, so there are no fortune-telling papers, called "Omikuji," here.

### In front of the steps to the Main Sanctuary

G: The Main Sanctuary is the place where Amaterasu-Ōmikami, the ancestral kami of the imperial family, is enshrined. The Holy Mirror, a symbol of Amaterasu-Ōmikami, is enshrined inside the Main Sanctuary. This architectural style is called "Yuiitsu-shinmei-zukuri." This building is made of **unpainted cypress wood** joined without nails. This is a "**post-in-ground**" **structure**. This **raised-floor style** is suited to Japan's wet climate. This style is said to be modeled on the **rice granaries** from the time when rice cultivation began in Japan — from the 10th century BC to around the 3rd century AD. You're not allowed to take pictures or speak in a loud voice after going up even one step. The Main Sanctuary of Ise Jingū is the most sacred area. It's important to **focus on** praying for the happiness of all and being grateful to be here. Later, I'll take you to Aramatsuri-no-miya, where you can pray for your own personal happiness.

G：通訳ガイド　T：観光客

## 手水舎でお清めして鳥居の前でお辞儀をした後、五十鈴川（お清め場）で

G：ここもまた、森から流れる川の水でお清めをする場所です。森林に降った雨水は
小さな流れを作り、川に流れ込むのです。

T：空気も水も透明ですね！　川底が見えますね！

G：瀧祭宮の神様にお祈りしましょう。この神様は五十鈴川を守る神様で、ここにお
祀りされています。

## 神楽殿の前で

G：個人的なお願い事があるなら、天照大神に舞を奉納してお祈りできますよ。神様
に喜んでいただくことはとても大切ですから。

T：ところで、私は未来を占う紙にとても興味があります。どこでいただけますか？

G：伊勢神宮に参拝しに来たので、あなたは大吉を手に入れたことになります。だか
らここには「おみくじ」と呼ばれる運命を占う紙はないのです。

## 正宮の前にある階段の前で

G：正宮は、皇室のご祖神の天照大神がお祀りされているところです。天照大神のシ
ンボルである神聖な鏡が、正宮の中にお祀りされています。建築様式は「唯一神
明造」と呼ばれています。釘を使わずに組まれた無彩色のヒノキ材で造られてい
ます。これは、「掘立式」建築です。この高床式は、日本の湿気の多い気候に適
しています。この様式は、日本で稲作が始まった紀元前 10 世紀から紀元 300 年
くらいの頃の米蔵が原型と言われています。階段を一歩でも上がると、写真を撮
ることも大きな声で話すことも許されません。伊勢神宮の正宮は最も神聖な場所
なのです。ここで皆の幸せを願うこと、そしてここに参拝していることに感謝し、
気持ちを集中させてお祈りすることが大切なのです。後で、あなた個人の幸せを
お祈りできる「荒祭宮」にお連れしますね。

## 単語の小箱

□ transparent 透明の　□ protect …を守る
□ unpainted cypress wood 無彩色のヒノキ材
□ post-in-ground structure 「掘建式」建築（地面に穴を掘って、そこに柱を立てる建築様式。
礎石を使用しない）　□ raised-floor style 高床式　□ rice granary 米蔵
□ focus on ... …に焦点を合わせる

# 2-3 伊勢神宮

 096

正宮の白い石、御稲御倉、荒祭宮、風日祈宮について

### After praying to Amaterasu-Ōmikami (in a low voice)

T: What are those white stones over there?
G: The white stones are like clouds. Imagine this sacred area is the **roof of heaven**.
T: It's not only sacred, but also romantic!
G: The white stones keep the sacred site clean by **preventing puddles from** forming and **weeds from** growing.

### In front of Mishine-no-mikura

G: Mishine-no-mikura is the shrine where **harvested rice** for **ritual offerings** to the kami is stored. The architectural style is similar to that of the Main Sanctuary. You can see the Shinmei-zukuri style here up close.

### In front of Aramatsuri-no-miya

G: This shrine is dedicated to the "**vigorous** spirit" of Amaterasu-Ōmikami. You can pray for your personal happiness here. Many people pray for **divine protection** before taking on new challenges.
T: I'll pray for success in my job.

### Looking at Isuzu River from the Kazahinomi-no-miya Bridge

G: Look at the autumn leaves reflected in the river. It looks like a rainbow.
T: I love this place! The air feels so crisp and clear.

### In front of Kazahinomi-no-miya

G: This is Kazahinomi-no-miya, which is dedicated to a couple of wind kami, Shinatsuhiko-no-mikoto and Shinatobe-no-mikoto. They control the wind and rain. Moderate wind and rain are necessary for growing crops. According to legend, a couple of gods saved Japan from a **Mongol invasion force** in the late 13th century by sending heavy rain and strong winds.
T: So they play a very important role!

G：通訳ガイド　T：観光客

## 天照大御神にお祈りした後で（小さな声で）

**T**：あちらに置かれていた白い石は何だったのですか？

**G**：白い石は雲のようですね。この神聖な場所が天空であると想像してください。

**T**：神聖であるだけでなく、ロマンチックですね！

**G**：白い石は、神域に水たまりができないように、そして雑草が生えないようにしてくれます。

## 御稲御倉の前で

**G**：御稲御倉は、儀式で神様にお供えするための収穫米を貯蔵する神社です。建築様式が正宮と似ています。こちらで神明造様式をじっくりとご覧になれます。

## 荒祭宮の前で

**G**：この神社には、天照大神の荒御魂がお祀りされています。あなた自身の幸福をここでお祈りすることができます。多くの人が新しいことに挑戦する前に、ここで神様のご加護をお祈りします。

**T**：仕事の成功を祈ります。

## 風日祈宮橋から五十鈴川を眺めながら

**G**：川に映る紅葉を見てください。虹のように見えますよ。

**T**：この場所が大好きです！　空気が澄み切っていますね。

## 風日祈宮の前で

**G**：こちらでは一組の風の神様、級長津彦命と級長戸辺命をお祀りしています。風と雨をつかさどっています。穀物を育てるには、適度の風と雨が必要です。伝説によれば、13世紀後半、モンゴルの侵略軍から豪雨と強風で日本を救ったと言われています。

**T**：とても重要な役割をされていますね！

### 単語の小箱

☐ roof of heaven 天空　☐ prevent A from *doing* A が〜するのを妨げる

☐ puddle 水たまり　☐ weed 雑草　☐ harvested rice 収穫したお米

☐ ritual offering 儀式でのお供え　☐ vigorous 活発な、激しい

☐ divine protection 神様のご加護　☐ Mongol invasion force モンゴルの侵略軍

4

日帰り旅行

263

# 2-4 伊勢神宮

 097

木除杭、おかげ参り、おかげ横丁、赤福餅について

### Looking at the wooden piles in the river

T: What are those **wooden piles** in the river?
G: Wooden piles prevent large pieces of **driftwood** or stones from hitting the bridge supports when the river rises or **floods** because of typhoons. This shows the wisdom of ancient people.

### To Okage-yokochō

G: The peaceful Edo period started at the beginning of the 17th century, after the battles of medieval times. People **longed to** visit Ise Jingū, the most sacred shrine in Japan, to express their **gratitude** to Amaterasu-Ōmikami. This was called "Okage Mairi." "Okage" is a word meaning "thankfulness." "Mairi" is "visit." Traveling to Ise was difficult. The local people of Ise welcomed their visitors with gratitude. They believed that treating visitors kindly was a good way to express their own gratitude to Amaterasu-Ōmikami. "Okage-yokochō" opened in 1993. Okage-yokochō means "Thankfulness Street." Okage-yokochō is modeled on buildings from mainly the Edo and Meiji periods from the 17th to the 19th century. You can enjoy the delicious local food, history, and culture. Okage-yokochō is full of the spirit of Ise people, who appreciate the blessings of nature and work with gratitude.

### In the Akafuku-mochi shop in Okage-yokochō

G: The "Akafuku-mochi" is a **specialty** of Mie. It is made with rice cake covered with red bean paste. The Akafuku-mochi **represents** the flow of the Isuzu River.
T: How does the Akafuku-mochi resemble the sacred Isuzu River?
G: Look at this Chinese character "Kawa." Kawa means river. Kawa consists of three **vertical lines**, which represent streams of water. Look at the three lines on the Akafuku-mochi.
T: That's interesting! The Akafuku-mochi is delicious!
G: There's a song about this sweet: "Ee ja nai ka! Ee ja nai ka! Ee ja nai ka!" which means "Very good! Very good! Very good!" (laughing)

G：通訳ガイド　T：観光客

## 川の中の木の杭を見ながら

T： 川にある木の杭は何ですか？

G： 木除杭は、台風による増水や洪水のときなどに、大きな流木や石が橋脚に当たることを防ぎます。木の杭は昔の人の知恵ですね。

## おかげ横丁へ

G： 中世の戦乱の時代の後、17世紀初めに平和な江戸時代が始まりました。人々は天照大神にお礼を言うために、日本で一番神聖な伊勢神宮に参拝したいと切望しました。これは「おかげ参り」と呼ばれました。「おかげ」は「感謝」を示す言葉です。「参り」は「訪問」を意味します。伊勢に旅行するのは困難でした。伊勢の地元の人たちは、感謝の気持ちを込めて参拝者を歓迎しました。彼らは訪問者を親切にもてなすことが、天照大神に感謝を示す良い方法だと信じていました。「おかげ横丁」は1993年にオープンしました。「感謝の横丁」を意味します。おかげ横丁は、17世紀から19世紀の、主に江戸時代から明治時代の建物をモデルにしています。おいしい郷土料理や歴史、文化を楽しめますよ。おかげ横丁には、自然の恵みに感謝し、おかげの心で働く伊勢人の精神が息づいています。

## おかげ横丁の赤福餅のお店で

G： 赤福餅は三重の特産品です。あんで覆われたお餅でできています。赤福餅は五十鈴川の流れを表現しています。

T： 「赤福餅」はどのように、神聖な五十鈴川と似ているのですか？

G： 「川」というこの漢字を見てください。「川」はriverを意味します。3本の縦線からできていて、水の流れを表しています。赤福餅の3本の線を見てください。

T： 面白いですね！　赤福餅はおいしいです！

G： このお菓子に関する歌があります。「ええじゃないか、ええじゃないか、ええじゃないか」、これはVery good! Very good! Very good! を意味します（笑）。

## 単語の小箱

□ wooden pile 木の杭　□ driftwood 流木　□ flood 洪水
□ long to do ～することを切望する　□ gratitude 感謝　□ specialty 特産物
□ represent …を示す　□ vertical line 垂直線、縦線

265

# 2-5 ミキモト真珠島

鳥羽、海女の実演について

G: Now we're in Toba. The Toba region has a "**ria**" **coastline**, where **coastal fishing** and **pearl farming** are thriving. It takes about 8 minutes to the Mikimoto Pearl Island, which is a pearl theme park. Mie Prefecture is world-famous as the birthplace of **cultured pearls**.

T: The vast, blue sea **stretches out** to the horizon. I like this seaside town!

### While watching an "Ama" diver show

G: You can see a 10-minute demonstration by female divers called "Ama."

T: I'm curious to know why the divers are women.

G: Women have an extra layer of **fat under their skin**, so it's said they can withstand cold longer than men. It's also said that while men were doing deep-sea fishing for many days, women were diving for seashells along the coastline.

T: I see. Why do the Ama wear white outfits?

G: It's said that the color white drives away sharks and jellyfish. It's also protection against sunburn.

T: I see. Are the Ama whistling that "Pyu-Pyu" sound to catch fish?

G: No. Many people think "Pyu-Pyu" is a signal, but it's to help them breathe. After a deep dive, **inhaling** deep breaths of air is dangerous for their hearts and lungs, so the women breathe slowly and quietly through **pursed lips**.

T: I see. That makes sense.

G: This sound has been selected as one of the "100 **soundscapes** of Japan."

T: Wow! An Ama caught something and put it into the basket! They're waving their hands! By the way, how many Ama are working in the pearl oyster business in Ise?

G: Because of the development of pearl cultivation techniques, Ama don't work anymore in this business. The Ama played a very important role in pearl cultivation until around 1960. Nowadays, this demonstration is performed to show appreciation for them. I'll talk about their work later.

G：通訳ガイド　T：観光客

G：鳥羽に到着しました。鳥羽地区には「リアス式」海岸があり、沿岸漁業や真珠養殖が盛んです。真珠のテーマパーク、ミキモト真珠島まで8分ほどで到着します。三重県は養殖真珠の誕生の地として、世界的に有名なのですよ。

T：広大な青い海が水平線まで広がっていますね。この海沿いの町が好きです！

## 「海女」の実演を見ながら

G：「海女」と呼ばれる女性ダイバーの10分間の実演をご覧いただけます。

T：なぜダイバーが女性なのかを知りたいです。

G：女性の方が男性よりも皮下脂肪が多いので、寒さに耐えられると言われています。それに男性が何日間も遠洋漁業に出る間、女性が沿岸で貝などを採取していたからだとも言われています。

T：なるほど。なぜ海女は白い服を着ているのですか？

G：白い色はサメやクラゲを追い払うと言われています。日焼けも防ぎますよ。

T：なるほど。海女は魚を捕まえるために「ピューピュー」と口笛を吹くのですか？

G：いいえ。多くの人が「ピューピュー」は合図だと思っていますが、呼吸をする補助なのですよ。深い潜水の後、深く息を吸うことは心臓と肺に危険なので、女性たちはすぼめた口からゆっくりと静かに呼吸するのです。

T：なるほど。理にかなっていますね。

G：この音は日本の「音風景百選」にも選ばれています。

T：わあ！　海女が何かを採ってかごに入れました。手を振ってくれていますね！ところで、伊勢には真珠貝の仕事をしている海女はどれくらいいますか？

G：真珠養殖の技術が向上したので、この仕事をしている海女はもういないのです。海女は1960年くらいまで真珠養殖に重要な役割を果たしました。今日、この実演は、彼女たちに感謝の気持ちを表すために行われているのです。後で海女たちの仕事について説明しますね。

**4**

日帰り旅行

## 単語の小箱

☐ ria coastline リアス式海岸線　☐ coastal fishing 沿岸漁業　☐ pearl farming 真珠養殖
☐ cultured pearl 養殖真珠　☐ stretch out 広がる　☐ fat under *one's* skin 皮下脂肪
☐ inhale …を吸い込む　☐ pursed lips すぼめた口　☐ soundscape 音風景

267

# 2-6 ミキモト真珠島

海女の歴史、御木本幸吉氏の努力、養殖真珠が作られる工程について

### Enjoying the beautiful scenery from the observation deck

G: There are about 600 Ama in Ise and they catch abalones, **turban shells**, seaweed, etc. You can visit an Ama hut and enjoy the fresh seafood. It's a lot of fun to hear about their experiences and lifestyle. They **range from** 20 **to** 80 years of age. I hope Ama culture will **survive**. It's said that the Ama have a history going back 2,000 years. The techniques of the Ama in Toba and Shima were designated as an Important Intangible Folk Cultural Property in 2017.

### In the Kōkichi Mikimoto Memorial Hall

G: In the case of natural pearls, a **grain of sand** or some other **particle** enters an oyster shell by chance, and it becomes a pearl after many years, unless the oyster shell **ejects** it. From this, Kōkichi got the idea of repeatedly **implanting** some kind of **nucleus**. Kōkichi was called a **con man** and made fun of by others. However, in 1893, he became the first person in the world to succeed in cultivating pearls.

T: I wish I had his enthusiasm and passion!

### After watching the demonstration in the Mikimoto Pearl Museum

G: They implant round nuclei into "Akoya" pearl oysters. That's why they can make large and round pearls. The Akoya pearl oysters are put into wire cages and cultivated in pearl farms with great care. For example, the **optimal** seawater temperature for the Akoya pearl oyster is from 18 to 23 degrees Celsius. They have to be cultivated in places with both good currents and abundant plankton. It takes about two years to grow a pearl.

T: Amazing! The pearls are raised with so much love!

G: In the past, the Ama had to dive to collect the pearl oysters and dive again to replace them on the seabed after the nucleus was implanted. The Ama also had to move the oysters to safe locations when a red tide or typhoon was approaching.

T: Cultured pearls are the beautiful fruits of human efforts!

G：通訳ガイド　T：観光客

## 展望台から美しい景色を楽しみながら

G：伊勢には約 600 人の海女がいて、アワビやサザエ、海藻などを採取しています。海女小屋を訪問し、新鮮な魚を召し上がれますよ。海女の経験や生活についてのお話を聞くことはとても楽しいですよ。海女の年齢幅は 20 歳から 80 歳位までです。海女の文化が存続することを願っています。海女には 2,000 年の歴史があると言われています。鳥羽・志摩の海女漁の技術は、2017 年に国の重要無形民俗文化財に指定されました。

## 御木本幸吉記念館にて

G：天然真珠の場合、真珠貝の中に砂やほかの小さなかけらが偶然に入り、貝がそれを吐き出さなければ、長い年月を経て真珠になります。そこから、幸吉は核となる物を繰り返し埋め込むアイデアを得たのです。幸吉はペテン師と呼ばれ、からかわれました。しかしながら、1893 年、彼は世界で初めて真珠の養殖に成功しました。

T：彼の熱意と情熱を見習いたいです。

## 真珠博物館で実演説明を見た後に

G：養殖真珠の場合は、丸い核をアコヤ貝に挿入します。だから、より大きな丸い真珠が出来上がります。アコヤ貝は網のかごに入れられて、養植場で大切に育てられます。例えば、アコヤ貝に適した海水温度はセ氏 18 度から 23 度です。潮の流れが良く、プランクトンの豊かな場所で育てる必要があるのですよ。真珠を育てるには約 2 年かかります。

T：すごいです！　真珠は愛情をもって育てられるのですね。

G：昔は海女が真珠貝を採集するために潜り、そして核を埋め込んだ後、それらを海底に戻すためにまた潜ったのですよ。さらに、赤潮や台風が近づくと、海女は貝を安全な場所に移し替えなければならなかったのです。

T：養殖真珠は、人間の努力の美しい結晶ですね！

### 単 語 の 小 箱

□ **turban shell** サザエ　□ **range from A to B** A から B の範囲である　□ **survive** 生き残る
□ **grain of sand** 砂粒　□ **particle** 小さなかけら、分子、粒子　□ **eject** …を吐き出す
□ **implant** …を埋め込む　□ **nucleus**（細胞の）核（複数形は nuclei）
□ **con man** ペテン師　□ **optimal** 最適な

# 瞬間英作文

1. 内宮には皇室のご祖神で、日本の総氏神としてあがめられている天照大神がお祀りされています。

2. 外宮には、私たちに豊作や、衣食住を授けてくださる豊受大御神がお祀りされています。

3. 御稲御倉は、儀式で神様にお供えするための収穫米を貯蔵する神社です。

4. 三重県は養殖真珠の誕生の地として世界的に有名です。

5. 「鳥羽・志摩の海女漁の技術」は、2017年に国の重要無形民俗文化財に指定されました。

解答例

1. The Naikū is dedicated to Amaterasu-Ōmikami, who is the ancestral god of the imperial family, and has been revered as the **universal tutelary kami** of Japan.

2. The Gekū is dedicated to Toyouke-no-Ōmikami, who blesses us with **abundant harvests** and gives us food, clothing, and shelter.

3. Mishine-no-mikura is the shrine where harvested rice for **ritual offerings** to the gods is stored.

4. Mie Prefecture is world-famous as the birthplace of **cultured pearls**.

5. The techniques of the Ama in Toba and Shima were designated as an **Important Intangible Folk Cultural Property** in 2017.

---

1. universal tutelary kami 総氏神　　2. abundant harvest 豊作
3. ritual offering 儀式の捧げもの　　4. cultured pearl 養殖真珠
5. Important Intangible Folk Cultural Property 重要無形民俗文化財

# 玉虫の宝庫

## 1 太古の歴史を刻む憧れの聖地、伊勢神宮はこう案内しよう

### ●伊勢の観光ルート

❶ 電車（JR）鳥羽駅→ミキモト真珠島→（バス）二見浦→（バス）内宮→（徒歩）おかげ横丁→（バス）外宮→（徒歩）近鉄伊勢市駅

❷ 観光バス　大阪→二見浦→外宮→内宮→おかげ横丁→大阪へ

### ●内宮のルート

❶ **宇治橋**　式年遷宮の4年前に架け替えられます。外側と内側に鳥居があります。床板と欄干はヒノキで、橋脚はケヤキです。

❷ **神苑**　宇治橋を渡ると参道両側に広がり、大相撲春巡業では横綱土俵入りの奉納があります。松の木が広がっています。

❸ **五十鈴川**　手水舎ができる前はここでお清めをしました。瀧祭神は五十鈴川を守る神様です。心も洗われます。

❹ **神楽殿**　宇治橋から正宮の中間点で、神様を喜ばせるために舞を奉納する場所です。

❺ **正宮（皇大神宮）**　皇室のご祖神様で、日本の総氏神である天照大神がお祀りされています。

❻ **御稲御倉**　神宮神田で収穫した稲を治める穀倉です。近くで神明造りを見られます。

❼ **荒祭宮**　天照大神御神の一面、荒御魂（活発で行動的な魂）が祀られています。個人的なお願いができます。

❽ **風日祈宮**　風雨をつかさどる神様です。風日祈宮橋から見る五十鈴川は素晴らしい眺めです。

❾ **参集殿**　参拝者向けの無料休憩所です。中央には能舞台があります。

※外宮から内宮に参拝するのが礼儀ですが、外国人観光客を案内する場合は内宮だけのことが多いので割愛しました。

# 2 通訳ガイドからのアドバイス

## アドバイス1　Kami とは？

伊勢神宮は神の英語表記を「god」から「kami」に改めたので、We call Shinto gods or deities "kami" in Ise Jingū と説明しましょう。ゲストが理解しにくいようなら、gods や deities を使っても OK です。

## アドバイス2　天照大神だけでなく他の神様の説明も！

Amaterasu-Ōmikami, the ancestral kami of the imperial family, is enshrined in the Main Sanctuary. Also, some (other) mythological kami are enshrined in associated shrines, such as Kazahinomi-no-miya.（皇室のご祖神の天照大神が正宮に祀られています。また、神話上の神が、別宮の風日祈宮などで祀られています）と説明して、瀧祭神や風日祈宮にもお連れしましょう。モンゴルの侵攻軍から豪雨と強風で日本を救った風日祈宮の kami、風も kami なんだなあと感じますね。

## アドバイス3　皇室、天皇について聞かれたら？

The imperial family has been in existence for more than 2,000 years. The emperor is the symbol of the state and of the unity of the people. Most Japanese highly respect him. He does not take part in government.（皇室は 2,000 年以上続いています。天皇は日本国の象徴であり、日本国民統合の象徴です。ほとんどの日本人は天皇を尊敬しています。天皇は国事行為のみを行い、参政はしません）と説明するとよいでしょう。

## アドバイス4　あらゆる物に生命が宿っている日本固有の神道の説明を！

Shinto is the indigenous religion of Japan. It is believed that kami live in many objects, such as mountains, rocks, gorges, ponds, rivers, and trees. It is said there are myriads of kami in Shintoism.（神道は日本固有の宗教です。山、岩、渓谷、池，川、木など、多くの物に神が宿ると信じられています。神道には万の神が存在すると言われています）と説明しましょう（春日大社 2-5 も参照）。春日大社には、屋根を突き抜けているシンパクの木があります。木を神と見なしているから切らないのです。

## アドバイス5　玉砂利でお浄めを！

It is said that the gravel represents a riverbed. Gravel purifies many things, so you can purify yourself by walking on this gravel path.（玉砂利は川底を表していると言われています。砂利は多くの物を清めるので、砂利が敷き詰められた参道を歩くことで自分自身を清めることができます）と伝えましょう。

## アドバイス6　五十鈴川でゆったりと

五十鈴川で Both the air and water are transparent.（空気も水も透明だ）と感動されるゲストが多いです。ここでも自然の生命力、川にも kami が宿っていることを感じてもらえるでしょう。

## アドバイス7　巨木に囲まれた緑深い神域で生命の息吹を感じる

The grounds of the Naikū are covered with cedars and Japanese cypresses, which are said to be from 400 to 900 years old.（内宮の境内は、樹齢 400 年から 900 年のスギやヒノキに覆われています）。こうした大きな木にも、生命力や kami を感じてもらえます。

## アドバイス8　スギの木に竹が巻かれている理由は？

Why are the lower parts of the cedar trees wrapped with strips of bamboo?（なぜスギの木の下部に竹が巻かれているの？）とよく聞かれます。This is to prevent the bark of the cedar tree from peeling off because worshippers touch the cedar tree too much.（参拝者がスギの木を触りすぎるので、スギの皮がはがれるのを防ぐため）と答えています。また、There is a rumor that cedar bark cures illnesses.（スギの木の皮が病気を治すといううわさがあります）ので、スギの皮を持ち帰ろうとする人がいるからだとも答えています。

## アドバイス9　観光客の心を読む

伊勢神宮におみくじがないことをがっかりされる方には、You've got the highest level of fortune because you came to pray at Ise Jingū.（伊勢神宮に参拝できたから、それだけで大吉）と伝えましょう。また、お守り（good lack talisman）をお勧めするのもよいでしょう。

## アドバイス10　古代からの三種の神器と現代の三種の神器

Mirrors, swords, and jewels have been considered to be the "three sacred treasures" since ancient times. Robot vacuum cleaners, fully automatic washer-dryer combos, and dishwashers are called the three sacred treasures of modern life.（鏡と刀と玉は古代からの三種の神器と見なされています。ロボット掃除機、全自動洗濯乾燥機、食洗器が現代の三種の神器と呼ばれています）などと比較することもできますね。これはジェネラルトピックとしても使えます。

## アドバイス11　夫婦岩が組み込まれているツアーもあるので、説明できるように！

Meoto Iwa means "Wedded Rocks." According to Japanese mythology, these two rocks represent Izanagi-no-mikoto and Izanami-no-mikoto, who are said to have created Japan. These two gods are often compared to Adam and Eve. You can enjoy the beautiful sunrise between these rocks at dawn.（夫婦岩は「夫婦の岩」を意味します。日本の神話によれば、これらの2つの岩は、日本をつくったと言われているイザナギノミコトとイザナミノミコトを表しています。この2人の神様はアダムとイブによく例えられます。夜明けには、2つの岩の間から美しい日の出を見ることができます）などと説明しましょう。

### アドバイス 12　おかげ横丁でおいしく楽しいものを！

おかげ横丁では、江戸時代タイムスリップしたような気分を味わえます。赤福餅の説明など、漢字を使って説明すると喜ばれます。

### アドバイス 13　世界初の養殖真珠を誕生させた御木本さん

In 1893, Kōkichi Mikimoto became the first person in the world to succeed in cultivating pearls.（1893年、御木本幸吉は世界で初めて真珠の養殖に成功しました）と、ペテン師（con man）とからかわれても、真珠養殖に成功した御木本さんの努力を称えましょう。

### アドバイス 14　海女を無形文化遺産に推奨する理由とは？

海女をユネスコ無形文化遺産へ登録すべきと勧める理由は5つあります。1つ目の理由は、海女がスキンダイビングという素潜り潜水の特殊技術を身につけた、自立した女性だということ。2つ目は、海女はどんな生業を営む民よりも長い歴史を持つということ。5,000年もの歴史があるかもしれないと言われています。3つ目は、持続可能な漁法を守り続けてきたこと。例えば、彼女たちは乱獲をしないというルールを守っています。4つ目は、海女の生き方が自然との共生を基本にしていること。彼女たちは、資源を守るために昔ながらの漁具や漁法を用いています。5つ目は、海女は他人を助け、教え、協力するので、地域の漁業共同体を活性化させるのに重要な役割を果たしていること。海女は自然と共存して積極的に明るく生きるようにと人々に勇気を与えてくれます。また、海女は鳥羽地区のシンボルであり、海洋環境を守っています。そして、日本と韓国にしか存在しません。

**英訳**

There are five reasons why Ama divers should be registered as a UNESCO Intangible Cultural Heritage. The first reason is that Ama divers are independent women who have mastered the special technique of skin diving. The second reason is that Ama diving has a longer history than any other way of making a living. They say that it may be 5,000 years old. The third reason is that they have maintained a sustainable fishing method. For example, they have followed the rules against overfishing. The fourth reason is that their way of life is based on living in harmony with nature. For example, they have used traditional fishing gear and methods in order to protect resources. The fifth reason is that Ama divers play an important role in revitalizing local fishing communities, mainly because they are willing to help, teach, and cooperate with others. Ama divers encourage people to live positively and cheerfully in harmony with nature. Also, Ama divers have long been a symbol of the Toba region. They help to protect the marine environment. Ama divers exist only in Japan and Korea.

## 3 通訳ガイド体験日記

### ◎擬宝珠は帰りのルートで説明する。

There are 16 bridge ornaments, called "Giboshi." Giboshi are in the shape of an onion.（16 個の擬宝珠と呼ばれる装飾品があります。擬宝珠は玉ねぎの形をしています）大鳥居に向かって左側の手前から 2 番目の擬宝珠の中には、橋の安全を祈って神札が納められており、触ると徳をいただけます。内宮は右側通行なので行きのルートで立ち止まって説明し、帰りのルートの人に迷惑をかけてしまいました。

## 4 通訳ガイドお役立ち英語表現

### ◎海女さんの磯笛は soundscape（音風景）。

人々が地域のシンボルとして大切にし続けたい音の聞こえる環境を「残したい日本の音風景 100 選」と呼びます。伊勢志摩の海女さんの磯笛は、その音風景 100 選に選ばれています。I hope Ama culture will survive.（海女さんの文化が存続することを願っています）などと感想を添えるとよいでしょう（2-6 参照）。

### ◎宇治橋を例として木の名前を覚えましょう。

Most of the Ujibashi Bridge is made of Japanese cypress, but the pillars in contact with the water are made of zelkova wood. Zelkova wood is water-resistant and durable.（宇治橋の大部分はヒノキでできていますが、水に接触する柱の部分はケヤキでできています。ケヤキは水に強く、耐久性があります）のように、宇治橋を例として木の名前を覚えておきましょう。

主な木の名前は以下の通り。
cypress（ヒノキ）　zelkova（ケヤキ）　camphor tree（クスノキ）　cedar（スギ）

# 3-1 白川郷

高山の古い町並み、合掌造りと呼ばれる理由とその利点について

**G**: Here we are in Takayama. Takayama is the largest city, in terms of area, in Japan, but 92% of the city **is forested**. Takayama is nicknamed "Little Kyoto." This area is called "Furui Machinami," which means "Old Street of Stores and Houses." The buildings keep the traditional style of the 17th to the 19th century: **latticed windows** and dark brown walls. Let's enjoy the traditional craft shops, sake shops, and local food.

### In a car on the way to Shirakawa-gō Ogimachi

**G**: I hope you enjoyed the views in this mountain town of Takayama. Did you like Takayama?

**T**: Yes! I especially liked the Hida beef skewers and sushi with raw beef on it! (laughing)

**G**: Me too. Next, we'll visit Shirakawa-gō village, which is surrounded by mountains. Ninety-six percent of the village area is forested. Shirakawa-gō is one of the snowiest areas in Japan. You can enjoy the Japanese landscape the way it used to be.

### After crossing the suspension bridge and praying at Myōzen Temple in Shirakawa-gō

**T**: Wow! The air is really fresh. I love Shirakawa-gō village.

**G**: Shirakawa-gō was registered as a UNESCO World Heritage Site in 1995. The famous architect Bruno Taut **was inspired by** this "Gasshō-style" of house and wrote about it in a book titled *The Rediscovery of Japanese Beauty* in around 1936.

**T**: So long ago! I'm impressed by this style, too.

**G**: This style is called "Gasshō-style." (smiling) Please look at my hands. Gasshō means joining your hands together in prayer, like this. The shape of the roofs resembles Gasshō.

**T**: I see. Why do the houses have such unique structures?

**G**: There are two benefits. Firstly, it snows heavily in this area in winter, so this 60-degree sloped roof helps the snow to **slide off** and **preserves** the roof for longer.

G：通訳ガイド　T：観光客

G：高山に到着しました。高山市は日本で一番面積の広い市ですが、その92％は森林です。高山には「小京都」というニックネームがついています。この通りは「古い町並み」と呼ばれ、「お店や家の古いストリート」を意味します。建物は格子窓や暗い茶色の壁など、17世紀から19世紀までの伝統的な様式を保っています。昔の工芸品店や酒屋さん、地元の食べ物を楽しみましょう。

### 白川郷・荻町への車中で

G：山の中にある高山の町並みを楽しまれたと思います。高山は気に入りましたか？
T：はい！　特に飛騨牛の串焼きと、生の牛肉がのったおすしが気に入りました！（笑）
G：私もですよ。次は、山に囲まれた白川郷村に行きますね。村の96％は森林で、日本で最も雪の降る場所の一つです。日本の原風景をお楽しみいただけます。

### 白川郷の吊り橋を渡り、明善寺を参拝してから

T：うわあ！　空気がとても新鮮ですね！　白川郷が大好きです。
G：白川郷は1995年にユネスコ世界文化遺産に登録されました。著名な建築家のブルーノ・タウトは合掌造りの家屋に感銘を受け、1936年頃に『日本美の再発見』というタイトルの本で白川郷のことを書きました。
T：そんなにも昔にですか！　私もこの建築様式にとても感動しています。
G：この様式は「合掌造り」と呼ばれています。（ほほ笑んで）私の手を見てください。合掌は、このようにお祈りの形で手を合わせることを意味します。あの屋根の形が「合掌」に似ています。
T：なるほど。どうしてこんなユニークな形をしているのですか？
G：利点が2つあります。1つは、この地域は冬に雪がたくさん降るので、この60度に傾いた屋根は雪が落ちるのを助けますし、屋根を長持ちさせるのです。

□ be forested　森林である、森林に覆われた　□ latticed window　格子窓
□ be inspired by ...　…に感銘を受ける　□ slide off　落ちる　□ preserve　…を保存する

# 3-2 白川郷

世界遺産に選ばれた理由、囲炉裏(いろり)の役割、蚕の生育に使っていた2階について

**G**: The other good thing about Gasshō-style houses is that they have a large **attic space**. The large attic space was used to **raise silkworms**. You can see it later.

**T**: I see. By the way, why do all Gasshō-style houses face in the same direction?

**G**: The **gables** of the roofs face north and south. This structure minimizes **wind resistance** and controls the amount of sunlight striking the roof. This makes for cool summers and warm winters.

**T**: That makes sense!

**G**: In his book, Bruno Taut **admired** Gasshō-style houses as "architecturally rational and logical."

### In Wada House, a typical Gasshō-style house

**G**: We're now in Wada House, which is 300 years old and designated as an Important Cultural Property. On the first floor, you can see Japanese-style rooms with paper screens, a Buddhist altar, and so on.

**T**: I'm curious about all of this. I've always wanted to sit in a tatami room!

**G**: Here's a **hearth** in the center of the living room. This hearth plays a very important role. The smoke rises and protects the **timbers** from insects and **corrosion**.

### On the second floor

**G**: This place was used for raising silkworms right up until 1970. Now, please look at some **cultivated** silkworms exhibited in this box. **Sericulture** was the **key industry** in this village. The large windows played an important role, because lighting and **ventilation** were necessary for raising silkworms. You can see various folk utensils, too.

**T**: This is the first time I've seen this type of structure. The timbers are held together with ropes.

**G**: Yes. No nails are used in the attic. This type of structure is constructed of timber and rope made from **witch-hazel saplings**. It's **resistant to** earthquakes and strong winds.

G：通訳ガイド　T：観光客

G：もう1つの利点は、合掌造りの家は大きな屋根裏のスペースを持てることです。広いスペースは蚕を生育するために使われていました。後で見ることができますよ。

T：なるほど。ところで、なぜ合掌造りの家は同じ方向を向いているのですか？

G：切妻側が南北を向いています。この構造は風の抵抗を最小限にし、屋根に当たる太陽光線の量をコントロールします。涼しい夏と暖かい冬にしてくれます。

T：理にかなっていますね。

G：ブルーノ・タウトは著書の中で、合掌造りの家は「建築学的に合理的かつ論理的である」と絶賛しましたよ。

### 典型的なの合掌造りの家、和田家住宅で

G：ここは、300年の歴史を持ち、重要文化財に指定されている和田家住宅です。1階では障子や仏壇のある典型的な日本の部屋をご覧いただけます。

T：すべてに好奇心がそそられます。私は畳の部屋に座りたいとずっと思っていたのです！

G：居間の真ん中に囲炉裏があります。囲炉裏はとても重要な役割を果たしています。立ち昇る煙は、虫や腐敗から木材を守ります。

### 2階で

G：この場所は、1970年まで蚕を育てるのに使われていました。この箱で飼育されている蚕の展示をご覧ください。養蚕業はこの村では基幹産業だったのです。蚕を育てる上で光と換気は不可欠だったので、大きな窓は大切な役割を果たしました。さまざまな民具もご覧になれますよ。

T：こんなスタイルの建造物を見るのは初めてです。木材が縄で縛られていますね。

G：そうです。屋根裏には釘が1本も使われていません。この様式の建物は、ネソという若木でできた縄と木を使って組み立てられています。地震や強風にも耐性があります。

## 単語の小箱

- □ attic space 屋根裏スペース　□ raise silkworms 蚕を育てる　□ gable 切妻
- □ wind resistance 風の抵抗　□ admire …を称賛する　□ hearth 囲炉裏　□ timber 木材
- □ corrosion 腐敗　□ cultivated 飼育された　□ sericulture 養蚕業
- □ key industry 基幹産業　□ ventilation 換気　□ witch-hazel ネソ（マンサクの一種）
- □ sapling 若木　□ be resistant to ... …に抵抗力がある

4

日帰り旅行

279

# 3-3 白川郷

原風景を楽しめる白川郷の歴史、世界遺産に選ばれた大きな理由「結」について

### While walking

T : I love this nostalgic, rural landscape. Carp and rainbow trout are swimming **leisurely** in the **irrigation canal**. It's nice to see a different side of Japan from the urban lifestyle. By the way, I'd like to know why they no longer raise silkworms.

G : Sericulture was one of Japan's main industries. After the **World Depression** of 1929, Japan lost its large foreign market. The times changed. The main reason is that **chemical fibers replaced** silks. However, they continued to grow silkworms until around 1970.

T : I see.

G : Actually, this village experienced ups and downs. When the **hydropower dams** were constructed from the 1940s to the 1960s, some areas **were submerged**. Some Gasshō-style houses were sold or demolished. There were around 300 Gasshō-style houses in 1924, but by 1961 the number had decreased to 190.

T : I'm sad to hear that.

G : However, people began a movement with the motto "Do not sell, do not rent, do not destroy." A new **association** to protect the natural environment was established.

T : Great! The residents' efforts also **led to** Shirakawa-gō being registered as a World Heritage Site in 1995!

G : Absolutely! Shirakawa-gō has **been thriving** as one of the most popular tourist spots for about 40 years. Gasshō-style houses were built in Shirakawa-gō from around 1700 to the early 1900s. There are 117 Gassho-style houses remaining now. The roofs need to **be rethatched** with **pampas grass** every 30 years. There's a system of **mutual assistance** among the villagers called "Yui," which means "**bond**." The Yui members voluntarily rethatch each other's roofs, and this creates a bond among them. Yui was one reason that Shirakawa-gō was chosen as a World Heritage Site. Local people are very proud of their Yui.

G：通訳ガイド　T：観光客

## 歩きながら

**T：** この懐かしい田園風景が大好きです。コイやニジマスがゆったりと用水路を泳いでいますね。都会の生活とは違った日本の一面を見られるっていいですね。ところで、なぜ蚕をもう育てていないのか知りたいです。

**G：** 養蚕業は日本の主要産業の一つでした。1929 年の世界恐慌の後、日本は外国の大きな市場を失いました。時代が変わりました。一番大きな理由は、化学繊維が絹に代わって使われるようになったことです。それでも、ここでは 1970 年頃まで蚕の飼育をしていました。

**T：** なるほどね。

**G：** 実はこの村は良い時代も悪い時代も経験しているのです。水力発電を行うダムが 1940 年代から 1960 年代に建設されたときに、いくつかの地域が水没しました。合掌造りの家は売却されたり、取り壊されたりしました。1924 年には 300 あった合掌造りの家が、1961 年には 190 に減ってしまったのです。

**T：** それを聞いてとても残念です。

**G：** しかしながら、人々が「売らない、貸さない、壊さない」をモットーに運動を始めました。自然環境を守る新しい組織が作られました。

**T：** 素晴らしいです！　住民の努力も、1995 年の白川郷の世界文化遺産への登録につながったのですね！

**G：** その通りです。白川郷は最も人気のある観光地として、約 40 年間栄えています。合掌造りの家は白川郷で 1700 年頃から 1900 年代初頭までに建てられました。今は 117 軒の合掌造りの家があります。屋根はススキで 30 年ごとにふき替えをしなければなりません。村人たちの間には、絆を意味する「結」と呼ばれる相互援助の制度が存在します。結のメンバーたちは自発的にお互いの屋根のふき替えをして、絆を作るのです。結の存在は世界遺産に選ばれた理由の一つです。地元の人々は自分たちの結をとても誇りに思っています。

4

日帰り旅行

## 単語の小箱

□ leisurely ゆったりと　□ irrigation canal 用水路　□ World Depression 世界恐慌
□ chemical fiber 化学繊維　□ replace …に取って代わる
□ hydropower dam 水力発電ダム　□ be submerged 水没する　□ association 組織
□ lead to ... …になる　□ thrive 栄える　□ be rethatched ふき替えをする
□ pampas grass ススキ　□ mutual assistance 相互援助　□ bond 絆

281

# 3-4 白川郷

### かやぶき、結、自然と人が手を取り合うことについて

T: Rethatching requires a lot of skill and **physical strength**, right?

G: Yes. Villagers think that it's important to **pass on** their skills to young people to preserve their Gasshō-style houses. One villager said to me, "I have a **sentimental attachment to** houses which I've rethatched." Now, in some cases, they outsource the preparatory work and then the Yui members rethatch the roof. This is called "Modern Yui."

T: I'm impressed to hear that residents cooperate with each other and love their houses. How long does it take to rethatch a roof?

G: One or two days. It had to be finished within a day in the old days because **household items** got wet if it rained. Three hundred people worked on a big house and 100 people worked on a small house.

**On the observation deck, after drinking tea**

T: What a nostalgic scene! By the way, I've been wondering why they began to thatch their roofs with pampas grass instead of using tiles or straw.

G: The village is located in a deep mountain valley, so they couldn't get tiles. People made use of the natural resources they could find. Luckily, pampas grass kept them cool in summer and warm in winter. It's more durable than straw.

T: I feel that these people try to work with the **harshness of nature** rather than go against it. They've built up a wonderful culture and lifestyle here by cooperating with each other!

G: Right! Gasshō-style houses have a weak point. They easily catch fire. If one house catches fire, the fire might spread to the others, so a large **simultaneous fire drill** is conducted every fall. Look at this picture. Sixty **water cannons** have been installed and they shoot out curtains of water. This drill also **brings** people **together**. I've talked with children here who love this village. One girl told me with shining eyes, "I want to work as a nursery school teacher here and live in Shirakawa-gō forever."

T: I want to live here, too. People in this village are very kind.

G：通訳ガイド　T：観光客

T：屋根のふき直しにはかなりの技術と体力を必要としますよね？

G：はい。村人たちは技術を若者たちに伝え、合掌造りを守ることが大切だと感じています。ある村人は、「私はふき直した家にはとても愛着があります」と語ってくれました。業者に準備作業を委託し、それから結のメンバーがふき直しをするケースもあります。これは「現代結」と呼ばれています。

T：住民がお互いに協力し、家を愛おしく思うお話を聞いて感動します。ふき直しをするにはどれくらいの時間がかかりますか？

G：1日か2日です。雨が降ると家財道具が濡れてしまうので、昔は1日で仕上げなければなりませんでした。大きな家は300人、小さな家では100人で作業します。

### お茶を飲んだ後、展望台で

T：ノスタルジックな風景ですね！　ところで、ずっと思っているのですが、人々はなぜ瓦やわらを使わず、ススキで屋根をふき始めたのですか？

G：村は山の深い谷間にあるので、瓦を手に入れることができませんでした。人々は手に入れることのできる自然資源を利用したのです。幸運なことに、ススキは夏を涼しく、そして冬を暖かくしてくれるのです。わらより耐久性があります。

T：人々は厳しい自然に逆らうよりも、自然と手を取り合っていると感じます。素晴らしい文化とライフスタイルが協力することで生まれたのですね！

G：その通りです！　合掌造りの家には短所もあります。火事になりやすいのです。一軒が火事になると他の家にも広がる可能性があるので、毎年秋に大規模な一斉火災訓練が行われます。この写真を見てください。60基の放水銃が設置されていて、水がカーテンのように放水されます。この訓練も人々を結びつけます。この村を愛する子供たちと話したことがあります。女の子が目を輝かして、「ここで保育園の先生として働き、ずっと白川郷で暮らしたい」と話してくれました。

T：私もここに住みたいです。この村の人達はとても親切ですね。

## 単 語 の 小 箱

☐ physical strength 体力　☐ pass on ... …を伝える
☐ sentimental attachment to ... …に対する愛着心　☐ household item 家財道具
☐ harshness of nature 自然の厳しさ　☐ simultaneous fire drill 一斉火災訓練
☐ water cannon 放水銃　☐ bring A together A を結びつける

# 瞬間英作文

1. 屋根の形は、このようにお祈り形で手を合わせることを意味する合掌に似ています。

2. この60度に傾いた屋根は雪が落ちるのを助け、屋根を長持ちさせます。

3. 養蚕業は白川郷では基幹産業でした。

4. 村人たちの間には「結」と呼ばれる相互援助制度が存在します。

5. 「結」のメンバーはさまざまな行事でお互いに助け合い、絆を築きます。

## 解答例

1. The shape of the roof resembles Gasshō, which means joining your hands together **in prayer**, like this.

2. This 60-degree **sloped roof** helps the snow to slide off and preserves the roof for longer.

3. **Sericulture** was a key industry in Shirakawa-go.

4. There's a system of **mutual assistance** among the villagers called "Yui."

5. The Yui members help each other with various events and create a **bond** among themselves.

---

1. in prayer 祈って　　2. sloped roof 傾いた屋根　　3. sericulture 養蚕業
4. mutual assistance 相互援助　　5. bond 絆

# 玉虫の宝庫

## 1 山中の町並みと田園風景を満喫してもらおう

❶ 行程の一例
大阪 8 時→高山 11 時 50 分→高山発 13 時→白川郷 14 時 30 分→ 16 時半→大阪到着 20 時

❶ 合掌造りと呼ばれる理由と利点、「結」を通しての村人たちの協力、伝統と自然を守る大切さを理解してもらいましょう。

## 2 通訳ガイドからのアドバイス

**自然に溶け込む明るい田園風景を楽しんでもらう！**

"I have a sentimental attachment to houses which I've rethatched." （私はふき直した家にとても愛着があります）の言葉の中に、白川郷の人々の愛情を感じ取ってもらいましょう。また人々は厳しい自然に逆らうよりも自然と手を取り合って生活しています。これからも明るい未来があります。The countryside has a brighter future!

## 3 通訳ガイド体験日記

合掌造りの家を見学する前に This is a home, so it's important for you to show good manners. （こちらは個人のお宅なのでマナーを良くしましょうね）とできるだけ優しく注意を促してから訪問することが大切です。団体客の場合、大声で騒ぐなどマナーの悪い人もいるので注意が必要です。

## 4 通訳ガイドお役立ち英語表現

◎「日本の原風景」は何と言う？
白川郷では日本の原風景である農村文化・生活・暮らしを深く感じ、楽しめますね。この「日本の原風景」は、英語で the Japanese landscape the way it should be と表現します。

## 霊場 高野山とは

### 高野山の地形、高野町の人口と仏僧の数

Kōyasan is a sacred place. Kōyasan is the central training center of Shingon Esoteric Buddhism, and was founded by Kōbō Daishi, also known as "Kūkai," in 816. Kōyasan was listed as a World Heritage Site in 2004, because it has been loved and used as a place of worship by many people for 1,200 years. The *National Geographic Traveler* selected it as one of the 20 destinations to visit in 2015 — the only Japanese destination chosen. **The population of Kōya-chō is about 2,600, of which about 600 are Buddhist monks.** There are 117 temples. It covers an area of about 137 square kilometers. Kōyasan is on an 800-meter-high basin surrounded by mountains of around 1,000 meters. This topography has been compared since ancient times to a lotus flower because of the resemblance. The lotus flower is a symbol of Buddhism.

\* \* \*

　高野山は霊場です。高野山は 816 年に「空海」の名でも知られる「弘法大師」によって開かれた真言密教の根本道場です。高野山は 1,200 年にわたって愛され、多くの人々に信仰の場とされていることから、2004 年に世界遺産に登録されました。2015 年に『ナショナルジオグラフィック・トラベラー』は、高野山を訪れるべき 20 の場所に選出しました。これは選ばれた日本の唯一の目的地でした。**高野町の人口は約 2,600 人で、そのうち約 600 人が仏僧です。**117 の寺院があります。面積は約 137 平方キロメートルです。高野山は 1,000 メートル級の山々に囲まれた、標高約 800 メートルの盆地です。高野山は古代より、地形が似ていることから、蓮の花に例えられてきました。蓮の花は仏教のシンボルです。

**アドバイス** ▶▶ かわいい蓮の花の写真を見せながら、楽しく説明しましょう。最後から 2 文目の This topography が通じにくい場合は The shape of Kōyasan に入れ替えて説明しましょう。

### 真言宗の開祖・弘法大師（空海）

Kōbō Daishi studied Esoteric Buddhism under the revered monk Keika and came back to Japan in 806, after having stayed in Tang Dynasty China for two years. In 816, Kōbō Daishi was granted permission by Emperor Saga to construct a monastery at Kōyasan. He devoted himself to **improving people's lives and contributed to making Japan a happy country**. Kōbō Daishi entered into eternal meditation at the age of 61, in 835. Still now, his spirit remains in this world, and he continues to pray for all living things. Kōbō Daishi, the founder of Shingon Buddhism, studied medicine, pharmacy, and civil engineering. He was also a famous calligrapher.

\* \* \*

　弘法大師は（空海）、尊敬する恵果の下で密教を学び、中国の唐に 2 年間滞在した後、806 年に日本に帰国しました。816 年に弘法大師は、嵯峨天皇から高野山の山中に僧院を建立する許可を得ました。彼は**人々の生活を向上させ、日本を幸福な国にする**ことに献身しました。弘法大師は 835 年、61 歳のときに入定されました（永遠の瞑想に入られました）。今もなお、弘

法大使の精神はこの世にとどまり、生きとし生けるもののために祈り続けてくださっています。真言宗開祖の弘法大師は、医学や薬学、土木工学などを学びました。また、有名な書道家でもありました。

**アドバイス** ▶▶ 「弘法大師は入定された（entered into eternal meditation）」が通じない場合は、肉体はなくても精神は生きておられると心を込めて話しましょう。

## 嵯峨天皇が弘法大師に信頼を寄せた出来事と信望が厚かった理由

There was an artificial pond for irrigation named Mannōike Pond in Shikoku. It wasn't functioning well, but Kōbō Daishi, who had studied the latest civil engineering in China, was chosen to be the overseer of the repair works for this pond, and **he successfully repaired Mannōike Pond in a short time**. Kōbō Daishi grew to be respected and loved not only by the common people but also by Emperor Saga, who entrusted him with Tōji Temple.

＊　＊　＊

　四国に満濃池という名前のかんがい用の人工池がありました。うまく機能していませんでしたが、中国で最新の土木工学を学んだ弘法大師が、この池の修繕工事の監督者として選ばれ、**見事に短期間で満濃池を修繕しました**。弘法大師は庶民だけでなく、東寺を彼に任せた嵯峨天皇にも、尊敬され愛されたのでした。

**アドバイス** ▶▶ 土木工学（civil engineering）を学び、修繕の監督者（overseer of the repair works）としても活躍した弘法大師が、庶民にも天皇にも愛されたことを強調しましょう。

## 真言宗

The founder of Shingon Buddhism in Japan was Kōbō Daishi. According to the doctrines of Shingon Buddhism, its main deity, Dainichi Nyorai, represents the absolute truth of the cosmos in which we live. Every single being in this world can be with Dainichi Nyorai. In other words, **Buddhahood inherently dwells inside us**. You can understand this better by doing Buddhist practices such as meditation and volunteer work. You are already enlightened. You need to realize it. This is called "Sokushin Jōbutsu" in Shingon Buddhism.

＊　＊　＊

　日本の真言宗の創始者は、弘法大師です。真言宗の教義によると、本尊である大日如来が、私たちが生きる宇宙の絶対的な真理を表しています。この世に存在するすべてのものが、大日如来と同体であると考えます。言い換えれば、**悟りは生まれながらに私たちの内面にあるのです**。あなたはそれを瞑想などの仏教の修行、ボランティア活動でより理解できるようになります。あなたはすでに悟っていて、それに気づくことが重要です。真言宗ではこれを「即身成仏」と呼んでいます。

**アドバイス** ▶▶ 曼荼羅は真言密教を絵画化しています。宇宙の真理そのものとされる大日如来を中心に、そ

287

の周りをさまざまな仏や菩薩が一定の秩序に従い描かれているのです。**両界曼荼羅の金剛界は悟りへの道筋、胎蔵界は慈悲の広がり**を表します。宇宙に**太陽と月**があるように、金剛界と胎蔵界の二つの曼荼羅が一つの世界を表すと説明しましょう。曼荼羅の塗り絵をし（do coloring）、ストレス解消になる説明を入れると楽しいです。

# 1. 高野山

## 大門

The gate to Kōyasan is called the "Daimon." The current Daimon was rebuilt in its current location in 1705. It is 25.1 meters tall. A pair of Deva Kings, one on either side, guards Kōyasan.

＊　＊　＊

　高野山への門が「大門」です。現在の大門は 1705 年に、現在の場所に再建されました。高さは 25.1 メートルです。両側の金剛力士像（仁王様）が高野山を守っています。

**アドバイス** ➡ 仁王の説明は p. 94 を参照してください。また、西側に淡路島と瀬戸内海が見えるフォトスポットであることも紹介しましょう。You can see Awaji Island and the Seto Inland Sea to the west!

# 2. 壇上伽藍

## 修学の場

The Danjō Garan is **a place where Buddhist monks practice Buddhism**. This is where Kōbō Daishi first began work when he established the monastery of Kōyasan. The construction of the monastic complex at Kōyasan started here in the early 9th century. The Danjō Garan is a monastic complex containing the Kondō and Konpon Daitō built by Kōbō Daishi. Kōyasan's major Buddhist services are held in this place.

＊　＊　＊

　壇上伽藍は**仏僧が仏教を学ぶ（修行する）場所**です。弘法大師が高野山の僧院を開創するにあたり、最初に着手された場所です。高野山の仏教僧院建設はここで 9 世紀初頭に始まりました。壇上伽藍は、弘法大師によって創建された金堂、根本大塔を含む、複合的な仏教僧院です。高野山の主要な法会が行われます。

288 ｜ 名所めぐり ✥ 高野山

## 中門

The gate to the Danjō Garan is called the "Chūmon." The Chūmon was burned to the ground in 1843. After a gap of 172 years, this one was built in 2015 to commemorate the 1,200th anniversary of Kōyasan's founding. The Shiten-nō, the Four Heavenly Kings, are protecting the four directions.

＊　＊　＊

　壇上伽藍への門は「中門」です。1843 年に焼失しました。この中門は 2015 年に高野山の開山 1,200 年を記念し、172 年ぶりに再建されました。四天王像が 4 つの方角を守っています。

**アドバイス** ➡ 四天王像の説明の中でも広目天と多聞天（p. 96,146 参照）に興味を持つ人が多いです。**増長天の胸にはトンボが、広目天の胸にはセミ**が止まっていることで有名です。解釈には諸説ありますが、トンボは遠くまで飛び回れる、セミは声が遠くまで響くことから、「遠くまで見渡せ、遠くまで声が届くように」を意味していると考えられます。

## 金堂

The Kondō Hall is Kōyasan's main hall. It has served a key role as **the central hall at Kōyasan** since the middle of the 9th century. It has been used for important Buddhist ceremonies. The Kondō Hall was originally built by Kōbō Daishi in 819. The present building is a reconstruction from 1932. The hall's principal Buddhist image is the Medicine Buddha.

＊　＊　＊

　金堂は高野山の本堂です。9 世紀半ばより、**高野山の中心的なお堂**として大切な役割を果たしています。仏教の大切な儀式に使われています。最初の金堂は 819 年に弘法大師によって建立されました。現在の金堂は、1932 年に再建されました。お堂の本尊は、薬師如来です。

## 三鈷の松（さんこのまつ）

After having studied Buddhism in China for two years, Kōbō Daishi came back to Japan. The legend goes that when leaving China, he threw a "Sankosho," which is a ritual implement, praying that he could find a place to build a practice hall. He found **the Sankosho stuck in the pine tree** here and decided to open his practice hall at Kōyasan.

＊　＊　＊

　中国で 2 年間、仏教を学んだのち、弘法大師は日本に帰国しました。伝説によると、弘法大師は中国を去るとき、修行道場を創建する場所を見つけるために、儀式の法具の三鈷杵を投げました。彼はこの場所の**松に刺さっている三鈷杵**を見つけ、ここに道場を建てることに決めたのです。

**アドバイス** ➡ 伝説なので楽しく話しましょう。**幸せを呼ぶ三つ葉の松の葉**を見つけられます（普通の松

の葉は二葉か五葉です）。

## 経蔵

This is a rotating storehouse for books in which important Buddhist scriptures are kept. Please try to push it round. It's said that by doing so you can earn **the same amount of merit as from reading all the sutras.**

\* \* \*

　これは、仏教の重要な経典が納められている回転式の本棚です。押してぐるっと回してください。そうすることで、**仏教のすべての経典を読むのと同じ徳を得られる**と言われています。

## 御社（みやしろ）

Kōbō Daishi prayed to Niu Myō-jin and Kōya Myō-jin, of Niutsuhime Shrine in Amano for **the protection of Kōyasan**, and enshrined them at Miyashiro in 819.

\* \* \*

　弘法大師は 819 年、天野の丹生都姫売神社の丹生明神・高野明神を**高野山の鎮守**として勧請（神様の来臨をお願い）し、御社に祀りました。

**アドバイス** ➡ 高野山は丹生都姫売神社の神領でしたので、勧請（神様の来臨のお願い）をしました。神道と仏教の密接な関係の一例です。

## 根本大塔

The Konpon Daitō is **a landmark of Kōyasan**. It often appears in Kōyasan sightseeing brochures. Kōbō Daishi began the construction of this pagoda in 816. It was completed in 887. It played the important role of the central training center for Shingon Esoteric Buddhism. It enshrines the "Buddha Vairocana of the Womb Realm," which is surrounded by four Buddhist figures from the "Diamond Realm." The sixteen pillars are painted with images of the Sixteen Great Bodhisattvas, and the Eight Patriarchs, who spread the teachings of esoteric Buddhism, are depicted in the four corners. The present Konpon Daitō is a 1937 reconstruction.

\* \* \*

　根本大塔は**高野山のランドマーク**です。高野山の観光用のパンフレットによく登場します。弘法大師は、816 年にこの仏塔の建設を始めました。完成は 887 年でした。真言密教の中心的修行場として重要な役割を果たしました。「金剛界」の四仏に取り囲まれた「胎蔵大日如来」が祀られています。16 本の柱には十六大菩薩が描かれ、四隅の壁には密教を伝えた八祖（はっそ）が描かれています。現在の根本大塔は 1937 年の再建です。

## 御影堂（みえどう）

The Miedō, or "Portrait Hall," was originally Kōbō Daishi's own meditation hall. Later, a portrait of Kōbō Daishi was enshrined here. The Miedō is considered one of the most sacred locations on Kōyasan. It is opened to the public only once a year.

\* \* \*

　「肖像堂」とも呼ばれる御影堂は、弘法大師自身の修行場（持仏堂）でした。後に、弘法大師の肖像が安置されました。御影堂は高野山で最も神聖な場所の一つだと考えられています。一般に公開されるのは、年に一度だけです。

# 3. 金剛峯寺

## 金剛峯寺・天水桶

Kongōbuji Temple is the headquarters of Kōyasan Shingon Buddhism. Kongōbuji was built by Hideyoshi Toyotomi in 1593. The present building is an 1863 reconstruction. **Only the emperor, members of the imperial family, and important Kōyasan officials could use this gate in the olden days.** ---Passing through the gate---
Please look at the **rain barrels** on the cypress bark roof. When it rains, water collects in them. When a fire broke out, the water in the buckets prevented the fire from spreading.

\* \* \*

　金剛峯寺は高野山真言宗の総本山です。金剛峯寺は 1593 年に豊臣秀吉によって創建されました。現在の建物は 1863 年の再建です。昔は、**この門を使えるのは天皇・皇族、高野山の重職だけでした。**
　…**門を通り抜けて**…檜皮ぶきの屋根の上にある**天水桶**をご覧ください。雨が降ると、水がこの桶の中に集まります。火事が起こった場合は、桶の水が延焼を防ぎました。

## 大広間・梅の間・柳の間

**Important rituals and ceremonies** are held in the "Ōhiroma" room. Kōbō Daishi is enshrined in the Buddhist altar in the Buddhist altar room. The mortuary tablets for successive generations of emperors of Japan are displayed on both sides. Cranes and pine trees are painted on the sliding doors called "Fusuma." Next to the Ōhiroma, there is the Plum Room and the Willow Room. They're named after the paintings on their sliding doors. Hidetsugu Toyotomi committed suicide in the Willow Room.

\* \* \*

**重要な儀式や式典**は「大広間」で行われます。弘法大師は仏壇部屋の仏壇に祀られています。両側には、歴代天皇の位牌をお祀りしています。「ふすま」と呼ばれる引き戸に、鶴と松が描かれています。大広間の隣には梅の間と柳の間があります。これらは、ふすまの絵から名付けられました。豊臣秀次は柳の間で自害しました。

**アドバイス** ▶ 大広間では鶴（longevity の象徴）と松（eternity の象徴）を説明しましょう。柳の間での秀次の自害の話は、日本史好きな人は興味を持たれますが、そうでない人には話すのを控えた方がいいでしょう。

## 新別殿

In 1984, the New Temple Annex was built to commemorate **the 1,150th memorial service of Kōbō Daishi's eternal meditation**. This is a reception room for the many visitors to the temple. You can listen to a **Buddhist monk's preaching,** and you will be served with tea. The New Temple Annex consists of two rooms. One room has 91 tatami mats and the other has 78. When the sliding doors are removed, the two rooms can be turned into one room of 169 mats.

＊　＊　＊

　1984 年、新別館は**弘法大師の入定 1,150 年の法要**を記念するために建てられました。お寺を訪れる多くの訪問者の応接場所です。**仏僧説法**を聞くことができ、お茶の接待もしてもらえます。新別館は 2 部屋から成り立っています。1 つの部屋は 91 畳で、もう 1 つは 78 畳の広さです。ふすまを取り除けば、169 畳の 1 つの部屋になります。

**アドバイス** ▶ It's easy to **enlarge the space available** by opening or removing the sliding doors!（ふすまを開けたり外したりすることで、**使えるスペースが広げられる**）と言って、日本家屋の部屋の利点をアピールできます。

## 蟠龍庭

Banryūtei Garden was also made in 1984. **This rock garden is the largest in Japan.** The two guardian dragons are emerging from the sea of clouds. A male dragon is on the left and a female dragon on the right. They're facing each other and protecting the Okuden. The dragon is considered to be one of the strongest animals and is revered. The dragons are made of 140 pieces of granite from Shikoku, where Kōbō Daishi was born, and the clouds are made of white sand from Kyoto.

＊　＊　＊

　蟠龍石庭も 1984 年に造られました。**この石庭は日本最大です。** 2 匹の守護龍が雲海から出現しています。オスの龍は左側に、メスの龍は右側にいます。お互いに向き合って、奥殿を守っています。龍は最も強い動物と見なされ、敬われています。龍は、弘法太師が生まれた四国の花崗岩 140 個でできていて、雲海は京都の白い砂でできています。

**アドバイス** ▶ Dragons are a symbol of evil.（龍は悪の象徴）と見なす国もあるので、文化の違いも考

えて興味を持ってもらえるように話しましょう。

## 別殿

The "Betsuden," or Temple Annex, was built in 1934 in commemoration of the 1,100th anniversary of Kōbō Daishi's eternal meditation. This room used to be used for the meetings of the Shingon Sect. It was also used as a rest area for worshippers until 1983. Flowers of the four seasons are depicted on the west side, and **scenes from the time of Kōbō Daishi's visit to China until the founding of Kōyasan** are depicted on the east side. Personally, I like the two dogs which accompanied Kōbō Daishi to Kōyasan.

＊　＊　＊

　別殿は 1934 年、弘法大師の入定 1,100 年を記念して建てられました。この部屋は、かつては真言宗の会議の場として使われていました。また、1983 年までは信者の休憩場所としても使われていました。西側には四季の花が描かれ、東側には**弘法大師の中国訪問から、高野山創建までの場面**が描かれています。個人的には、高野山まで弘法大師にお供した 2 匹の犬が好きです。

## 書院上段の間・武者隠し

The Shoin Jōdan-no-ma is now used as a place where Kōyasan's major ceremonies are conducted. In the olden days, this room was used as a reception room when emperors and retired emperors visited Kōyasan. The walls are covered in gold leaf. There is a bodyguard's room named "**Musha Kakushi**" behind the sliding doors with the beautiful tassels. Actually, **several armed guards were on standby there**. The bodyguards were prepared to jump out at intruders.

＊　＊　＊

　現在、書院上段の間は高野山の重要な儀式を行う場所として使用されています。かつては、天皇や上皇が高野山を訪問された際の応接間として使用されました。壁は金箔で覆われています。美しい房の付いたふすまの奥には、「**武者隠し**」と呼ばれる護衛たちのための部屋があります。実際に、**複数の武装した護衛たちがそこで待機**していました。護衛は侵入者の前に飛び出してくる準備ができていたのです。

## 台所

This was a kitchen for preparing food for a great number of monks. Look at the three large iron pots. One kettle is capable of cooking 98 kilograms of rice. When all three pots are used, **rice can be cooked for 2,000 people**. Look up at the rack hanging down from the ceiling. Food was preserved on the rack. Hanging it from the ceiling improves the ventilation. Also, the hanging paper stops the mice from getting down to the food rack. It's cool here in Kōyasan, so, luckily, there are almost no cockroaches trying to get into the kitchen.

\* \* \*

　ここは多くの僧侶たちの食事を準備する台所でした。3つの大きな鉄の釜を見てください。1つの釜で98キログラムのお米を炊くことができます。3つの釜をすべて使うと、**2,000人分のお米を炊くことができます**。天井からつり下ろした棚を見上げてください。食べ物はこの棚の上で保存されていました。天井からつるすことで換気が良くなります。また、つるされている紙は、ネズミが食べ物の棚に来るのを防ぎました。高野山は涼しいので、幸運なことに、台所に侵入するゴキブリはほとんどいません。

アドバイス ▶ The kitchen feeds up to 2,000 people! と驚く方もいます。棚は「ネズミ落とし」と呼ばれていて、観光客に喜ばれます。現場での方が説明しやすいですね

# 4. 奥之院

## 弘法大師と奥之院・一の橋

In the Okunoin there is the mausoleum of Kōbō Daishi, the founder of Shingon Buddhism. Kōbō Daishi is one of the most revered people in the religious history of Japan. Lining the approach, there are about 200,000 tombstones for people ranging from famous historical figures to commoners. The cemetery at Okunoin is **the largest in Japan**. I think this is probably because many people want to be close to Kōbō Daishi. You have to walk two kilometers and cross three bridges to get to **Kōbō Daishi's mausoleum**. There are more than 1,300 cedar trees, which are registered as "Prefectural Natural Monuments." Ichinobashi Bridge is the entrance to the Okunoin. Please bow and pray with both hands together before crossing this bridge.

\* \* \*

　奥之院には真言宗の創始者、弘法大師の霊廟があります。弘法大師は日本の宗教史上で最も尊敬されている人物の一人です。歴史的な人物から一般の人まで、約20万基のお墓が参道に沿ってあります。奥之院の墓地は**日本で一番大きいです**。きっと、多くの人が弘法大師のそばにいたいからだと思います。**弘法大師の霊廟までは2キロ歩き、3つの橋を渡らなければなりません。**そこには1,300本以上の杉の木があり、「県の天然記念物」に指定されています。一の橋は奥之院への入り口です。この橋を渡る前にどうぞおじぎをして、両手を合わせてお祈りください。

アドバイス ▶ 弘法大師についての詳しい説明はP. 286にあります。上記は一の橋からのコースです。中の橋台駐車場からのコースでは企業のお墓を見ることができます。企業のお墓はとてもユニークな形をしています。新明和工業（航空機の部品会社 巨大なロケット）、福助（靴下の製造・販売 福助人形）、キリンビール（聖獣・麒麟）、UCCコーヒー（コーヒーカップ）、ヤクルト（ヤクルトの容器）、日産自

294　名所めぐり ❖ 高野山

動車（物故者の像）、パナソニックなど。日本の企業と従業員の関係や、社員が企業墓を誇りに感じていることなどを話しましょう。

## 汗かき地蔵・姿見の井戸

"Asekaki Jizō" literally means "Sweating Jizō." It's said that this Jizō always seems to be perspiring, because this Jizō **works for others and suffers pain on behalf of all**. Please look into this well; if you don't see your own reflection, you'll die within three years.

\* \* \*

「汗かき地蔵」は「汗をかいている地蔵」を意味します。この地蔵は**いつも他人のために働き、人の代わりに痛みを受けているため、汗をかいているように見える**と言われています。この井戸をのぞき込んでください、あなたが映った姿が見えなければ、3年以内に亡くなります。

**アドバイス** ➡ 中の橋を渡ると汗かき地蔵と、その隣に姿見の井戸があります。姿見の井戸は誰が見ても姿が映りますよ。汗かき地蔵、水向け地蔵に興味を持つ外国人観光客が多いです。

## 水向け地蔵

In front of Gobyōbashi Bridge, there is a line of 15 Buddhist statues. They're collectively called "Mizumuke Jizō." Worshippers **offer wooden sutra tablets and pour water over the tablets or on the feet of the statues** to pray for the repose of their departed relatives. The clear water of the Tamagawa River flows behind the line of statues.

\* \* \*

御廟橋の前には15体の仏像が並んでいます。総称して「水向け地蔵」と呼びます。参拝客は**経木を奉納し、経木または仏像の足元に水を手向けて**、亡くなったご先祖様の魂が安らぐことを祈ります。仏像の列の後ろには玉川の清水が流れています。

## 御廟橋

**Please take off your hat or cap, bow, pray by placing both hands together, and cross the Gobyōbashi Bridge**. After crossing the bridge, you'll enter the most sacred area. Taking pictures, speaking in a loud voice, and eating and drinking are not allowed. It is said that Kōbō Daishi comes to welcome you at the bridge. The Gobyōbashi Bridge is made up of of 37 stone slabs. The 37 stones represent the 37 deities of the "Diamond Realm."

\* \* \*

**脱帽してから、一礼して合掌し、お祈りをして御廟橋を渡ってください**。橋を渡ったら、一番の聖域に入ります。写真撮影、大声で話すこと、飲食は許可されていません。弘法大師が橋までお迎えに来てくださると言われています。御廟橋は、37の石板からできています。37の石板は、「金剛界」の37尊を意味しています。

## 燈籠堂

There are **20,000 lanterns** in the Tōrōdō Hall and the Tōrōdō Memorial Hall. Visitors pray for the safety of their families and the repose of the dead. In the basement of the Tōrōdō Hall, there are about **50,000 tiny statues of Kōbō Daishi**. After praying at Kōbō Daishi's mausoleum, we'll pray at Kōbō Daishi's image in the basement.

＊　＊　＊

　燈籠堂と記念燈籠堂には **2 万基の燈籠**があります。訪問者は家内安全や亡くなった人の平穏を祈ります。燈籠堂の地階には、**5 万体もの弘法大師の小さな像**があります。弘法大師の御朝でお祈りした後、地階の弘法大師の御影にお祈りします。

## 弘法大師御廟

This is Kōbō Daishi's mausoleum. **Kōbō Daishi rests in eternal meditation to save mankind.** Meals are ritually offered to Kōbō Daishi twice a day.

＊　＊　＊

　こちらが弘法大師の御廟です。**弘法大師が人々を救済するために、入定されています。**弘法大師のためにお食事が毎日 2 回、儀式的に運ばれます。

# 5. 宿坊

## 宿坊について（一例）

A Shukubō is a temple which offers lodgings to guests. You can experience the monks' lifestyle by staying overnight. You can **experience silent meditation, copy sutras, and listen to a sermon preached by a monk.** The morning religious service begins at about 6, and you can chant a sutra or listen to it and observe the Buddhist rituals, etc. It's up to you whether you participate in it. We have to arrive at the Shukubō before 5 p.m., because dinner is usually served at around 6 p.m. You can experience vegetarian dishes named Shōjin Ryōri.

＊　＊　＊

　宿坊はお客様に宿を提供するお寺の施設です。一晩滞在し、仏僧の生活を経験できます。**座禅や写経を体験できますし、僧侶による説法を聞くこともできます。**朝の礼拝は 6 時頃に始まり、お経を読むか、聞くかしたり、仏教の儀式を見たりできます。参加するかはあなた次第です。夕食は午後 6 時頃に出されるので、宿坊には午後 5 時前には到着しなければなりません。精進料理という名の、菜食主義者向け料理を食べることができます。

## 写経

"Shakyō" is a kind of **Buddhist training through copying Buddhist sutra texts**. It began in around the 7th or 8th century, when there was no printing technology. Now people practice it to concentrate and purify themselves. Please sit up straight and breathe deeply. Even if you do not know any Chinese characters, it's OK. A Buddhist sutra is printed lightly on a sample copy. All you have to do is trace it with an India ink brush.

＊　　＊　　＊

　写経は**お経の文を書き写す、仏教の修行**のことです。印刷技術がなかった 7 世紀から 8 世紀に始まったと言われています。今日では精神を集中させ、自分自身を清めるために行われます。背筋を伸ばして座り、深呼吸をしてください。漢字をまったく知らなくても大丈夫です。お経は見本のコピーに薄く印刷されています。あなたそれを筆でなぞればよいのです。

## 精進料理と和食

"Shōjin Ryōri" was originally a vegetarian dish for Buddhist monks. Shōjin means **"improving the soul."** It contains neither fish nor meat. It is the origin of Japanese cuisine, which applies the basic concept of "Five Flavors, Five Ways, Five Colors." The five flavors are sour, bitter, sweet, salty, and hot. The five ways are serving food raw, stewed, grilled, deep-fried, and steamed. The five colors are red, blue, yellow, black, and white. Shōjin Ryōri consists of a grilled dish, a deep fried dish, a pickled dish, a tofu dish, and a miso soup dish. **"Washoku"** was registered on **the UNESCO Intangible Cultural Heritage List** in 2013. The ingredients are carefully chosen and beautifully arranged according to the season. It's a healthy, nutritious, and well-balanced meal.

＊　　＊　　＊

　「精進料理」は元は仏僧のための菜食料理です。「精進」は**「精神を向上させること」**を意味します。料理には魚も肉も含まれません。「五味、五法、五色」という基本理念を駆使した日本料理の元祖です。五味は、酸っぱい、苦い、甘い、しょっぱい、辛いです。五法は生で出す、煮込んで出す、焼いて出す、揚げて出す、蒸して出すです。五色は、赤、青、黄、黒、白です。精進料理は焼き物、揚げ物、漬物、豆腐料理、みそ汁で構成されています。**和食**は 2013 年に**ユネスコ無形文化遺産**に登録されました。食材は季節に合わせて注意深く選ばれ、季節に従って美しく盛り付けられます。健康的で栄養価が高く、バランスの取れた食事です。

**アドバイス** ▶▶ 和食がユネスコ無形文化遺産に登録された話はぜひ、説明に入れてください。

## 豆腐・高野豆腐の起源・ごま豆腐

Tofu is an important source of protein. Let me tell you about the origins of Kōya Tofu (Dofu). According to legend, about 800 years ago a young monk dropped some tofu accidentally on a very cold night in winter and found it frozen the next morning, and when it thawed out it was delicious. Later, in order to preserve tofu, a freezing and drying process was developed. "Goma Tofu (Dofu)" has a unique, sticky taste because it is made with **roasted and ground sesame seeds**.

＊　＊　＊

　豆腐は重要なたんぱく源です。高野豆腐の起源について説明させてください。伝説によると、約800年前、冬のとても寒い夜に若い僧が誤って豆腐を落としてしまい、翌朝、それが凍っているのを見つけました。氷が解けると、とてもおいしかったのです。後に、豆腐を保存するために、冷凍と乾燥のプロセスが発達しました。「ごま豆腐」は、**焼いて細かく砕いたゴマ**とともに作られるので、こくのある独特な味がします。

## 朝の勤行体験と護摩祈祷（ごまきとう）

The Buddhist service in the morning involves **chanting sutras** in front of the principal image of the Buddha as we pray. In the "Goma Fire Ritual," a monk burns pieces of wood with the participants' wishes written on them and asks for the Buddha's blessings.

＊　＊　＊

　朝の勤行体験とは、本尊の前で**お経を読み**、お祈りすることを含みます。「護摩祈祷」では仏僧が祈願者の望みを書いた護摩木を燃やし、仏の加護を願います。

## お風呂（温泉）の入り方

Please take off your clothes and put them in a basket on the rack. Please enter the bathroom with a small towel. Rinse your body and sit on a stool, wash your body and rinse off all the soap from your body **outside the bathtub**. Then you can **soak yourself in the bathtub** as long as you like. Before leaving the bathroom, rinse your body again and wipe off your body with a towel.

＊　＊　＊

　服を脱いで、棚のかごに入れてください。小さなタオルを持って浴室に入ってください。体を流し、いすに座り、体を洗い、そして**浴槽の外**で体のせっけんを洗い流してください。それから、いくらでも好きなだけ**浴槽に浸かって**ください。浴室を出る前に体を流し、タオルで拭いてください。

# 索　引

この索引には、本書に登場した約 250 のキーワードが分野別・五十音順に掲載されています。
数字はページ番号を表しています。英語表現や説明の仕方を調べる際にご活用ください。

## 城に関する語彙

石打ち棚………216
石落とし………212, 214
大手門………44
釘隠し………212
刻印石………56
桜門………48
狭間（さま）………206
残念石………56
鯱（しゃちほこ）………52
白い城と黒い城………227
千貫櫓………42
西の丸………46, 220
廃城令………204
姫路城が白い理由………204
武者隠し………214
武者だまり………222

## 神仏共通の語彙

絵馬………183
おみくじ………182
擬宝珠（ぎぼし）………275
七五三………84, 89
朱印………84
手水舎でのお清めの方法………74

## 神道（神社）に関する語彙

天照大神と豊受大御神………258
ウサギが持つ意味………74
神楽殿と舞の奉納………260
Kami とは………272
こま犬………72
酒樽と神様………160
三種の神器（古代と現代）………273
式年遷宮………258
しめ縄の持つ意味………78

神道………70
神道の祈り方………76
太鼓橋………72
玉砂利の持つ意味………160, 272
茅（ち）の輪くぐり………82
月見………72
鳥居………72
巫女………76
みこし………130

## 仏教（寺）に関する語彙

お水取り………152
合掌が持つ意味………96
経木流し………98
経蔵（きょうぞう）………290
華厳宗………148
講堂………98
弘法大師（空海）………286, 287, 288, 289,
　　290, 291, 294, 296
香炉………94
52 の意味………184
五重塔………98, 184
極楽往生………98
護摩祈祷（ごまきとう）………298
金堂………96
金銅八角燈籠………142
西国三十三所………184
33 の意味………184
鴟尾（しび）………140
写経………297
舎利出し法要………109
精進料理………297
真言宗………287
僧侶の剃髪………154
即身成仏………287
大仏殿………140

# 索 引

転法輪………94
蓮の花………144
彼岸………92
108 の除夜の鐘………150
仏教の伝来………90
曼荼羅………287
和宗………100

## 仏像

仏像の種類は、大まかに 4 つに分類されます。如来、菩薩、明王、天部で、位としては悟りを開いた如来が一番上となります。

### 1. 如来

阿弥陀如来………98
東大寺大仏（盧舎那仏）………136, 144
如来と菩薩の違い………96
薬師如来………186

### 2. 菩薩

救世観音菩薩………96, 108
虚空蔵菩薩………144
地蔵菩薩………104
（おもかる地蔵………100）
十一面観音菩薩………98
日光・月光菩薩………186
如意輪観音菩薩………144
不空羂索観音菩薩………184
薬王・薬上菩薩………188

### 3. 明王

不動明王………22

### 4. 天部

広目天………96, 146
金剛力士（仁王）………94
三面六臂の阿修羅像………188
四天王と邪鬼………96
十二神将………186
持国天………96

増長天………96
大黒天………188
多聞天………96, 146
弁才天………133

## その他　羅漢

賓頭盧（びんずる）………100

## 日本事象の一般的な用語

### あ

赤福餅と五十鈴川の関係………264
馬酔木（アセビ）………168
海女………266, 268, 274

### い

池田輝政………204
石燈籠………84, 162
一寸法師………80
一粒万倍（いちりゅうまんばい）………82
厳島神社の大鳥居が立つ理由………236
厳島神社の回廊の床板の隙間の理由
………238
厳島神社の寝殿造り………238
厳島神社の高舞台と舞楽………240

### え

江崎グリコと看板………16, 18
遠足………46

### お

大阪・京都・神戸人の比較………20
大阪市立中央公会堂（大阪商人の魂）
………128
大阪城天守閣の虎のレリーフの意味
………69
大阪・中之島公園………128
大阪のシンボルの木・イチョウ………129
大阪の名産物コイン………58
大阪の薬品と繊維産業………12
大阪弁………34
おかげ参り………264
お好み焼きとたこ焼きの人気が大阪で出た
理由………30

300

織田信長………65
お風呂（温泉）の入り方………298
お礼をする日本文化………89
温泉………232

**か**

柿の葉ずし………154
風見鶏の館………198
合掌造りの利点………276, 278
カップヌードル………14, 16
家紋………44, 69
唐獅子ボタン………170
冠位十二階と十七条の憲法………90

**き**

北野異人館街………196
木の名前………275
鬼門………58
行基………136

**く**

くいだおれ太郎………20
串カツ………30
黒門市場………26

**け**

遣隋使派遣………92
遣唐使………70
景観条例………191
健康を増進する笑い………24
原爆死没者慰霊碑とオバマ氏………250
原爆ドームが保存された理由………248
原爆の子の像が造られた経緯………252, 254

**こ**

好古園………222
高野山の地形………286
高野町の人口と僧侶の数………286
高野豆腐の伝説………297
高度経済成長期………122
交番………114

**さ**

佐々木偵子………252
三鈷の松（幸せを呼ぶ松の葉）………289

**し**

シカ………154, 176, 178
鹿戸がある理由………236
食品サンプルと講習会………26
将軍とは………67
十二支………86
聖徳太子（8つの耳を持つと言われた理由
　など）………90
聖武天皇………136
真珠（養殖真珠）が作られる行程………268
ジンベエザメの不思議………120

**せ**

世界初が多い大阪………35
世界初の缶コーヒー（神戸）………196
世界初のパイプ構造の建物・神戸ポートタ
　ワー………230
世界初の連結超高層ビル・梅田スカイビル
　………110
関ケ原の戦い………40
戦国三英傑（織田・豊臣・徳川）の表現
　………36, 40
千畳閣（豊国神社）………244
千羽鶴の意味………254
千姫………40, 56, 220

**そ**

造幣局………58

**た**

太陽の塔………122, 124
田植えと水田栽培の理由………82
たこ焼きの食べ方の注意………22
だるま………133

**ち**

忠犬ハチ………114

**つ**

通天閣………28
鶴と亀の寿命………89

**て**

鉄砲の伝来………65
天下の台所の意味………20
天神祭………130

# 索　引

天皇と皇室………272

## と
徳川家康が平和な時代を築いた理由………66
徳川家と豊臣家の関係………40
豊臣秀吉とナポレオン………65
豊臣秀吉の生い立ちと織田信長との関係………36, 54
豊臣秀吉の政策………38

## な
灘の酒がおいしい理由………228
七種寄木と風宮神社………172

## に
日本のキリスト教の歴史………208
日本のコーヒー、チョコ、靴の歴史………196, 200
日本の自動販売機………203
日本初のジャズバンド………198
忍者………58

## の
能………242

## は
白鶴酒造資料館………228, 229
柱の穴くぐり………146
花嫁の綿帽子………174
パワースポット………46, 100, 164

## ひ
ヒノキの効能………193
ビリケン………28
広島の名産品………244
広島平和記念資料館の形………250
広島・平和の灯の意味………248

## ふ
フジと春日大社………166
藤原氏………160, 166
武士が生まれた理由………68
文楽………22
文楽とセサミストリート………20

## へ
ペットブームと少子高齢化………114
ヘビが神様である理由………174

## ほ
豊國神社とヒョウタン………46
法善寺横丁と不動明王………22
母衣（ほろ）：兵士が担ぐ袋の役割………69

## ま
町屋………192
松下幸之助………14
招き猫………78
漫才………24

## み
身代わり申………193
御木本幸吉………268, 274
水の都………12
ミックスジュースの起源………30

## め
夫婦岩………273
メリケンパークやメリケン粉の名前の由来………230

## も
もみじまんじゅう………244
桃太郎………218

## よ
養蚕業と化学繊維………280

## ら
落語………24

## り
龍………292
林檎の庭と林檎の持つ意味………166

## ろ
良弁杉………150, 152
路面電車………84, 254

<著者略歴>
**柴山かつの** Katsuno Shibayama

日米英語学院梅田校講師。元京都産業大学非常勤講師。多くの企業、大学のエクステンションコースなどでもTOEIC® L&Rテスト、英検®、ビジネス英語、通訳ガイドの講師を務めた経験を持つ。著書に『あなたも通訳ガイドです 英語で案内する京都 [新装版]』（ジャパンタイムズ出版）、『世界中使える 瞬時に使える旅行英会話大特訓』、『全業種で使える 瞬時に使える接客英会話大特訓』（以上Jサーチ出版）、『英語のWEB会議 直前3時間の技術』、『英語の会議 直前5時間の技術』（以上アルク）、海外翻訳出版8冊など多数。

<英文校閲>
**Paul Dorey** ポール・ドーリー

セント・アンドリュース大学中世史学部修士課程修了。TEFL（英語教授法）資格取得。ケンブリッジ大学検定協会現代語学口頭試問・EFL（外国語としての英語教授法）部門にて勤務の後、日米英語学院にて勤務、現在英国在住。

本書のご感想をお寄せください。
https://jtpublishing.co.jp/contact/comment/

あなたも通訳ガイドです
## 英語で案内する大阪・奈良・神戸

2025年3月20日　初版発行

著　者　柴山かつの　© Katsuno Shibayama, 2025
発行者　伊藤秀樹
発行所　株式会社ジャパンタイムズ出版
　　　　〒102-0082 東京都千代田区一番町2-2 一番町第二TGビル2F
　　　　ウェブサイト https://jtpublishing.co.jp/
印刷所　日経印刷株式会社

本書の内容に関するお問い合わせは、上記ウェブサイトまたは郵便でお受けいたします。
定価はカバーに表示してあります。
万一、乱丁落丁のある場合は送料当社負担でお取り替えいたします。
（株）ジャパンタイムズ出版・出版営業部宛てにお送りください。

ISBN978-4-7890-1888-3　Printed in Japan